CW01430272

ETHICS IN SOCIAL RESEARCH

STUDIES IN QUALITATIVE METHODOLOGY

Series Editor: Chris J. Pole

Recent Volumes:

Volume 1:   Conducting Qualitative Research

Volume 2:   Reflection on Field Experience

Volume 3:   Learning about Fieldwork

Volume 4:   Issues in Qualitative Research

Volume 5:   Computing and Qualitative Research

Volume 6:   Cross-Cultural Case Study

Volume 7:   Seeing is Believing? Approaches to Visual Research

Volume 8:   Negotiating Boundaries and Borders

Volume 9:   Qualitative Urban Analysis: An International Perspective

Volume 10: Qualitative Housing Analysis: An International Perspective

Volume 11: New Frontiers in Ethnography

STUDIES IN QUALITATIVE METHODOLOGY   VOLUME 12

ETHICS IN SOCIAL RESEARCH

EDITED BY

KEVIN LOVE
Nottingham Trent University, UK

Emerald

United Kingdom – North America – Japan
India – Malaysia – China

Emerald Group Publishing Limited
Howard House, Wagon Lane, Bingley BD16 1WA, UK

First edition 2012

Copyright © 2012 Emerald Group Publishing Limited

Reprints and permission service
Contact: booksandseries@emeraldinsight.com

British Library Cataloguing in Publication Data
A catalogue record for this book is available from the British Library

ISBN: 978-1-78052-878-6
ISSN: 1042-3192 (Series)

ISOQAR certified
Management Systems,
awarded to Emerald for
adherence to Quality
and Environmental
standards ISO 9001:2008
and 14001:2004,
respectively

ISOQAR
REGISTERED

UKAS
MANAGEMENT
SYSTEMS
0026

Certificate Number 1985
ISO 9001
ISO 14001

INVESTOR IN PEOPLE

CONTENTS

LIST OF CONTRIBUTORS   *vii*

OPEN QUESTIONS: ETHICS AND SOCIAL RESEARCH
Kevin Love   *ix*

PART I: ELABORATIONS

HOW DID WE EVER GET INTO THIS MESS? THE RISE
OF ETHICAL REGULATION IN THE SOCIAL
SCIENCES
Robert Dingwall   *3*

KNOWLEDGE AND ITS INTEGRITY WITHIN A
KNOWLEDGE ECONOMY: ETHICS AND
WISE SOCIAL RESEARCH
John Harrison and David Rooney   *27*

PUBLIC SOCIOLOGY, CRITICAL SOCIOLOGY, AND
THE SOCIOLOGICAL ENTERPRISE
Richard A. Courtney   *51*

PART II: ENCOUNTERS

ETHICS AND SOCIAL CONFLICT: A FRAMEWORK
FOR SOCIAL RESEARCH
Marco Marzano   *73*

THE POLITICS OF TELLING: BEYOND SIMILARITY
AND DIFFERENCE IN THE INTERVIEW
RELATIONSHIP
Michael Keenan   *91*

TRUST, COERCION AND CARE: RESEARCHING
MARGINALISED GROUPS
Andrew Wilson and Philip Hodgson   *111*

IMPROVISATION, ETHICAL HEURISTICS AND THE
DIALOGICAL REALITY OF ETHICS IN THE FIELD
Mark Edwards and Sam Hillyard   *129*

CONSENT, CONFIDENTIALITY AND THE ETHICS
OF PAR IN THE CONTEXT OF PRISON RESEARCH
James Ward and Di Bailey   *149*

PART III: INTENSIFICATIONS

LISTENING TO VOICES: AN ETHICS OF
ENTANGLEMENT
Lisa Blackman   *173*

THE AGENCY OF ETHICAL OBJECTS
Joost van Loon   *189*

TOWARD A SPECULATIVE ETHICS
Kevin Love   *207*

LIST OF CONTRIBUTORS

Di Bailey	Nottingham Trent University, Nottingham, UK
Lisa Blackman	Goldsmiths, University of London, London, UK
Richard A. Courtney	University of Leicester, Leicester, UK
Robert Dingwall	Dingwall Enterprises and Nottingham Trent University, Nottingham, UK
Mark Edwards	University of Bristol, Bristol, UK
John Harrison	University of Queensland, Brisbane, Australia
Sam Hillyard	Durham University, Durham, UK
Philip Hodgson	Nottingham Trent University, Nottingham, UK
Michael Keenan	Nottingham Trent University, Nottingham, UK
Kevin Love	Nottingham Trent University, Nottingham, UK
Marco Marzano	University of Bergamo, Bergamo, Italy
David Rooney	University of Queensland, Brisbane, Australia
Joost van Loon	Katholische Universität Eichstätt-Ingolstadt, Eichstätt, Germany
James Ward	Durham University, Durham, UK
Andrew Wilson	Nottingham Trent University, Nottingham, UK

OPEN QUESTIONS: ETHICS AND SOCIAL RESEARCH

The relationship between ethics and knowledge must surely be one of the most fraught and interesting in human history. Without wishing to overly dramatise matters, it is possible to identify this particular theme at or around the crux of a number of major cultural narratives retrospectively over a few thousand years at least. One will recall, for instance, the play of morality and knowledge that provides the basic plot for the myth of the fall from grace: human kind required to recognise the moral imperative issued with respect to the tree of the knowledge even before they had acquired knowledge of good and evil! Or again, the conjunction of knowledge and the Good in Plato's *Republic*, most emphatically in the metaphor of the sun (1974). It is not perhaps necessary to track the relation further, through the enlightenment, modernity and the increasing scientisation of ethics, to make the point. Far from having resolved matters, however, the tensions for us today are no less pronounced. Simply casting a lay-eye across contemporary events one observes the same difficult juxtaposition of knowledge acquisition and morality, in apparently ever more prominent forms. From stem cell research and 'Frankenstein foods', to nanotechnology and 'God particles', we remain unable to divorce the epistemological from the ethical, even though the ethical often appears to bump along uncomfortably in the wake of scientific advance . The social sciences sit at a crucial intersection in the contemporary manifestation of this relation, owing to the ethical status of their disciplinary objects certainly, and also thanks to their particular course of development and more critical relation to both knowledge and ethics alike.

To explicate the first of these factors, one might note that while there remain controversies concerning the direction of scientific enquiry and the epistemological veracity of its conclusions, few would object on ethical grounds to the analysis and cataloguing of natural scientific objects per se. Whatever the reasons, philosophical or cultural, it is clear that only certain beings attract moral considerability. At this point in history those beings called 'human' and to a lesser extent certain other higher-order animals *do*, whereas elementary physical particles *do not*, notwithstanding the fact that (we are reliably informed) the latter nonetheless constitute all material reality, presumably ethics included. For the natural sciences, it is only when research and its applications interact with morally considerable beings that the specific relation between ethics and knowledge becomes visible. The same remains true in principle for social research, but of course morally considerable beings figure as the object of study much more frequently, and typically by design rather than coincidence. It is moot whether such anthropocentrism is justifiable, a point some contributors raise. Nonetheless, the exposure to ethical issues that results has led to a heightened sense of the ethical, and a degree of reflexivity in these disciplines designated 'social', that are valuable in themselves. Social research accordingly situates itself at the juxtaposition of science and philosophy, knowledge and ethics, attentive to both empirical and theoretical dimensions and perhaps for that reason provides a crucible where ethical questions can be most grittily confronted and creatively addressed. This collection attempts to follow the same rationale, examining and interrogating current conjunctions theoretically and in practical terms. Exposing theory to practice and *visa-versa*, it is hoped the collection responds in a critical and philosophically enlivened manner to contemporary issues in ethics and social research.

I have entitled this introduction *Open Questions* partly in recognition of the many interesting avenues of thought my fellow authors broach in their respective discussions. Some of these I have attempted to indicate below, albeit in the limited context of an introduction, but many more remain undisturbed by my efforts to scope what I take to be some of the key shared themes. For those familiar with 20th-century moral philosophy, however, the term 'open question' will immediately call to mind G.E. Moore's famous argument pertaining to the nature of the good. In this respect my titular decision is a little more self-serving (for which I rather sheepishly apologise), in that this argument figures prominently in my own contribution. Nonetheless, it seemed appropriate to me to so title the introduction, in order to capture the highly contestable nature of the subject matter. I am pleased to say that there is a good measure of shared sentiment amongst the contributors to this work; I am equally pleased that there is a decent amount of disagreement.

As far as structure is concerned, the volume organises itself into three parts, primarily to assist the reader. This demarcation is not intended to be reductive or restrictive, however, and many of the contributions fortunately overflow the internal boundaries of the book. Nonetheless, broadly speaking, the first section elaborates key arguments/issues regarding ethics in, and the ethics of, social research. Part II engages more noticeably with empirical encounters in social research and the final section seeks to extend and intensify ethical theory, with potential consequences for the mode, nature and role of social research. The remainder of this introduction will therefore aim to illustrate how the structure unfolds while articulating some apparent emergent themes.

ELABORATIONS

Part 1, then, begins with Dingwall's analysis and evaluation of ethical regulation in the social sciences. Following a socio-historical account of the present regulatory regime, which concludes that ethical regulation has been and remains largely a matter of reputation management, he proceeds to consider the costs and benefits of ethical regulation. Dingwall argues that far from being indicative of anarchic and now largely anachronistic administrative regimes, autonomy and decentralisation were in fact finely evolved structural responses to facilitate innovation and creative knowledge generation within institutions of higher education. The spasms of centralisation that have accompanied the rise of ethical regulation reflect a wider managerialism and corporatism that not only inhibit innovation, but are also largely inward-facing and therefore more concerned with shielding the institution than protecting vulnerable research subjects. The costs of ethical regulation in its present form may well outweigh the benefits. Examining research ethics in the context of a knowledge economy, Harrison and Rooney reach remarkably similar conclusions in relation to ethical autonomy and decentralisation. Introducing the main traditions of western moral philosophy, they progress to a discussion of research ethics in the context of normative ethical positions in society more broadly. After examining three seminal, social research projects, they point up the failure of traditional approaches and again indicate the importance of organisational structures. Rather than unreflexively policing abstract codes of conduct, which by implication are thoroughly outflanked by the complexities of a contemporary political economy of knowledge, research institutions they argue must generate wise ethical cultures through the production of institutional ethical spaces. Here autonomous reflection, individual engagement and ethical dialogue form an organic base for wise organisation. Rather than a 'tickbox' approach to satisfy legal and professional obligations, one imagines an institutional culture of ethical deliberation that extends to consider the furthermost implications for society.

Taking emancipation as his guiding theme, and writing from within sociology specifically, Courtney nonetheless begins to illuminate and question some of the inherent ethical norms that inform our respective disciplines. In so doing the chapter provides something of a bridge to Part II (where ethical dilemmas faced by the social researchers 'in the field' take centre-stage), and also gestures to the final section in asking how sociology might justify its normative stance. Posing a four-fold distinction between professional, policy, critical and public sociologies, Courtney highlights a dilemma afflicting the lattermost: in its properly libertarian form the priority of 'giving voice' to the subject can leave the public sociologist ethically impotent in the face of illiberal constructions of reality. Courtney draws upon his own research experiences of racialised discourses amongst the British white working class to illustrate this. Despite its expository force, he continues, critical sociology cannot furnish the discipline with normative principles that remain ideologically neutral and therefore immune to interminable critical analysis. Courtney thus argues for a closer link between public and professional sociology which, while incorporating the critical tendency, nonetheless aims to generate positive ethical principles to inform the discipline. Commending the re-engagement with (political) philosophy, he looks for rational foundations, evidentially supported, to justify a set of normative ethical principles that will hold sway beyond the mere relativity of 'voice'. At the same time, however, he defends the micro-sociological focus of the discipline, and so in sum argues for a more theoretically articulate form of emancipatory sociology.

ENCOUNTERS

The central section of the collection affords active researchers in the social sciences an opportunity to write about the ethical issues that have arisen as a result of, or during the course of, their research. I have explicitly encouraged an honest and reflective approach to issues, rather than a sanitised 'text book' account, and have certainly not been disappointed in this respect. The following chapters manifest candour, sensitivity and theoretical dexterity in equal measure. Marzano reflects on his efforts to gain access to the Catholic religious organisation *Cammino Neocatecumenale*, and instead of taking 'voices' at their word urges a more investigative attitude. He argues for a Weberian notion of responsibility that seeks to accommodate the dialectical complexities of conflict theories in a purposive framework for social research. If Harrison and Rooney favour a virtue ethics watched over by the principle ethic of wisdom, Marzano by contrast argues for an ethics that combines consequentialist and deontological elements. Themes of moral autonomy again seem crucial, however, as this is no rule-bound deontology but a full acceptance of responsibility for the consequences of one's action, in pursuit of a final good. Perhaps this represents a step beyond a cognitive model of wisdom to a more strategic ethics based upon ontological calculation; then again, perhaps an ethics of wisdom would demand nothing less. In any event, notwithstanding the similarities in contextual and methodological terms, one is struck by the contrast between Marzano's piece and that of Keenan which follows.

In an admirably frank and sensitive account of the interview process, Keenan demonstrates how quickly the intricate play of difference and identity begins to structure and influence a research project. Here the relation between researcher and researched seems very different to that proposed by Marzano. If the model suggested by the latter can be typified (crudely no doubt) by the image of an active, thrusting, investigator, Keenan by contrast presents a picture of research as a responsive accord between researcher and participant. Despite the complexities of difference and identity (he mentions sexuality, ethnicity, age, class, gender and work, but no doubt one could add ideological, religious and moral difference, the better to include Marzano and Courtney in the conversation), Keenan calls for greater recognition of the collaborative nature of narrative production. The interview represents an event of coalescence, where a thousand threads of relational interaction crystallise in a text. On this account, qualitative research is to be considered a particular negotiation and crystallisation of difference, rather than the unveiling or application of an independent truth. Thus debates concerning the ontological status of 'voice' and the consequent ethics emerge once more. Even here, however, where research is viewed in strictly consensual terms, it is difficult to guarantee complete transparency. As Keenan implies in his discussion of first impressions, one may ask whether even the most sympathetic research exchange will not be shadowed by irreducible moments of instrumentally covert practice.

Keenan's honesty in this respect opens questions regarding the very nature of coercion. If one dissimulates in an interview context, concealing a personal dislike, disdain or even revulsion in order to facilitate an interview is this not a form of coercion, a use of force to secure compliance? Is there some manner of Derridean economy at play here (see for instance Derrida, 1992) that prevents one distinguishing in principle between paying a fee and paying a compliment? Research ethics as presently configured appears to remain dismissive of the micropolitics of everyday coercion and subterfuge on the one hand, and seemingly unconcerned by the wider social issues on the other: as Harrison and Rooney indicate, in a knowledge economy y instrumentalised towards commercial/policy ends, and a sector similarly aligning itself in terms of personal career, status and reward, research ethics presently hardly reconcile the production of knowledge with notions of exploitation and coercion. Wilson and Hodgson, criminologists working with socially marginalised groups, respond that it must always be the interests of the participants that provide the lead in this respect. Joining with Dingwall, they express scepticism in relation to the role and objectives of the now ubiquitous Research Ethics Committee (REC), favouring instead an ethics of care. Wilson and Hodgson go further, however, arguing that at least procedurally and possibly functionally RECs are in fact complicit in the marginalisation of those social groups that, for ethical reasons, most demand our attention. To make their point they adopt a case study approach and utilise excerpts from their fieldwork with drug-dependent offenders, sex workers and those convicted of violent crimes. Drawing on Noddings and others, they argue for a less bureaucratic approach to research ethics resting on situated principles of trust and care, rather than abstract conceptions of risk, rights and justice.

Edwards and Hillyard would agree on the importance of a situated response, but are less critical of the existing systems of administration. Relating their experiences of research in primary education they make clear the importance of improvisation in the field. Professional and institutional guidelines, however, are presented as assistive rather than prescriptive, providing reassurance and safe-quarter for early-career researchers in particular. This perspective offers a valuable counterweight in the emerging debate, but Edwards and Hillyard do not thereby gainsay the theme of moral autonomy other contributors favour. Guidelines can never be entirely comprehensive and the authors accordingly propose a pragmatic, situational ethics, where the field researcher draws upon all resources at his or her disposal to respond to ethical challenges as they arise. Depending on the specificity of the situation, they suggest, such resources may well include (but not perhaps be limited to) codes of ethics, disciplinary training and individual discretion. Immediately one notes the resonances and possible dialogues emerging relative to Keenan and Courtney, especially as regards accepted norms and the negotiation of difference through improvisation. With Edwards and Hillyard's less than complimentary account of the 'stage-management' of a research scenario by the management of an organisation, Marzano also joins the debate.

Ward and Bailey complete the second section of the book with an account of participatory action research (PAR) in a prison context. Again issues of coercion figure prominently, given a distinctive twist by the particularity of the research context, and again the appeal to participant empowerment and emancipation is central to the discussion. PAR clearly distinguishes itself as a research approach in its relationship to knowledge production. First of all it is a problem-based mode of research, one less concerned with deducing generalisable principles than with solving specific problems. Second, the emphasis on participatory action imbues the approach with a specific ethic of its own. Ward and Bailey provide a valuable discussion of the limits and risks of the participative approach in a prison environment that engenders reflection on the relationship between emancipation and research more broadly.

INTENSIFICATIONS

The final section of the book is perhaps the most ambitious. The aim is to expose debates relating to ethics in social research to contemporary work in philosophy and social/cultural theory—and of course *visa versa*. Writing at the intersection of critical psychology and cultural theory, Blackman seems to pose us three questions that interject with both force and relevance: (1) in all of our preceding references to 'voice', what counts as a voice and which voices count; (2) if all voices signify, even the resolutely silent voices, how might one articulate that which eludes vocalisation, or how does one 'do justice' to the unvoiced, and therefore; (3) what do we take the ontological and ethical status of the vocalic itself to be? It is vital to note that Blackman wishes to extend notions of voice and listening well beyond the boundaries of the human perceptual system, giving voice (and with that some measure of moral considerability, if not a right to be heard) to phenomena (or aphenomena) that typically remain aphonic within social research. In so doing she joins with an increasing number of theorists from a great variety of backgrounds who question the anthropocentrism, not just of ethics, but of thought generally, and provokes us to think the ethical beyond the limits of humanism.

Tackling a distinction that sits at the heart of Western metaphysics, that between subjects and objects, van Loon similarly challenges and extends our notion of the ethical. The question of what constitutes subjects and objects does not, for van Loon, turn on questions of essence. He proposes instead an empirical enquiry concerning modalities of 'having' in contrast to modalities of 'being'. In a gesture compellingly close to Blackman's, van Loon rejects both the ontological primacy of perception and its anthropo-centric monopolisation. Immediately the notion of 'research' becomes much more experimental in character. Research is about inserting oneself into particular assemblages of things in experimental mode and (as a thing amongst things) mediating the assemblage from a specific conjuncture within. Favouring elements of Actor Network Theory, van Loon has things themselves display varying and variable qualities of agency/passivity in the encounter, and would no doubt be happy to extend these qualitative modalities into the middle-voice also. The researcher amounts to a 'being-affected', where that term resonates across both nominal and verbal registers and would ideally incorporate the entire spectrum of possible affect: cognitive and noncognitive; human and posthuman. Keenan's implicit conception of research as the negotiation of difference sits well in this context and, as Blackman states, one begins to envisage forms of emergent social research that would utilise all manner of artistic and scientific 'sensors' to facilitate the mediation. van Loon returns to the question of ethics at the end of his piece with an illustrative discussion of pornography.

My own contribution adopts a more traditionally philosophical approach to the question of ethics, but intriguing despite this is the point of intersection between Blackman's vocative and van Loon's affective. The ethical in van Loon might be interpretable in one of two ways: (1) as a modality of affect; (2) as an overarching injunction to 'be-affected', reminiscent of Deleuze (see for instance Deleuze, 2004). The final chapter gravitates around G.E. Moore's naturalistic fallacy and, in particular, his open question argument. It radicalises the latter to resist the all but obsessive tendency in philosophy to reduce the ethical to an ontological foundation. Drawing upon recent developments in continental philosophy the chapter attempts to isolate some properly ethical principle on which to base a meta-ethics. The notion of *exhortation* is proffered for speculative absolutisation, a subjunctive mood that avoids both (onto-epistemological) description and (political) prescription; more colloquially, is *and* ought. In van Loon's terms, exhortation would be a modality of affect that resisted all reduction to being: ontology, epistemology, politics, that is to say, are separate modalities, and the modal itself cannot be formulated as an encompassing metaphysics without again committing the ontological fallacy. Drawing a little on Heidegger, the chapter formulates these modalities as specific questions (the question of ethics as opposed to the question of being) that prestructure the mode of enquiry. It is perhaps a small step to reconfigure these questions in the vocative form, given that one is able to distinguish sufficiently well a free-standing form of the vocative from Levinas's humanistic, and arguably theistic, dyad.

Notwithstanding, however, the various conversations initiated by this collection progress, it has been a pleasure to have been involved this far. All that remains is for me to thank my fellow authors for their excellent contributions, which lend the volume such substance and variety, and the series editor for the opportunity to work on this project with an interdisciplinary field of talented academics.

Kevin Love
Editor

REFERENCES

Deleuze, G. (2004). *Difference and repetition* (P. Patton, Trans.). London: Continuum.
Derrida, J. (1992). *Given time: 1. Counterfeit money* (P. Kamuf, Trans.). Chicago, IL: University of Chicago Press.
Plato. (1974). *The republic* (D. Lee, Trans.). London: Penguin.

PART I
ELABORATIONS

HOW DID WE EVER GET INTO THIS MESS? THE RISE OF ETHICAL REGULATION IN THE SOCIAL SCIENCES

Robert Dingwall

ABSTRACT

Purpose – *To outline the history of ethical regulation in the social sciences and to question the proportionality of its costs and benefits.*

Methodology/approach – *Secondary analysis of primary literature.*

Findings – *Ethical regulation in the social sciences has been driven more by institutional reputation management than human subject protection. It has a range of social and economic costs that have not received adequate critical appraisal.*

Social implications – *Ethical regulation in the social sciences may be highly damaging to a society's ability to understand itself, particularly by constraining scientific research relative to journalism or imaginative forms of communication.*

Ethics in Social Research
Studies in Qualitative Methodology, Volume 12, 3–26
Copyright © 2012 by Emerald Group Publishing Limited
All rights of reproduction in any form reserved
ISSN: 1042-3192/doi:10.1108/S1042-3192(2012)0000012004

Originality/value of paper – *Review of the most current research and an explanation of the positive case against regulation.*

Keywords: Research ethics; social science; human subjects; regulation; innovation; knowledge

Once upon a time, not so long ago, social scientists worked in a world where research ethics was entirely a matter for their professional judgement, as individuals or as members of a community of peers. Today, most social scientists who work in universities, and many contract research organisations, in the Anglophone world and the Nordic countries must pass through a process of regulatory approval from an institutionalised ethical review committee before they can begin to collect many kinds of data. This applies equally to large-scale, externally funded projects that have passed a scientific peer review and small-scale curiosity-driven work in personal research time. Typically, it applies to student projects as much as to those by experienced professional researchers. There are, though, still parts of the world, particularly Mainland Europe, that retain and cherish traditions of professional autonomy, offering an alternative to the Anglo-Saxon movement towards a system of command and control. What did Anglo-Saxon social scientists do that was so catastrophically wicked that it justified this change? Has it produced identifiable social benefits or are these outweighed by the direct and indirect costs?

This chapter tells the story of the rise of ethical regulation in the social sciences. How did bodies like IRBs, REBs and URECs – every country has its own alphabet pasta to describe social science research governance – come to be created? Why were they created? What was the problem to which they were responding? There are four main sections: a review of the 'origin myths' cited by advocates for regulation; a sketch of the evidence for reasonably effective self-regulation; a discussion of the movement for change; and an assessment of the consequences.

THE CREATION MYTH OF RESEARCH ETHICS

Israel and Hay (2006, pp. 23–39) present the conventional story about the rise of ethical regulation to protect human subjects, from the Nuremberg Code (1947) through the Declaration of Helsinki (1964), the Belmont Report (1979) and the CIOMS/WHO statement (1982). Although they acknowledge that the historical record is more complex, they focus on these events as a sufficient justification for the regulation of social science research that emerged from the late 1970s onward. Two points need to be made. The first is that the historical record is indeed more complex, as will be demonstrated, and the second is that, although their avowed readership is social scientists, all of these documents, with very limited exceptions in the Belmont Report, are directed at biomedical research. This has a very different matrix of knowledge, risks and benefits from social science research, which will be explored later.

The statement promulgated by the prosecution at the Nuremberg Doctors Trial in 1947 as a basis for the charges against doctors, whose experiments had indeed involved the grossly inhumane treatment of human subjects, has subsequently acquired a mythic quality (Annas & Grodin, 1995). Regulation is often held to be the only defence against the possibility of such atrocities recurring. However, historical scholarship has established a very different story.

First, Germany was the only country in the 1930s with an explicit regulatory regime for biomedical research, which had been introduced in administrative regulations by the Prussian state government in 1900, reinforced by similar action from the German national government in 1931. The latter, in particular, anticipate, and in some respects go beyond, the Nuremberg Code. Unfortunately, many German biomedical researchers simply did not accept the legitimacy of the regulations and they lacked enforcement (Dingwall & Rozelle, 2011). Elsewhere, standards were effectively maintained by informal social controls – refusing to share data or correspond with peers whose practice was considered questionable (Halpern, 2004). This meant that the prosecution at Nuremberg had to invent a set of 'generally accepted' principles rather quickly in order to prosecute the case (Hazelgrove, 2002). This is underlined by the questions that have been raised about the Tuskegee and Guatemala studies by US researchers on minority populations infected with sexually transmitted diseases, where it is not clear that research judged unacceptable with hindsight clearly breached the standards of the 1930s and 1940s (Jones, 1981; Reverby, 2009, 2011; Shweder, 2004; Walter, 2012).

Second, the Allied Powers did not seem to perceive that the Code might also apply to them. The *Manchester Guardian*, England's leading liberal newspaper, did not report the Nuremberg Doctors Trial at all. Their first reference to the Code (17 July 1947) is in the context of a meeting of the British Medical Association (BMA), the UK doctors' professional association, being asked to endorse a draft of what became the 1948

Declaration of Geneva, the precursor of the Declaration of Helsinki. The story makes little of the trial and presents the problem as something to be addressed within the profession itself. When, in 1951, the BMA asked the General Medical Council, the licensing body for UK doctors, to consider requiring UK medical graduates to affirm their adherence to the Declaration of Geneva, the latter declined to take any position on the matter (28 November 1951). There are no further references until the end of the decade. This indifference was reflected in a lack of attention to the Allies' own wartime experiments and in the acceptance of biomedical research practices that eventually provoked sharp attacks from Maurice Pappworth (1962, 1967) in the United Kingdom and Henry Beecher (1959, 1966) in the United States.

Change emerged, however, from the early 1950s within the US National Institutes of Health (NIH) in-house research programme, as Stark (2012) describes. The construction of the NIH Clinical Center, a new research hospital at Bethesda, a northern suburb of Washington, DC, which opened in 1953, and the increasing use of healthy volunteers as experimental subjects, led to a review of the existing organisational model. This had emphasised the independence of the various research programmes or institutes. Expert group review provided a means of developing a common approach while respecting the autonomy of each programme and the specific needs of its research. In this respect, it was a straightforward evolution from the informal controls described by Halpern (2004). A model crafted to preserve professional discretion was exported to NIH contractors in a quite different form by the US Surgeon-General as policy in 1966 and then as Federal regulation in 1974. Hedgecoe (2009) shows that this also drove UK developments because of the number of UK research centres receiving NIH funding.

This initiative had very little to do with human subjects protection as such, but was the outcome of an internal struggle between government lawyers over the management of litigation risks and institutional reputation. It was then used to address the legal problems that had emerged from the research programmes funded by NIH in universities and other centres, particularly a cancer research study at the Jewish Chronic Disease Hospital in Brooklyn, New York, in 1964. By requiring institutions receiving funding to create their own internal review committees, NIH hoped to avoid being held ultimately liable for any claims made by participants. Nevertheless, this was a system that was still intended to allow a good deal of local flexibility in defining acceptable standards. Although it was mandated in 1974, as Federal officials scrambled to respond to the breaking news about the

Tuskegee study, the original regulations carried over much of the spirit of local discretion and flexibility to respond to the circumstances of different disciplines and their research traditions.

Stark emphasises that this administrative history substantially predates the conventional history of bioethics that has been laid over it. It was an organisational model that was applied to solve certain organisational problems. However, this does not preclude the adoption of the parallel story told about bioethics as a story about the cultural developments that afforded legitimacy to the solution (Rothman, 2003). As Stark notes, the emergence of the legal challenges, and the scandals charted by Rothman, Reverby (2009) and others, reflect wider shifts in American culture towards a more inclusive community that was less deferential to historic hierarchies and sources of authority. Although she does not put it quite this way, scandals are not self-evident. The Jewish Chronic Disease Hospital study acquired a particular resonance through the rediscovery of the Holocaust in the 1960s as a solution to problems facing Jewish people in the United States (Novick, 1999). The Tuskegee study resurrected the historic injustices towards Black people that had preoccupied US society and politics throughout much of the 1960s. Bioethics offered a cultural neutralisation of these concerns under a set of principles and doctrines that could be applied to all groups within US society on an impartial basis, although its emphasis on autonomy rather than justice would cause problems when it came to be exported to communities that did not share the American Dream of self-fulfilment through personal achievement in a non-discriminatory marketplace (Benatar, 1997).

From the outset, then, ethical regulation was primarily about the protection of organisations rather than human subjects. Damaging trial participants could be costly, both economically and reputationally, but a well-crafted procedure would minimise these risks or, at least, reposition them away from NIH and the US government. However, risk management is not a good story about an organisation. It does not supply legitimacy as effectively as a story about disinterested altruism and public benefit (DiMaggio & Powell, 1983). Consider the connotations of 'Institutional Reputation Management Board', compared with 'Institutional Research Ethics Review Board'. A group of conceptive ideologists (Cain, 1983) was needed to devise a better legitimation in the form of an origin myth: 'a narrative that explains how a culture came into being ... It infuses everyday life and relations with significance by explaining why things are as they are and by providing guidance for how things should evolve based on what we already understand about our world (Silbey, 2008)'.

Origin, or creation, myths seem to be a ubiquitous feature of human social organisation (Eliade, 2005). Christians, Muslims and Buddhists all have accounts of the world's creation and the introduction of their religion to humans. Ancient Romans described the foundation of their city and empire by the twins, Romulus and Remus (Tudor, 1972). However, the phenomenon is found in many contemporary social groups, as nurses tell stories about Florence Nightingale (Whittaker & Olesen, 1964), patent lawyers about intellectual property (Silbey, 2008) and bioethicists about bioethics (Gaines & Juengst, 2008). As the latter comment: 'It seems that in Bioethics, different origin myths do not necessarily serve as markers of self-identity, but may act as markers of the bioethicist's audience and the task at hand on a particular occasion' (Gaines & Juengst, 2008, p. 324). In effect, bioethicists frequently serve as conceptive ideologists supplying legitimations for biomedicine and the institutional settings within which it is practiced (Elliott, 2004, 2005, 2010).

ETHICAL REGULATION AND THE SOCIAL SCIENCES

Neither NIH research governance nor bioethics had much to say about social science research in the early years. However, it was clarified within NIH in December 1966 that the expectations for external contractors also included the review of behavioural research (Stark, 2012, p. 155). The model here appears to be that of the psychological experiment, which has many parallels with other clinical and experimental investigations that do things to sick people or healthy volunteers. Then, as now, NIH carried out a substantial amount of research, both internally and externally, on mental health issues, which drew in psychologists and, to a lesser extent, sociologists and anthropologists. Erving Goffman (1968), for example, was partly supported by external NIH funding for the research reported in *Asylums*, and some of the fieldwork was carried out in the NIH Clinical Center. Nevertheless, the language that was adopted in the late 1960s covered both social and behavioural sciences in the search for a bureaucratically tidy uniformity (Schrag, 2010). This extension occurred in the face of early mobilisation by sociologists, anthropologists and political scientists against its implications. Only psychologists were reasonably supportive, partly because they recognised the parallels with biomedical research and the need for a defence against emerging concerns in the US Congress about studies that addressed sensitive issues, like sexuality, or involved children.

If we look back to social science before the 1960s, though, we can see that certain conventions were established very early in the development of the empirical social sciences. The principles of confidentiality and anonymity designed to protect the privacy of informants – and the security of researchers – are evident from the beginnings of institutionalised social science. Classic ethnographies invariably conceal the identities of informants and, often, the detail of locations within which fieldwork was conducted. Cressey's (2008) *The Taxi-dance Hall*, first published in 1932, introduces these premises, where patrons bought tickets to dance with young women, through a composite description. The book does not identify either the women or their patrons except in broad age and ethnic categories. It was, however, carried out without the co-operation of the owners, and in the face of outright opposition from some. Investigators were 'instructed to mingle … and to become as much a part of this social world as ethically possible' (Cressey, 2008, p. xx). Shaw's (1966) *The Jack Roller*, first published in 1930, based on a life history written by a young delinquent, assigned him a pseudonym, respected by Snodgrass (1983), when he tracked the man down in the 1970s with the help of Shaw's son. The clash between Boelen (1992) and Whyte (1992) over the authenticity of Whyte's (1993) classic *Street Corner Society*, first published in 1943, maintained the use of pseudonyms except where informants had clearly given consent to their names being used or had died. Anthropologists were a partial exception, although distance obviously offered a degree of protection to their informants and they frequently chose to anonymise a particular village and use pseudonyms for its residents even when naming a tribe.

So what were the scandals? Prior to 1974, three main issues were discussed among social scientists: covert observation, data linkage and political manipulation. The first debate actually embraces two of these issues since it describes the covert observation of the occupational socialisation of US Air Force recruits by an officer for research purposes (Sullivan, Queen, & Patrick, 1958). Sullivan et al. discuss the practical challenges involved but seem to have considered the practice uncontentious. The study provoked a sharp attack from Lewis Coser, who considered it amounted to spying in the interests of authority (Coser, 1959), although it was supported by Julius Roth, who was one of the most accomplished ethnographers of the 1950s and 1960s (Roth, 1963). Covert observation has always been an issue which social scientists have approached with caution (Erikson, 1967). Many have, however, strongly defended it as a justifiable means of generating data on oppressed or marginalised groups, provided that it was coupled with a commitment to articulating their claims and world view, rather than as part of a strategy for control. Although Cressey's work was carried out in response to a social problem mandate – concern over the recruitment of young women into prostitution through the dance halls – covert research made it possible to explore the complexity of the reasons why both the women and their clients ended up in these locations and to defy the simple prescriptions of moral reformers.

This justification was also a critical defence for supporters of Laud Humphreys' (1975) *Tearoom Trade*, first published in 1970. Claiming to have taken the established role of lookout, Humphreys observed anonymous sexual contacts between gay men in a park toilet in a Midwestern US city at a time when such practices were criminal.[1] In fact, university management tried to withhold his PhD for failing to report the offences that he had witnessed and there were organisational issues about the absence of IRB approval, given that the work was funded by NIMH (Galliher et al., 2004). Most concerns among other social scientists, however, were raised by the fact that he logged the participants' car numbers, identified them through deception of the campus police (Humphreys, 1980) and then slipped their names into a wider public health survey. This produced data of considerable social value in demonstrating the extent to which many of these men had 'normal family lives' with their wives and children, but also potentially placed them at risk of arrest and prosecution. Humphreys initially moved the linkage data out of the reach of the local criminal jurisdiction and later destroyed it altogether. Following the publication of various commentaries, some of which are collected in an enlarged edition of *Tearoom Trade* (Humphreys, 1975), Humphreys did concede that he had not given the implications of his actions sufficient thought, and would now seek to cultivate more informants for interviews based on explicit consent, at some cost in methodological rigour. Nevertheless, he remained proud of his findings and their contribution to the greater social acceptance of the gay community. Of course, it is also arguable that his findings would have had less impact if they had been more easily dismissed as a self-selected sample.

The third area of concern focussed on the association between social science and various US government agencies looking to counter opposition to various commercial and strategic interests in Central and South America. The best-known example is Project Camelot (Horowitz, 1967; Sjoberg & Sjoberg, 1969). This was an initiative launched by the US

Department of Defense in 1964 to fund anthropologists, sociologists and political scientists to study social conflicts in Central and South America. The source of funding was not acknowledged and it became clear that the objective was to provide a social scientific basis for counter-insurgency work. Given that many social scientists were generally critical of the conduct of the US government's policies in the region, and their deference to corporate interests rather than local democracy, this rapidly provoked a hostile response and was cancelled after congressional hearings in 1965. This issue has continued to provoke debate within US anthropology, in particular, with a re-examination of the role of anthropologists in the Second World War and the Cold War of the 1950s, continuing through to the Human Terrain programmes of more recent conflicts (Price, 2004, 2008, 2011). The concern reflects both the way in which social science had been covertly co-opted for highly contested social goals and the degree to which such co-option put other colleagues at risk because it would promote suspicion that anyone claiming to be a social scientist was really a secret agent. Journalists have often raised similar concerns about the use of their profession as a cover for undercover work. UK social science has given less attention to such issues, at least in part because of the state's relative indifference to the work of anthropologists, many of whom were strongly committed to challenging the, implicit or explicit, racism of colonial administrations (Kuper, 1996). This neglect was exemplified by the readiness, in 2006, of the Economic and Social Research Council (ESRC) to accept Foreign Office funding for a near-clone of Project Camelot to investigate Islamic fundamentalism in support of counter-terrorism policy. This programme was substantially revised under pressure from the social science community, but it is notable that it was given serious consideration by ESRC, which appeared to be wholly unaware of the Camelot controversy.

Taken together, these examples suggest that the sorts of mechanisms described by Halpern (2004) in the biomedical sciences worked reasonably effectively in the social sciences. The basic principles of confidentiality and anonymity were identified from a very early date, as was the conditional legitimacy of covert research. Where these boundaries were pushed, the community was capable of self-policing and articulating a professional consensus that was responsive to external criticism. Indeed, it could be argued that these mechanisms were more effective than institutional controls when it came to the political manipulation of research – while ESRC were pressing UK universities to install internal ethical regulation, they were uncritically accepting funding from homeland security sources. If ethical regulations were genuinely about ethical matters, questions about the propriety of this funding would have been asked before rather than after a deal had been done.

Two other studies may be worth mentioning because they are frequently cited as justifications for regulation. One is the series of experiments conducted by Stanley Milgram to investigate obedience to authority, where participants were induced by the experimenter to administer what they thought were increasingly powerful electric shocks to a confederate (Milgram, 1963, 1974). This provoked considerable ethical debate over the element of deception and the stress created for participants by the pressure from the experimenter to continue with the shocks (e.g. Baumrind, 1964). I happened to meet one of the participants in another context in the 1980s and he admitted to continuing anger about the experience, despite subsequent debriefings and personal discussions with Milgram. This work predated any requirement for ethical review so it was not cleared by any regulatory body. However, Milgram (1963) notes that a methodologically comparable study (Buss, 1961) was completed at around the same time – there seems to have been a priority issue in relation to publication – which suggests that his work would not have been seen as lying outside a professional consensus. It clearly gave an impetus to the regulatory movement. By the time Philip Zimbardo (2008, p. 236) came to conduct the Stanford Prison Experiment, in 1971, approval was required from the sponsor (US Office of Naval Research), a departmental review committee, and the university's IRB. This study involved a group of students who were randomly assigned to the role of 'prisoner' and 'guard'. The 'guards' became so abusive that the project was terminated by Zimbardo after six days instead of the intended two weeks. Zimbardo (2008, pp. 168–171) admits that his own ethical sensibility was dulled by the fact of approval and that the trigger for termination was his girlfriend's concern that what he was doing was simply wrong.

Both of these projects underline a fundamental difference between most biomedical, and some psychological research, and other social science research methods, namely the relative power relationship between investigator and participants (Murphy & Dingwall, 2007). Biomedical research draws on the authority of medicine to carry out procedures that may have physically damaging and irreversible consequences that are difficult to predict in advance. Psychological experiments draw subjects into an experimental situation under the control of the researcher, which is difficult to leave once the protocol has begun, as both the Milgram and Zimbardo studies demonstrate in extreme form. Most other social science research rests on the courtesy of the informants in granting time and access. Sometimes it involves people who are more powerful than the researcher, as in large areas of political science, where political leaders and their advisers may be interviewed. Often it involves moment-to-moment negotiation with people who are being observed in everyday situations that they would not normally share with outsiders. Social scientists are usually guests in other people's lives. The risks run by informants are relatively straightforward – and straightforward to manage. Informants do not have to make complex scientific judgements about the risks of an experiment but simply assess the likely consequences of their secrets becoming public knowledge – and the degree to which they trust the promises of the person who they are dealing with. This is the sort of assessment that we all make every day.

THE RISE OF REGULATION

When we come to look at the rise of ethical regulation in the social sciences, it is, then, hard to identify any obvious precipitating scandals of the kind that provoked regulatory intervention in the biomedical sciences. The US National Research Act 1974, which was a legislative response to the exposure of the Tuskegee study, maintained the language of biomedical and behavioural research, so that it would clearly embrace psychological experiments. In this sense, it might be thought to reflect the concerns raised by Milgram's work, although there is no clear evidence of this. However, its implementation in Federal Regulations extended the coverage to any work involving human subjects. Moreover, these required any institution receiving federal funds to review all its research, whether or not it was supported from this source. The development of the regulations by a National Commission took very little account of the distinctive concerns of social scientists, despite the efforts of some staff members to get commissioners to attend to the evidence that was being submitted (Schrag, 2010, pp. 54–95). Initially, enforcement was not particularly rigorous in the social sciences but it became increasingly controversial. Schrag (2010, pp. 45–53) describes early conflicts at Berkeley and at the University of Colorado at Boulder. Berkeley proposed to extend the protection of individuals to cover groups and institutions, whose reputation might be damaged. Boulder sought to regulate the use of publicly available data. Both were seen as threatening censorship and the institutions retreated in the face of internal and external criticism, particularly as both had gone beyond the expressed requirements of the regulations and struggled to legitimate the actions of their review boards.

By the end of the 1970s, there was a much more direct and organised confrontation between the federal bureaucracy and representatives of the social sciences, which led to a number of significant concessions in 1981, exempting most survey and observational research (Schrag, 2010, pp. 116–119). However, almost immediately, the office created to oversee the regulatory system began to undermine the concessions, with the enthusiastic support of many of the administrators hired by universities to administer their IRBs. From the mid-1990s, the federal administrators began to demand greater enforcement and net-widening to encompass disciplines like anthropology and oral history, which had previously largely ignored IRB jurisdiction. Universities hired more IRB staff, who formed their own professional association and developed accreditation for their training and programmes. Although this crackdown provoked a further response, Schrag (2010, pp. 143–160) argues that the social science community was less united and effective than it had been 20 years before. There was now a significant bloc of interests vested in the present system, from federal bureaucrats down to university administrators keen to have an extra tool for managing their independent-minded faculty. Social science association leaderships were reluctant to compromise their wider lobbying relationships in Washington, DC, and prominent scholars did not want to risk their own research funding under federal programmes.

Outside the United States, developments pursued a slightly different course. The impact of US regulation was felt directly only in the biomedical field, where there were substantial areas of international collaboration and funding that required other countries to create parallel systems. However, because biomedical funders also supported behavioural and social scientific research, these fields were swept into the net as far as work in the health field was concerned. Both Canada and the United Kingdom, for example, initially created systems that were restricted to the regulation of research within healthcare settings. However, once created, these systems generated isomorphic pressures on other parts of the research enterprise to extend regulation. In Canada, much of the impetus came from the Medical Research Council, leading to the publication of the *Tri-Council Policy Statement on Ethics Involving Human Subjects* in 2001, which all Canadian universities were required to accept as a condition of receiving research grants (van den Hoonard, 2011). In the United Kingdom, the initiative was more strictly confined to the National Health Service (NHS), which developed its own ethical regulatory process as a gateway to research on patients and organisations within the system (Hedgecoe, 2009). There were widespread complaints from social scientists, and some groups of health professionals, about biases within this process, particularly where qualitative research was concerned, although Hedgecoe (2008) argues that these may have been exaggerated. Nevertheless, there was sufficient concern to generate heavy lobbying of ESRC by UK social scientists to negotiate for a more flexible approach to the review of social science proposals by the NHS committees. In retrospect, this was probably an ill-advised strategy. Over the last 30 years or so, ESRC has increasingly seen itself as a manager of the UK social science community on behalf of government rather than as an advocate for its interests (Savage, Bradley, & Smith, 2011). Its response was, then, to develop its own institutional framework for ethical regulation, although it rapidly became clear that the NHS would not defer to any decisions taken within this. With the publication of the ESRC *Research Ethics Framework* in 2005 (now the *Framework for Research Ethics*), UK social scientists suddenly found themselves caught up in an IRB-type system, with universities required to create ethical regulation committees as a condition of receiving ESRC funding. As Hedgecoe (2008) and Dingwall (2008) have noted, there are already signs that these committees are more concerned with institutional risk and reputation management than with the support of social scientific research.

The international push for regulation continues to evoke criticism and resistance, but this lacks organisation and leadership. In the United States, law schools were late to experience the incursion of IRBs, possibly because institutions were slow to recognise the growth of empirical research by law professors and the implications of hiring social scientists to teach a broader curriculum. Some of the most vocal critics in recent years have come from this background. The prestige and revenue streams attached to law schools in many US universities confer a certain measure of protection from bureaucratic pressures for conformity. Malcolm Feeley (2007) used his presidency of the Law and Society Association to campaign for change and Philip Hamburger (2004, 2007) has argued that prior review of social science research by IRBs may, in fact, be unconstitutional as conflicting with First Amendment rights to freedom of speech. However, it is a basic observation of socio-legal studies that rights are only made real by enactment and enforcement, which can be costly in both human and economic terms – taking a case to the Supreme Court could cause major damage to an academic career and a bank balance. While it is possible that similar claims could be made in other countries with a written constitution, like Canada, the absence of such protections in the United Kingdom makes legal challenges hazardous. The European Convention on Human Rights has a much more qualified approach to freedom of speech, which can be understood in the United States to include research, than does the US Constitution (Dingwall, 2008). UK opposition is much more fragmented and tends to concentrate on moral outrage which can easily be dismissed as the self-interested complaints of a professional group. In the political climate of recent years, professions have tended to be seen as sources of resistance to democratic changes intended to enhance their responsiveness to consumers of their services rather than as disinterested servants of the public welfare. Ethical regulation, it might be argued, is merely another means of holding irresponsible professionals to account.

This may, however, understate the wider social interest in free inquiry and the justifications for supporting an approach that maximises the liberty of empirical researchers within the general framework of law on matters like privacy and libel.

THE COSTS OF REGULATION

The growth of ethical regulation has taken place within a wider context of organisational transformation in universities. Indeed, it could be argued that this is one of the drivers for change. The informal mechanisms of social control within the professional community described by Halpern (2004) simply do not work at the global scale of modern biomedical, and social science. Where research is a matter for a limited number of elite scholars in small and densely networked universities, withdrawal of goodwill is a serious sanction. This may still be the case in some emerging or niche fields but, in general, professional ostracism is no longer a realistic sanction. The academic profession is no different from other professions in this respect (Dingwall, 1999). This might be an argument for strengthening discipline-based processes of control but it is not necessarily an argument for organisation-based processes like IRBs. For the sources of this, we may need to look at the changing nature of universities as organisations.

Fifty years ago, most universities might reasonably have been described as co-operatives of professionals. They were, on the whole, run by the faculty for the faculty, even where they received public funding. Faculty were supported by administrators but supplied the institutional leadership, often on a rotating basis so that no senior officer could consolidate power. Over the last half century, in many developed countries, faculty have been progressively displaced from this role by a cadre of professional managers. Some of these are drawn from the ranks of the professoriate but this now tends to be a career move rather than a temporary diversion from research or teaching. Others are from fields like accounting, estates or human resources and bring skills, attitudes and career orientations into the university that look to the wider field of management in corporate environments rather than the historically distinctive nature of universities. New university-level institutions have been created from training or educational organisations that had always been governed in a bureaucratic fashion. The culmination of these changes has been a shift, particularly in those countries where ethical regulation has grown fastest, towards more corporate forms of university organisation (Ginsberg, 2011; Tuchman, 2011).

Shweder (2006) encapsulates this when he describes the change at the University of Chicago between 1967, where a high-level faculty committee articulated two fundamental principles of research autonomy, and the terms of an ethics training course run by the IRB. In 1967,

> The first principle entrusts the university with the defense of the 'autonomy' of its faculty and students 'in the discovery, improvement and dissemination of knowledge' (including critical and even unpopular inquiry into all aspects of social life) ... . The second academic-freedom principle ... is a justification for the idea of 'institutional neutrality' and the notion that a university is a 'community' in only a very limited and special sense, namely, one that promotes and defends the intellectual autonomy of its faculty and students ... the university thrives because of the freedom of its members to hold unpopular or eccentric views ... the university must avoid the temptation to make institutional or collective judgments concerning matters that have an impact on the activities of its faculty and students in the discovery, improvement, and dissemination of knowledge (Shweder, 2006, p. 511).

By the end of the century, the university's IRB is declaring that 'Conducting research is a privilege and NOT a right' (Shweder, 2006, p. 514). As Shweder recounts the episode, the University of Chicago was quick to respond to faculty concern and to look for ways of mitigating the impact of federal requirements on non-federal research. However, he nurtures the suspicion that things are less happy elsewhere, which is essentially van den Hoonard's (2011) conclusion on his study of ethical regulation in Canada.

This may sound like precisely the kind of special pleading for which academics are criticised. It is, though, an important context because only by understanding the evolution of the tradition of research freedom can we properly appraise the consequences of the regulatory system. Three of these seem to be important: the diversion of resources; the promotion of ignorance; and the stifling of innovation. All of these contribute to a more positive case against regulation than mere professional autonomy. Professions are afforded autonomy because there is a societal benefit for this, not simply because they have captured legislatures and obtained favourable legislation (Dingwall & Fenn, 1987).

There is an emerging body of work on the costs of ethical regulation in biomedical research. Van den Hoonard (2011, pp. 75, 288) suggests that the annual direct expenditures for Canada alone are CAD 35 million (GBP 22 million at 2011 rates) and that the combined bill for Canada, Australia, United Kingdom and United States may be CAD 432 million (GBP 273 million). This excludes the salary costs of committee members and the time consumed in preparing applications, for example. All of this is money diverted from the actual business of doing research. If a new drug is delayed or abandoned because of the burden of IRB requirements, the costs of the lives that may be impaired or lost as a result should be set against any lives saved by the scrutiny (Silberman & Kahn, 2011; Whitney & Schneider, 2011). Although the methodology is not yet robust, the emergence of this work reflects the basic principle that the costs of regulation should be proportionate to the benefits. The social sciences rarely present the potential for economic losses on a comparable scale to those of the biomedical sciences. There is, then, an urgent challenge to break out and specify the costs that can be allocated to the social sciences and to define the benefits. This may be a relatively small proportion of research expenditure but when resources are short there is a particular obligation to evaluate the effectiveness with which they are being used. Every administrator involved in regulation will be roughly equivalent to one fewer research assistant: whose labour is more productive?

Ethical regulation may also create perverse incentives. Understandably, investigators are likely to develop projects which minimise trouble for them and which are likely to pass smoothly through the regulatory process. The result is likely to be growing and systematic ignorance about population groups whose circumstances may be precisely those about which we should at least want to be ignorant or who most need to have their voice articulated by reasonably disinterested advocates. White (2007), for example, notes the creativity with which ethical regulators may define 'vulnerable populations' in ways that justify their oversight role. He quotes Yan and Munir (2004, p. 45) on the consequences:

> The parens patriae doctrine by legal guardians and IRBs should not only work in the direction of protection by exclusion, but by protection through inclusion. Often the risks are minimal, and the arguments that such participants are unable to consent are overstated. Furthermore, the conflicts of commitment by IRBs also may inadvertently

prioritize institutional precautions and legal concern. ... As it stands, urgent action is needed as most children and individuals with DD [developmental disabilities] receive less mental health care, poorer quality of care, and are underrepresented in mental health research.

White (2007, p. 558) concludes

... board actions are not really aimed at protecting vulnerable research subjects from dangerous research, but at protecting vulnerable institutions from potential lawsuits and public-relations fiascos hastened by a growing cultural obsession with zero-risk lifestyles, an ever-drifting concept of harm, and growing regulatory tentacles.

Whole sectors of society may be abandoned to social scientists' competitors in social investigation and commentary – journalists, novelists, creative artists (Strong, 1983). All of these have important contributions to make – but each explores a topic in relation to their own motivations, interests and institutional location, which are different from those of the social scientist seeking generalisable and disinterested knowledge as a basis for improvement. Consider, for example, how an investigative journalist might write about the outrages of the taxi-dance hall and the thin boundary between this work and outright prostitution. Compare this with Cressey's sympathetic exploration of the co-production of a social organisation from the intersecting lives of low-income women and men with few opportunities to create other kinds of relationship. Which has more to contribute to the development of public policies that address causes rather than effects?

Finally, we should note the potential for the inhibition of innovation. For Shweder (2006) and others, research is a right and, in some contexts, a duty of academics, to go where others do not dare, and to bring back the results for the benefit of society. This is not a call for social irresponsibility or the creation of an ivory tower. Notice the emphasis, in the 1967 report that he quotes, on dissemination, well before the current fashion for 'impact'. This is all part of the same mission to discover and improve, wherever this may take a member of the university's faculty. By the end of the century, research has changed into an activity done under contracts with specified processes and outcomes. In United Kingdom, and European Union, funding, it is the language of 'deliverables'. Researchers are expected to describe in advance what they expect to find and to be evaluated on that basis. This is a recipe for incremental rather than breakthrough science. The conceptual knots in which some governments have tied themselves to promote the marketisation of research and higher education while delivering centrally planned outcomes deserve fuller treatment than they can receive here. However, the basic problems were identified many years ago by Hayek (2001) in *The Road*

to Serfdom, first published in 1944. Although the policy prescriptions are
less straightforward than some subsequent enthusiasts for this work
assumed, the diagnosis, reflecting the work on the social distribution of
knowledge for which he later won the Nobel Prize, raises critical questions
about many countries' direction of travel in research policy.

Essentially, Hayek's argument is that central planning can only ever be as
good as the judgement of the central planners and this is limited by their
capacity to handle information. As Hayek (1945) demonstrates, this is
achieved by coding devices, of which the most important is price.

> Fundamentally, in a system where the knowledge of the relevant facts is dispersed among
> many people, prices can act to coordinate the separate actions of different people in the
> same way as subjective values help the individual to coordinate the parts of his plan
> (Hayek, 1945, p. 526)

We do not need to know the entire history of the development, production and distribution of some good or service because this is all encoded
in the price we are asked to pay for it. Complex societies, and organisations,
can only function because such devices reduce the amount of information
that any actor is required to deal with. This is not a perfect system: it does
not deal well with issues of moral judgement; it may fail to internalise all the
externalities of a product or service; and it may conceal malpractice.
However, Hayek rightly describes it as a 'marvel' in the way that it can
spontaneously generate order by means that are much more flexible and
responsive to change than any form of central direction. It creates space for
innovation and incentives for this to take place. Under stress, however,
institutions tend to seek stability through centralisation and planning –
Hayek does not dispute its short-term value under the exceptional
conditions of wartime. This does, though, tend to be inimical to success
when revolutionary changes are happening (Tushman & O'Reilly, III, 1996).
The historically decentralised nature of universities, with faculty grouped in
small, relatively autonomous, production units in close proximity to their
distinctive markets is an evolved solution to the challenge of innovation very
much of the kind currently envisaged by leading management theorists.
There is a certain paradox in that the strengthening of central control, by
measures like ethical regulation, quality assurance, and research performance management is introducing the sort of corporate model that has
clearly failed to sustain and profit from innovation. One of the most
important arguments against ethical regulation may then relate to its place
in a wider structure of command and control that is actually inimical to one
of the most important institutional goals of a research-oriented university

system – if universities cease to generate revolutionary science, what is the point of universities?

DOES IT HAVE TO BE THIS WAY?

Advocates of ethical regulation tend to present this as an historical inevitability. All countries will, and should, adopt this practice. There are certainly strong pressures within the biomedical sciences to achieve this goal, from international research funders, regulatory agencies, international organisations and associations of scientific journal editors and scientific publishers. Implementation is, however, subject to a continuing degree of national variation – ethical review of biomedical research in France, for example, remains much more professionally dominated than the IRB system in the United States. Social science research in healthcare has been sucked into this system, although the leading journals vary in their demands for evidence of prior review and it is still feasible to carry out unfunded research and publish it without becoming entangled with the regulatory system. This reflects the weak international organisation of the social sciences and the persistence of national traditions. Although ethical regulation has penetrated the countries that have the greatest contact with the United States, and there are discussions at the European Commission about trying to compel universities to introduce such processes as a condition of funding, major players in social science like France, Germany and Italy have made no moves to adopt such controls.

French sociologists have discussed possible mechanisms for strengthening professional codes but have been reluctant to create a system that might lead to the imposition of any particular intellectual hegemony. Indeed, this is a common anxiety in European countries, reflecting the sectarian struggles of the 1960s between various Marxist and non-Marxist groups within the universities and the intellectual crises that followed the collapse of the revolutionary movements of 1968. German social scientists have suggested that the strong guarantees of academic freedom in their national constitution – designed to block the kind of political interventions that characterised both the fascist regime of the 1930s and 1940s and the communist regime in East Germany until 1989 – would make it legally impossible to regulate their research in this way. This may be an excessively optimistic view but it would certainly form a basis for mobilisation if such proposals were mooted. A number of post-communist constitutions in Eastern and Central Europe entrench similar guarantees for similar reasons.

Italian universities face such a wide range of organisational challenges that ethical regulation does not seem to be high on anyone's list of priorities, particularly given the strong traditions of professorial autonomy. There is no good evidence that any of these countries are conducting social science research in a less ethical fashion than is the case in the Anglo-Saxon world, although it is probably fair to say that there is more self-consciousness in postgraduate training about the need for explicit ethical discussion than would have been the case, say, 30 years ago.

If there are alternatives to the US model, what are the prospects of them being adopted elsewhere? There are now powerful interests vested in the present regulatory system. It has created a substantial administrative bureaucracy with its own supporting associations and lobbies. It is culturally integrated with the growth of managerialism and corporatism within universities. It is wrapped in a powerful origin myth which de-legitimises critics as amoral and self-interested dinosaurs. Nevertheless, there are serious objections. There is a lack of evidence on the proportionality of the costs of regulation to the benefits achieved. There are indications that the consequences will be socially damaging in the promotion of ignorance about important social issues, or the abandonment of investigations to people outside the academy whose particular motives and voices will go unquestioned and unchallenged by the disciplined evidence-gathering of the social sciences. Finally, there must be concern that ethical regulation is merely a symptom of a more general shift to organisational practices that undermine the very reasons for the existence of universities.

Truly, the road to hell is paved with good intentions.

NOTE

1. Questions have subsequently been raised about whether Humphreys could have acted as a lookout or whether he was, in fact, a participant in the acts he described (Galliher, Brekhus, & Keys, 2004). However, the ethical debate has always focussed on his published account of his role in the setting, although there might be other issues to explore if he had been a more central agent in the setting.

ACKNOWLEDGEMENT

I am grateful to Zachary Schrag for his comments and corrections. Any remaining errors are mine.

REFERENCES

Annas, G. J., & Grodin, M. A. (Eds.). (1995). *The Nazi doctors and the Nuremberg code: Human rights in human experimentation*. New York, NY: Oxford University Press.

Baumrind, D. (1964). Some thoughts on ethics of research: After reading Milgram's 'Behavioral Study of Obedience'. *American Psychologist, 19,* 421–423.

Beecher, H. K. (1959). *Experimentation on man*. Springfield, IL: Thomas.

Beecher, H. K. (1966). Ethics and clinical research. *New England Journal of Medicine, 274,* 1354–1360.

Benatar, S. (1997). Just healthcare beyond individualism: Challenges for North American bioethics. *Cambridge Quarterly of Healthcare Ethics, 6,* 397–415.

Boelen, W. A. M. (1992). Street Corner Society. *Journal of Contemporary Ethnography, 21,* 11–51.

Buss, A. H. (1961). *The psychology of aggression*. New York, NY: Wiley.

Cain, M. E. (1983). The general practice lawyer and the client: Towards a radical conception. In R. Dingwall & P. S. C. Lewis (Eds.), *The sociology of the professions: Lawyers, doctors and others* (pp. 106–130). London: MacMillan Press.

Coser, L. (1959). Participant observation and the military: An exchange 'A question of professional ethics?'. *American Sociological Review, 24,* 397–400.

Cressey, P. G. (2008). *The taxi-dance hall: A sociological study in commercialized recreation and city life* (new ed.). Chicago, IL: University of Chicago Press.

DiMaggio, P. J., & Powell, W. W. (1983). The iron cage revisited: Institutional isomorphism and collective rationality in organizational fields. *American Sociological Review, 48,* 147–160.

Dingwall, R. (1999). Professions and social order in a global society. *International Review of Sociology, 9,* 131–140.

Dingwall, R. (2008). The ethical case against ethical regulation in humanities and social science research. *Twenty-First Century Society, 3,* 1–12.

Dingwall, R., & Fenn, P. (1987). 'A Respectable Profession'? Sociological and economic perspectives on the regulation of professional services. *International Review of Law and Economics, 7,* 51–64.

Dingwall, R., & Rozelle, V. (2011). The ethical governance of German physicians, 1890–1939: Are there lessons from history? *Journal of Policy History, 23,* 29–52.

Eliade, M. (2005). *The myth of the eternal return*. Princeton, NJ: Princeton University Press.

Elliott, C. (2004). Six problems with pharma-funded bioethics. *Studies in History and Philosophy of Science. Part C: Studies in History and Philosophy of Biological and Biomedical Sciences, 35,* 125–129.

Elliott, C. (2005). The soul of a new machine: Bioethicists in the bureaucracy. *Cambridge Quarterly of Healthcare Ethics, 14,* 379–384.

Elliott, C. (2010). *White coat, black hat: Adventures on the dark side of medicine*. Boston, MA: Beacon Press.

Erikson, K. T. (1967). A comment on disguised observation in sociology. *Social Problems, 14,* 366–373.

Feeley, M. M. (2007). Legality, social research, and the challenge of Institutional Review Boards. *Law & Society Review, 41,* 757–776.

Gaines, A. D., & Juengst, E. T. (2008). Origin myths in bioethics: Constructing sources, motives and reason in bioethic(s). *Culture, Medicine, and Psychiatry, 32,* 303–327.

Galliher, J. F., Brekhus, W. H., & Keys, D. P. (2004). *Laud Humphreys: Prophet of homosexuality and sociology*. Madison, WI: University of Wisconsin Press.

Ginsberg, B. (2011). *The fall of the faculty: The rise of the all-administrative university and why it matters*. New York, NY: Oxford University Press.

Goffman, E. (1968). *Asylums: Essays on the social situation of mental patients and other inmates*. Harmondsworth: Penguin.

Halpern, S. (2004). *Lesser harms: The morality of risk in medical research*. Chicago, IL: University of Chicago Press.

Hamburger, P. (2004). New censorship: Institutional review boards. *The Supreme Court Review*, *2004*, 271–354.

Hamburger, P. (2007). Getting permission. *Northwestern University Law Review*, *101*, 405–492.

Hayek, F. A. (1945). The use of knowledge in society. *The American Economic Review*, *35*, 519–530.

Hayek, F. A. (2001). *The road to serfdom* (2nd ed.). London: Routledge.

Hazelgrove, J. (2002). The old faith and the new science: The Nuremburg code and human experimentation ethics in Britain 1946–73. *Social History of Medicine*, *15*, 109–136.

Hedgecoe, A. (2008). Research ethics review and the sociological research relationship. *Sociology*, *42*, 873–886.

Hedgecoe, A. (2009). 'A form of practical machinery': The origins of Research Ethics committees in the UK, 1967–1972. *Medical History*, *53*, 331–350.

Horowitz, I. L. (1967). *The rise and fall of project camelot: Studies in the relationship between social science and practical politics*. Cambridge, MA: MIT Press.

Humphreys, L. (1975). *Tearoom trade: Impersonal sex in public places*. New York, NY: Aldine de Gruyter.

Humphreys, L. (1980). Social science: Ethics of research. *Science*, *207*(4432), 712–714.

Israel, M., & Hay, I. (2006). *Research ethics for social scientists*. London: Sage.

Jones, J. H. (1981). *Bad blood: Tuskegee syphilis experiment*. New York, NY: Free Press.

Kuper, A. (1996). *Anthropology and anthropologists: The modern British school* (3rd ed.). London: Routledge.

Milgram, S. (1963). Behavioral study of obedience. *The Journal of Abnormal and Social Psychology*, *67*, 371–378.

Milgram, S. (1974). *Obedience to authority: An experimental view*. New York, NY: Harper & Row.

Murphy, E., & Dingwall, R. (2007). Informed consent, anticipatory regulation and ethnographic practice. *Social Science & Medicine*, *65*, 2223–2234.

Novick, P. (1999). *The holocaust in American life*. New York, NY: Houghton Miflin.

Pappworth, M. H. (1962). Human guinea pigs: A warning. *Twentieth Century* (171), 66–75.

Pappworth, M. H. (1967). *Human guinea pigs: Experimentation on man*. London: Routledge.

Price, D. H. (2004). *Threatening anthropology: McCarthyism and the FBI's surveillance of activist anthropologists*. Durham, NC: Duke University Press.

Price, D. H. (2008). *Anthropological intelligence: The deployment and neglect of American anthropology in the Second World War*. Durham, NC: Duke University Press.

Price, D. H. (2011). *Weaponizing anthropology: Social science in service of the militarized state* (reprint). Oakland, CA: AK Press.

Reverby, S. M. (2009). *Examining Tuskegee: The infamous syphilis study and its legacy*. Chapel Hill, NC: University of North Carolina Press.

Reverby, S. M. (2011). 'Normal exposure' and inoculation syphilis: A PHS 'Tuskegee' doctor in Guatemala, 1946–1948. *Journal of Policy History*, *23*, 6–28.

Roth, J. A. (1963). *Timetables: Structuring the passage of time in hospital treatment and other careers.* Indianapolis, IN: Bobbs-Merrill.

Rothman, D. J. (2003). *Strangers at the bedside: A history of how law and bioethics transformed medical decision making.* New York, NY: Aldine de Gruyter.

Savage, M., Bradley, H., & Smith, D. (2011). Symposium on the ESRC, BSA, and HAPS international benchmarking review of UK sociology. *The Sociological Review*, *59*, 149–164.

Schrag, Z. M. (2010). *Ethical imperialism: Institutional review boards and the social sciences 1965–2009.* Baltimore, MD: Johns Hopkins University Press.

Shaw, C. R. (1966). *The Jack-Roller: A delinquent boy's own story.* Chicago, IL: University of Chicago Press.

Shweder, R. A. (2004). Tuskegee re-examined. *Spiked.* Retrieved from http://www.spiked-online.com/articles/0000000CA34A.htm

Shweder, R. A. (2006). Protecting human subjects and preserving academic freedom: Prospects at the University of Chicago. *American Ethnologist*, *33*, 507–518.

Silberman, G., & Kahn, K. L. (2011). Burdens on research imposed by institutional review boards: The state of the evidence and its implications for regulatory reform. *Milbank Quarterly*, *89*, 599–627.

Silbey, J. M. (2008). The mythical beginnings of intellectual property. *George Mason Law Review*, *15*, 319–379.

Sjoberg, G., & Sjoberg, G. (1969). Project Camelot: Selected reactions and personal reflections. In *Ethics, politics and social research* (pp. 141–161). London: Routledge and Kegan Paul.

Snodgrass, J. (1983). The Jack-Roller. *Journal of Contemporary Ethnography*, *11*, 440–460.

Stark, L. (2012). *Behind closed doors: IRBs and the making of ethical research.* Chicago, IL: University of Chicago Press.

Strong, P. M. (1983). The rivals: an essay on the sociological trades. In R. Dingwall & P. S. C. Lewis (Eds.), *The sociology of the professions: Lawyers, doctors and others* (pp. 59–77). London: Macmillan.

Sullivan, M. A., Queen, S. A., & Patrick, R. C. (1958). Participant observation as employed in the study of a military training program. *American Sociological Review*, *23*, 660–667.

Tuchman, G. (2011). *Wannabe U: Inside the corporate university.* Chicago, IL: University of Chicago Press.

Tudor, H. (1972). *Political myth.* New York, NY: Praeger.

Tushman, M. L., & O'Reilly, C. A., III. (1996). The ambidextrous organization: Managing evolutionary and revolutionary change. *California Management Review*, *38*, 8–30.

van den Hoonard, W. (2011). *The seduction of ethics: Transforming the social sciences.* Toronto, ON: University of Toronto Press.

Walter, M. (2012). Human experiments: First, do harm. *Nature*, *482*(7384), 148–152.

White, R. F. (2007). Institutional review board mission creep: The common rule, social science, and the nanny state. *The Independent Review*, *11*, 547–564.

Whitney, S. N., & Schneider, C. E. (2011). Viewpoint: A method to estimate the cost in lives of ethics board review of biomedical research. *Journal of Internal Medicine*, *269*, 396–402.

Whittaker, E. W., & Olesen, V. L. (1964). The faces of Florence nightingale; functions of the heroine legend in an occupational sub-culture. *Human Organization*, *23*, 123–130.

Whyte, W. F. (1992). In defense of street corner society. *Journal of Contemporary Ethnography*, *21*, 52–68.

Whyte, W. F. (1993). *Street corner society: Social structure of an Italian slum* (4th revised ed.). Chicago, IL: University of Chicago Press.

Yan, E. G., & Munir, K. M. (2004). Regulatory and ethical principles in research involving children and individuals with developmental disabilities. *Ethics & Behavior*, *14*, 31–49.

Zimbardo, P. (2008). *The Lucifer effect: How good people turn evil*. New York, NY: Random House.

KNOWLEDGE AND ITS INTEGRITY WITHIN A KNOWLEDGE ECONOMY: ETHICS AND WISE SOCIAL RESEARCH

John Harrison and David Rooney

ABSTRACT

Purpose – *The purpose of this chapter is to discuss the roles of ethics and wisdom in knowledge economies and specifically the place of ethics and wisdom in social research in knowledge economies.*

Approach – *It does this through examining traditional theories of ethics, their application in the context of research ethics, and the origins of the current institutional ethics approval regimes. The limitations of consequentialist and deontological approaches to ethics in social research are articulated, as is the rise of neo Aristotelian virtue ethics – to which wisdom is integral. Questions are posed about several high-profile cases of past social research, and the extent to which these might be considered both unethical and unwise. Attention is then given to the place of wisdom in the practice of social research. Aristotle presents practical wisdom as an executive virtue that coherently integrates intellectual and ethical virtues to create deliberative excellence.*

Ethics in Social Research
Studies in Qualitative Methodology, Volume 12, 27–50
ISSN: 1042-3192/doi:10.1108/S1042-3192(2012)0000012005

Findings – *Practical wisdom is thus seen as a way of performing as an educated, skilled, and ethical social actor with carefully constructed predispositions which automatically seek excellence and well-being. Furthermore, a wise social researcher considers the needs of others carefully to try to find the right thing to do, but in understanding others emotionally, intellectually, or otherwise, is not manipulative. The conclusion poses the question as to how practical wisdom might be developed applied to the practices of contemporary social research.*

Keywords: Research ethics; social science; human subjects; regulation; innovation; knowledge

Integrity without knowledge is weak and useless, and knowledge without integrity is dangerous and dreadful.

Samuel Johnson

This quote from Samuel Johnson could have been pointing towards the role of wisdom and ethics in research and knowledge economies by linking knowledge to the integrity of outcomes. Very little has been said about the roles of ethics and wisdom in knowledge economies (Rooney, McKenna, & Liesch, 2010), and even less has been said about the place of ethics in research in knowledge economies. Van Loon (2005) has noted that there is an inward spiral of knowledge production in that every time new knowledge opens our eyes to new understandings of reality, it also makes us more aware of our ignorance. He argues further that this continual exposure to the depths of ignorance creates a climate of anxiety. The circuit breaker for this spiral is not more knowledge, but greater wisdom. We also argue that it is the social sciences (including humanities and economic research) that must take the lead in developing understanding of how to make knowledge production (and consumption) more wise, and by extension, more ethical.

But why focus on social research? One reason is that knowledge economies are heavily dependent on services sector innovation. Creative industries, well-being professions, law firms, the finance sector, and other sectors that draw on social research to innovate, are more economically important now than ever (Howells, 2001; Miles, 2008; Rooney & Mandeville, 1998). A second and related reason is that some now argue that developed economies are increasingly understood to rely on the development of equality and fairness rather than technology and Gross Domestic Product growth to increase well-being and quality of life (Engelbrecht, 2007; Wilkinson & Pickett, 2009). Social research directly influences equality through its contribution to fields of practice such as human rights law, equal opportunity employment, social inclusion policy, anti-discrimination policy, social welfare policy, child protection, welfare economics, education, and so on. In an age in which evidence-based public policy is a growing phenomenon, ethical social research takes on greater importance.

This chapter has four elements. First, we provide an overview of the major philosophical theories of ethics. Second, we discuss the role of ethics in contemporary life as rights and responsibilities, and law and justice. Third, we set out the application of ethics in contemporary social research. Finally, we explore the explicit tensions and challenges created for a research ethics practice that is backed by a wisdom-informed view that also considers institutional issues.

FOUNDATIONAL THEORIES OF ETHICS

The intellectual history of the West has produced three principal philosophical theories of ethics: *virtue ethics, consequentialism* and *deontology*. Each of these theoretical approaches has influenced ethics in social research. Of these, deontology, the theory based on principles, duties and rights, has had the strongest institutional influence on ethics in social research.

Virtue Ethics

Moral virtues are centrally about values such as honesty, integrity, empathy, good judgement and a sense of social responsibility. Importantly, Aristotle distinguished between intellectual virtues and moral virtues; he identified intelligence, practical wisdom, understanding and good sense as intellectual virtues. Alasdair MacIntyre says virtues are 'dispositions not only to act in particular ways, but also to feel in particular ways' (1984, pp. 149–150). Dispositions, in this formulation, are habits. Thus, a virtuous person is habituated to *act* and *feel* in particular ways. Moral virtue, therefore, is a state of being and doing, developed in the course of living one's life; that is, through experience, rather than through conscious, rational, cognitive decision-making processes. Furthermore, as Mintz says, 'Virtues are acquired human qualities, the excellences of character, which enable a person to achieve the good life' (1996, p. 827).

Three important points emerge here. First, virtues are *acquired* human qualities. How are they acquired? Aristotle believed that virtues were habits acquired by experience. Second, virtues are *excellences* of character. Such excellences (Gr: *arete*) are achieved by seeking the middle way, not the extremes of action and feeling. Finally, virtues enable the individual to achieve *the good life*. Here we come back again to the ancient Greek concept of 'human flourishing', 'happiness', 'pleasure' or the 'good life' (Gr: *eudaimonia*). Unlike utilitarianism, which seeks the greatest good for the greatest number, seeking virtue provides the good life for the individual.

Aristotle's approach to ethics is very much a middle-way approach, one that weighs and balances decisions and actions. Fig. 1 is a representation of Aristotle's doctrine of the mean that guides this balancing act between the cardinal virtues.

Virtue, then, works in the space between two equally undesirable outcomes: one an excess, the other a deficit. Thus, between cowardice and rashness is courage. Aristotle says in *Nichomachean Ethics* (Aristotle, trans. 1908, II: IV):

> With regard to giving and taking money the mean is liberality, the excess and the defect prodigality and meanness. In actions people exceed and fall short in contrary ways; the prodigal exceeds in spending and falls short in taking, while the mean man exceeds in taking and falls short in spending ...
> With regard to money there are also other dispositions – a mean, magnificence ... an excess, tastelessness and vulgarity, and a deficiency, niggardliness; these differ from the states opposed to liberality. With regard to honour and dishonour the mean is proper pride, the excess is known as a sort of 'empty vanity', and the deficiency is undue humility.

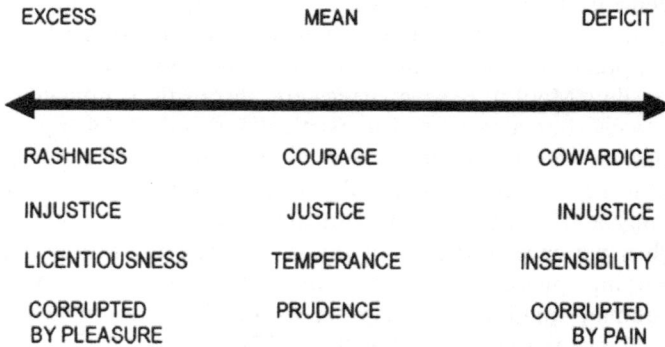

EXCESS	MEAN	DEFICIT
RASHNESS	COURAGE	COWARDICE
INJUSTICE	JUSTICE	INJUSTICE
LICENTIOUSNESS	TEMPERANCE	INSENSIBILITY
CORRUPTED BY PLEASURE	PRUDENCE	CORRUPTED BY PAIN

Fig. 1. Artistotle's Virtues and the Doctrine of the Mean.

What is also important for Aristotle is the teleological emphasis on virtue to achieve *eudaimonia* (the good life, human flourishing, well-being). Virtue is not just a social practice, but also one that aims specifically for the long-term good of society.

Adam Smith (1723–1790) was the philosopher whose ideas became important elements of modern capitalist thought. He studied Aristotle and was influenced by virtue ethics, which is central to his *Theory of Moral Sentiments* that precedes his famous work on economics, *The Wealth of Nations*. Smith valorised the principal virtues: *self-command* (an individual virtue) and *justice* (a social virtue). Self-command combines Aristotle's courage and temperance, and its consequent virtue, prudence. Justice, says Smith, is the glue that prevents a society descending into anarchy. Smith was also concerned with another virtue, *universal benevolence*, a virtue which, 'while not an imperative virtue, reflects the character of the benevolent and all wise Being, who directs all the movements of nature' (in Calkins & Werhane, 1998, p. 54). Commerce and trade is impossible without human interaction. For this interaction to occur in a 'parsimonious' way, justice is essential so that commercial interaction is conducted fairly; injustice hinders commercial progress (Calkins & Werhane, 1998, p. 56). Smith is also famous in economics for his notion of the invisible hand. This is the hand of justice and it is central to his theory of economic behaviour. It is useful to note that contemporary neo-liberal economic theory claims Smith as its intellectual originator, but Smith would abhor neo-liberalism's absolute denial of the importance of virtue and ethicality. What is true of Smith, though, is that he does not accept Aristotle's *eudemonic* teleology. According to Smith, we act virtuously for rewards – not necessarily financial rewards – and the utility those rewards provide.

Weakness of Aristotelian Virtue Ethics
Aristotle's concept of virtue ethics is dependent on the good character of individuals, but what if some, even many, people are not of good character? There is relativism in virtue ethics that requires people to have good judgement. But who can always make good judgements, particularly under the stresses of contemporary life? As MacIntyre says, 'The virtues ... are necessary if practitioners are to defend internal goods against corruption by the institutionalized pursuit of external goods' (Knight, 2009, p. 117), and who is totally immune from this institutional corruption? Furthermore, Bauman (2000) asks if Aristotle's four cardinal virtues are sufficient for a world characterised by 'liquid modernity'?

Consequentialism

The concept of consequentialist ethics is based on outcomes. Consequentialism in its simplest explanation is concerned with the consequences of actions and ultimate goals. Consequentialists assess the rightness of an action only in relation to the consequences or outcomes it produces. In consequentialism, there are three main theories: egoism, altruism and utilitarianism. The origins of egoism and altruism are ancient, and egoism has similarities with modern libertarian and neo-liberal philosophies; however, utilitarianism is the most commonly applied consequentialist theory.

Utilitarianism begins with the premise that all human beings seek happiness and that ethical actors seek the greatest good for the greatest number. Jeremy Bentham saw utilitarianism as based on the principle of utility, which he defined as:

> [T]hat principle which approves or disapproves of every action whatsoever, according to the tendency it appears to have to augment or diminish the happiness of the party whose interest is in question: or, what is the same thing in other words to promote or to oppose that happiness. I say of every action whatsoever, and therefore not only of every action of a private individual, but of every measure of government. (Bentham & Bowring, 1843, I: II)

Moreover, Bentham argues that:

> An action then may be said to be conformable to the principle of utility, or, for shortness sake, to utility (meaning with respect to the community at large) when the tendency it has to augment the happiness of the community is greater than any it has to diminish it. (Bentham, 1823, I: II)

Rather naively, Bentham argued that utility or happiness should be measured using a moral–mathematical calculation of pleasure and pain. In doing so, one could accurately tell what was a right or a wrong action. This utility calculus involved notions of: intensity; duration; certainty; propinquity (proximity); fecundity (the chance that a pleasure is followed by other ones, a pain by further pains); purity (the chance that pleasure is followed by pains and vice versa); and extent (the number of persons affected) (Bentham & Bowring, 1843, I: IV). Bentham's disciple John Stuart Mill (1806–1873) dispensed with Bentham's utility calculus as unworkable, but reasserted the egalitarian character of utilitarianism in that the views and interests of all, irrespective of location, class, religion, race, or gender, are considered as part of the whole. The difference between Bentham and Mill is that while Bentham treated pleasure as the desired consequence, Mill focused on the quality or value of the outcome or consequences, so that some pleasures were more desirable than others.

Utilitarian versions of consequentialism have many recent variations. The attraction of utilitarianism is that it provides a simple principle for making decisions and producing the greatest balance of pleasure over pain for everyone – and it purports to be democratic. Critics of utilitarianism say that it is not democratic but majoritarian; that is, it is based on the interests of the majority and prejudices the interests of minorities. Therefore, utilitarianism is predisposed towards an outcome that is likely to be popular rather than right and just. Like egoism, utilitarianism needs to be tempered by deontological and virtue approaches to protect the position of minorities. It is arguable that certain research outcomes, particularly in public health research, advance the health and well-being of the majority, and that despite deleterious consequences for a minority, the outcomes of such research should become public policy. Immunisation against diseases such as small-pox, diphtheria, cholera and tetanus are examples of such.

Institutional ethics committees (IECs) have addressed such possibilities by mandating the reporting of adverse events. Regulatory authorities, such as the Food and Drug Administration (FDA) in the United States and the Therapeutic Goods Administration (TGA) in Australia, require extensive clinical trials, disclosure of potential conflicts of interest between researchers and funding sources, and warnings of potential adverse effects as part of the general use approval of new therapeutic agents. While this contestation is not as acute in social research as it is in scientific research, there are quite clearly challenges in both the approval and dissemination of social research, not least of which is the almost limitless capacity of interest groups and the mass media to create moral panics based on (mis)readings of research data. Criminology, political science, cultural studies, industrial relations, issues management in professional communication and language studies are some of the fields of social research that are especially vulnerable.

Deontology

The central concern of deontology is duty; understandings and choices about what is right and wrong are determined by duty to ourselves and to others. Being ethical is linked to the roles that each of us is required to fulfil because of our position. The three principles underpinning deontology are duty (or responsibility), rights and justice.

We examine two widely recognised approaches to duty: the classical theory of duty based on Immanuel Kant's principle of Categorical

Imperatives, and W.D. Ross's idea that there exists a prima facie moral duty. Kant's reason-based theory of duty focuses on moral obligation determined from the exercise of reason. Starting with the question 'What ought I do?' Kant developed a major principle of moral reasoning, which he called the Categorical Imperative. The first formulation of the imperative can be stated as: 'Act as if ... your action were to become ... a universal law of nature' (Kant, trans. 1895, p. 48). This is the principle of universalisability, the notion that an action is only right if it can be made universal and reciprocal. The second formulation is about respect for people. This principle is best understood as 'treat people as ends not means'.

W.D. Ross based his theory of duty on a critique of utilitarianism. Ross argued that an action that produces the maximum good is not necessarily right and that good is promoted by certain self-evident duties, which he calls *prima facie duties*. These duties, argues Ross, are as axiomatic as the laws of mathematics. The prima facie duties are those of *fidelity*, *reparation*, *gratitude*, *justice*, *beneficence*, *self-improvement* and *malfeasance* (see Table 1).

These prima facie duties are founded on morally significant relationships, such as parent–child, friend–friend, employer–employee and creditor–debtor relationships. While the application of each of the duties depends on the situation, Ross argues that the duty of malfeasance – of not harming others – is the primary duty. He writes, 'We should not in general consider it justifiable to kill one person in order to keep another alive, or to steal from one in order to give alms to another' (Ross, 1930, p. 22). A reading of these duties provides insight into how the principles expressed in codes of professional ethics are developed.

Table 1.   Prima Facie Duties after Ross (1930, p. 21).

Duty	Description
Fidelity	A duty based on a promise
Reparation	A duty arising from a previous wrongful act
Gratitude	A duty arising from previous acts of charity or service
Justice	A duty arising from the redistribution of pleasure or happiness according to merit
Beneficence	A duty to improve the lot of others with respect to virtue, intelligence or pleasure
Self-improvement	Our duty to improve ourselves with respect to virtue, intelligence or pleasure
Malfeasance	A duty not to injure others

In sum, duty is the responsibility to act in accordance with certain universal principles: universalisability and respect for others in the case of Kant's Categorical Imperative, or in prima facie duty in the case of Ross.

Rights and Responsibilities, Law and Justice
Notions of rights are deeply embedded in our culture and legal system. The conflict of competing rights – crudely put as the right of an individual to privacy in the face of the public's right to know – is often at the core of ethical dilemmas faced by media and communication professionals. The ideas of rights, and particularly of natural rights, originated from the idea of natural law. According to the principles of natural law, there is a definable natural order to the world. The basic principle of natural law was 'we ought to do good and not evil', a principle with which Kant's Categorical Imperative resonates. The idea of natural law had itself given birth to the notion of natural rights. Rights are entitlements to be, and to act, without interference from others, or entitlements that oblige others to act positively to assist you. More recently, rights not only are universal, but also include situation-specific rights such as civil rights and legal rights that belong to those living in a particular legal jurisdiction.

In general terms, any discussion of rights recognises the existence of at least two different sorts of rights: negative rights and positive rights. Negative rights are those rights that require others to restrain from action. For example, to exercise rights such as freedom of speech, assembly and worship, others have to refrain from actions such as violence and intimidation, which might impinge on those rights. Others must also refrain from passing and enforcing laws that proscribe any of those rights. Positive rights can only be exercised if others undertake a positive action to allow this. For example, the right to education and healthcare requires positive actions by individuals and the community to provide the opportunity to access those services.

The contemporary world has seen the widespread embedding of rights into the legal and constitutional fabric of democratic communities. In December 1948, the newly formed United Nations agreed on a Universal Declaration of Human Rights, which spoke of the 'inherent dignity and of the equal and inalienable rights of all members of the human family [which] is the foundation of freedom, justice and peace in the world' (United Nations, n.d.).

Thus, the twentieth-century saw the universalisation of rights and their expansion to groups not previously perceived to have rights, or who were previously denied their rights: women, children, indigenous peoples, people with disabilities and the unborn.

Yet the notion of rights as the fundamental principle underlying social relations has not been without its critics, both philosophical and political. For the utilitarians such as Jeremy Bentham the idea that rights could be a starting point for the construction of a political theory was 'wild and pernicious nonsense' (Bentham & Bowring, 1843, p. 491). For Karl Marx, rights were a manifestation of individual egoism. He wrote, 'None of the so-called rights of man goes beyond egoistic man ... an individual withdrawn behind his private interests and whims and separated from the community' (Marx & McLellan, 1977, p. 54).

There have been two schools of opposition to the rights-based society. The first argues that rights do not need to be abandoned, but must be balanced by responsibilities. In her critique, *Rights Talk: The Impoverishment of Political Discourse*, Mary Ann Glendon writes of the legalistic character, exaggerated absoluteness, hyperindividualism, insularity, and silence with respect to personal, civic and collective responsibilities within the current discourse on rights (Glendon, 1991, p. x). The second oppositional argument is that asserting the rights of individuals can place at risk the greater good of the wider community, which is a utilitarian argument. Amartya Sen (b. 1935), winner of the 1998 Nobel Prize for Economics, identified a fundamental flaw in the argument that collective decisions can preserve individual rights. Sen asserts that to produce justice, there must be a balance between responsibility and rights.

Justice is a concept that means not only doing what is right (that is, acting with justice), but doing so with fairness and equity, respecting the interests of all parties. Justice comes in a number of forms: retributive, compensatory, procedural and distributive. Retributive justice is based on the idea of punishment for wrongdoing, for example, the ancient principle of 'an eye for an eye'. The use of imprisonment and the death penalty in the criminal justice system are examples of retributive justice. Compensatory justice is about providing compensation to atone for wrongdoing. The concept of damages in civil law is an example of compensatory justice at work. Procedural justice is the notion that the process of dispensing justice has to be fair and transparent, which leads to principles such as the presumption of innocence, the right to representation, and the right to appeal a decision. Distributive justice is all about the allocation of resources, raising questions about scarcity and equality of opportunity, and the ethics of benefit from distributive justice.

Discontent with the imperfections of utilitarianism in a democratic society led John Rawls (1921–2002) to develop a theory of distributive justice consistent with the principles of the liberal democratic state. First published in 1971, Rawls' *A Theory of Justice* had a wide social impact and it argued that he provided a philosophical foundation for the welfare state. Underlying Rawls's theory is the idea of a social contract that draws from Locke, Rousseau and Kant. The basic idea of Rawls's approach to justice, which he defines as fairness, is that:

> All social primary goods – liberty and opportunity, income and wealth, and the bases of self-respect – are to be distributed equally unless an unequal distribution of any or all of these goods is to the advantage of the least favoured. (Rawls, 1973, pp. 60–62)

Rawls has reduced his statement of justice to two principles: the first is that each person has an equal right to liberty so long as that liberty or system of liberties is equally available to all; and the second argues the priority of justice over both efficiency and welfare. Rawls posits that social and economic inequalities must provide the greatest benefit to the least advantaged, and can only be justified if they advantage the most disadvantaged. For Rawls, liberty is more important than justice is, and the principles are not intended to be applied to the making of specific ethical decisions, but to social structures.

Sen has addressed both the theory and practice of distributive justice. He contends that while ethical theory assumes equality among individuals, the capacity of individuals to exercise that equality is in fact unequal. So while Rawls argues for an equality of opportunity, Sen argues for the development of an equality of capability. This differs from equality of opportunity, in that the equality of opportunity means little if the individual does not have the capacity to avail themselves of the opportunity. Sen does recognise that some individuals make decisions that influence or determine their subsequent capacities. So for Sen, the function of distributive justice is to develop the capacity of individuals to take advantage of equality of opportunity (Sen, 2009).

Nozick argues that Rawls's theory of justice treats people's natural talents as social resources. According to Nozick, this violates Locke's notion of the ownership of property, that a person was entitled to the ownership of the fruit of his or her labour. In addition, Nozick says Rawls violates Kant's Categorical Imperative in relation to respect for people: by treating people's natural talents as social resources, they are being treated as a means to an end, and not as an end in their own right. Consistent with libertarian principles, Nozick argues for a minimalist state; he says that because the state maintains a monopoly on the use of force and the protection of those within its territory, the state violates the rights of individuals, and 'hence is intrinsically immoral' (Nozick, 1974, p. xi). To counter the notions of distributive justice promoted by Rawls, Nozick develops what he terms an entitlement theory, which permits the re-distribution of resources under certain defined circumstances, such as rectification of the effects of theft.

What is ethical, good and right, and how to achieve it, is contested, often guided by ideological commitments. But where does this leave social research ethics?

APPLIED ETHICS IN RESEARCH

The application of deontological ethics is most clearly seen in the development of behavioural codes such as codes of ethics, codes of conduct, and codes of practice, including those that regulate research ethics. Such codes set down the duties of those who are subject to the codes, the principles guiding their actions (such as honesty, integrity and fairness), and sometimes, the rules through which those duties and principles are given effect. Those duties and principles, however, are not a modern idea, but have been developed over millennia; the commands in the ancient Scriptures contain the genesis of our contemporary codifications of our responsibilities to others.

In the application of deontological approaches to ethics not just in social research, but also more broadly in scientific research, two principles are foundational: first, the duty of the researcher to treat the subject as the researcher would wish to be treated; and second, historically more recent development of the notion of rights. This second principle means that the research subject has rights, and in particular, the right to be properly and adequately informed about the nature, impact and outcomes of the research and to consent to participation in the research.

In the context of IEC approvals for research projects, the application of this second principle has become problematic in relation to securing informed consent from vulnerable human populations. Minors, potential subjects with permanent or temporary cognitive impairment, potential subjects in emergency medicine research who are not conscious, the unborn, indigenous populations, in fact any population for whom an ordinary lay description of the proposed research is inadequate or insufficient to obtain their consent can be deemed to fall into this category of vulnerable subjects. The not always satisfactory solution to this problem has been for IECs to more closely scrutinise research that involves vulnerable populations, to have enhanced protocols for particular classes of subjects, and to require more detailed information from researchers in their applications about research involving vulnerable populations. This solution depends on the integrity of the researcher and the vigilance and diligence of the members of the IEC. It depends, effectively, on the members of the IEC having dispositions of character that make them alert to injustice, imprudence, or rashness on the part of the researchers whose activities they are sanctioning.

THE ORIGINS OF CURRENT RESEARCH ETHICS MANAGEMENT REGIMES

Evidence to the Nuremburg war crimes trials about medical experiments on humans in Nazi Germany saw a concerted attempt after the war to regulate medical and scientific research using human subjects, and subsequently, animals. The Nuremberg Code of 1947 was a general statement of principles governing medical research, such as informed consent, research design, and public benefit (NIH, n.d.).

These principles were the basis for the World Medical Association's Geneva Declaration of 1948 (subsequently revised in 1968, 1984, 1994, 2005 and 2006) and the Helsinki Declaration of 1964 (amended in 1975, 1983, 1989, 1996, 2000 and 2008), which focused on clinical research protocols. The Helsinki Declaration thus became the foundation for legislated research ethics regimes in national jurisdictions (WMA, n.d.).

The proliferation of IECs to ensure compliance with statutory require-ments for clinical research saw a diminution of the functions of pre-existing ethics committees in healthcare settings. This affected the ethics education of staff as well as the institutional policies and protocols relating to issues such as the end of life, and subsequently, the beginning of life. That is to say, compliance with clinical research protocols took precedence over the processes of moral reasoning surrounding issues of clinical practice such as the point of brain death (a central question for transplant surgery), the implementation of 'do not resuscitate' requests, palliative care regimes and the ethicality of various forms of human fertility treatment. Arguably, discussions about these clinical practices were about the wisdom of fol-lowing, or not following, particular clinical pathways (DeRenzo, Silverman, Hoffmann, Schwartz, & Vinicky, 2001). It is important to consider the reasons for devaluing moral reasoning relative to policies and protocols in this context.

Schwartz and Sharpe (2006) argue that moral reasoning and wisdom are challenged by the contemporary politico-economic context. The implication here is that the context inhibits wise judgement and behaviour. Theories of wisdom are closely linked to ethics theory. In the Greek tradition, the most salient expression of wisdom for promoting the application of ethics is practical wisdom (*phronesis*). Practical wisdom is often seen as an executive virtue that governs judgement and practice in particular situations. Moreover, practical wisdom acknowledges the value of both practical (atheoretical) experience and abstract (generalisable) theory as useful in dealing with particular problems. Our variant of practical wisdom is social practice wisdom, which places high importance on understanding the discursive and sociological dimensions (including institutional contexts) of wise praxis (the application of virtue and knowledge in social endeavour). We will consider the impact of contemporary social research institutional conditions below, but before that, we consider three vignettes in the social sciences in which ethics have been questioned, featuring anthropology (Margaret Mead), psychology (Stanley Milgram) and economics (Fischer Black, Myron Scholes and Robert Merton).

These three vignettes are examples of research which was ethically unproblematic for the institutions that facilitated them at the time it was done, but whose outcomes, and in some cases treatment of research subjects, has been contested with the passage of time. This contestation may come from a greater contemporary understanding of what constitutes ethical and even 'wise research' and of the consequences of research, or it may result from the more diligent application of the rules and principles governing research practice, or indeed, a combination of both.

The vignettes come from three different time periods. While the controversy over Margaret Mead's anthropological research only emerged in the 1980s, the research itself was conducted in the 1920s, before the post-War development of institutional frameworks for reviewing ethics in social research. Stanley Milgram's psychology experiments were conducted in the 1950s, in the post-war period when the frameworks of institutional ethics were still developing. And the applications of economic theory that contributed to the global financial crisis (GFC), come at the end of the first decade of the twenty-first century.

Margaret Mead

In 1983, anthropologist Derek Freeman published *Margaret Mead and Samoa: The Making and Unmaking of an Anthropological Myth*. Freeman's contention is that the conclusions drawn by Mead in her 1928 classic *Coming of Age in Samoa*, were in error, and her original sources were not credible. Even though the scholarly community of anthropologists largely rejected Freeman's conclusions (Côté, 1999, 2000, 2005; Orans, 1996, 1999) the furore has continued. However, behavioural geneticist N.G. Martin (1984, p. 320) asks social researchers 'to reflect on the extent to which twentieth-century thought has been shaped by the fibbing of a few Samoan schoolgirls!'.

The controversy raises two interesting questions. The first: Would a twenty-first century institutional ethics committee approve such research? Probably yes, given that Freeman went to Samoa in the 1970s to revisit the original research. And the second: Would peer reviewers ask questions about the validity and reliability of the research if submitted for publication today? Sadly, one suspects that given the ideological context of the original research, the answer is no. But this does not exclude the possibility, indeed the probability, that Mead's original research was flawed.

Stanley Milgram

Milgram's experiments involved subjects who believed that they were teachers delivering an electric shock to learners (who were the experimenter's confederates) when they failed to give correct answers on a test. Subjects who wished to desist from causing pain were encouraged to continue and to deliver increasingly higher voltages as the experiment continued, despite the protestations of the 'learners'. The object of the experiment was to measure obedience to authority (Milgram 1963, 1974). The ethicality of these experiments has been debated since (Blass, 2004; Miller, 1986). Even the moral philosophers (Herrera, 1997, 2001) have come to Milgram's aid. However, De Vos (2010, p. 156) recently problematised the issue succinctly:

> [I]f both Milgram and Zimbardo claim that their work has emancipatory dimensions – a claim maintained within mainstream psychology – does a close reading of the studies not then reveal that psychology is, rather, the royal road to occurrences such as Guantanamo and Abu Ghraib?

Black, Scholes and Merton

The credibility of a number of economic theories applied to the operations of the financial markets has been called into question following the GFC that commenced in 2008 (Morgenson & Rosner, 2011; Schulz, 2010). In 1973, economists Fischer Black and Myron Scholes, and Robert Merton, published their work on a formula to calculate the value of particular types of financial instruments (Black & Scholes, 1973; Merton, 1973; Taleb, 2007; Van Loon, 2005). The Black–Scholes formula, as it is known, 'prices the value of a European option on a financial asset, given its price, the exercise price, the time to maturity, the risk-free interest rate and the asset's expected standard deviation/volatility' (OECD, 2007, p. 72). An interesting footnote to the original Black and Scholes paper is its acknowledgement of some financial support from the Ford Foundation (Black & Scholes, 1973, p. 637). How ironic that a philanthropic foundation would support a project whose ultimate end would be the collapse of the global financial markets.

In 1997, Merton and Scholes were awarded the Nobel Prize for Economics. Only a year later, in 1998, Long-Term Capital Management, a hedge fund whose board Merton and Scholes had joined at the inception of the company in 1994, crashed with losses of $4.6 billion dollars (Lowenstein, 2000). It would be reasonable to think that a decade before the GFC such a result would have given the financial markets, and their regulators, reason to pause for thought. In January 2011, the Final Report of the National Commission on the Causes of the Financial and Economic Crisis in the United States (FCIC) found: 'Financial institutions and credit rating agencies embraced mathematical models as reliable predictors of risks, replacing judgment in too many instances' (FCIC, 2011, p. xix).

There are no prizes for guessing which mathematical models had been found wanting. The FCIC also articulated the economic and social cost:

> As this report goes to print, there are more than 26 million Americans who are out of work, cannot find full-time work, or have given up looking for work. About four million families have lost their homes to foreclosure and another four and a half million have slipped into the foreclosure process or are seriously behind on their mortgage payments. Nearly $11 trillion in household wealth has vanished, with retirement accounts and life savings swept away. Businesses, large and small, have felt the sting of a deep recession. The collateral damage of this crisis has been real people and real communities. The impacts of this crisis are likely to be felt for a generation. (FCIC, 2011, pp. xv–xvi)

Who bears moral responsibility for this systemic failure? Are those economics and business school academics who propagated the theories as much to blame as those who executed them? Is it a sufficient defence for practitioners using those devices to say 'everyone was doing it' or 'in a competitive environment you have to try every possible advantage'? Does the ethical imperative of medical practice – first, do no harm – apply to financial markets? As with Mead and Milgram's case, Black, Scholes and Merton were lauded by their profession for their new insights into the discipline. Victims of the GFC – the jobless, the homeless, the bankrupt – may have expected more virtuous dispositions of both individual and institutional character, such as prudence, temperance and justice.

In each of these three cases, the ethics of social research was subsequently legitimated and normalised by the community of practice *ex post facto*. So, implicit in each of these vignettes are not only issues about individual and professional dispositions and wisdom, but also questions of institutional and organisational character, or virtue, and indeed, organisational culture.

Petrick, Scherer, Brodzinski, Quinn, and Ainina (1999), for example, have developed a matrix of virtues that he sees as necessary in the modern organisation for the building and maintenance of reputational capital. The term 'reputational capital' describes the idea that the reputation of an organisation is an intangible asset that helps to sustain its competitive market position. For research institutions, reputational capital is critical to the ongoing funding of their work by government agencies, industry partners and philanthropists. There is a very real sense in which institutional ethics committees have a critical role to play in safeguarding the institutional reputation for integrity and rigour in research. Public disclosure of unethical behaviour in research organisations has impacts on reputational capital. Therefore, the reputational capital of an organisation needs to be supported, not only by example, but also by internal structures. Table 2 shows a number of the virtues, which, according to Petrick et al. (1999), enhance the reputational capital of an organisation.

The problem encountered with such a wide diversity of virtues is the difficulty of keeping them all in focus and in balance, as well as the potential for virtues to clash. For example, how congruent are the intellectual virtues of visioning, foresight and innovation with the moral virtue of prudent stewardship of resources?

Social research presents particular problems for ethics, particularly when its findings are applied in social practice. The practical application of social research is always contestable because it is not always strongly generalisable (or universalisable) and because its subject matters are familiar and accessible to many citizens who may have their own strongly held opinions. An inescapable result of public contestation and weak generalisability is that applying social science research findings for the good and the right (*eudaimonia*) is never clear and is always political. If this is true, an important question for social science, and for those who apply it in practice in knowledge economies (in industry, policy, NGOs and so on), is: What is a wise, ethical and eudemonic institutional setting for research?

Table 2. Building Reputational Capital (Petrick et al., 1999).

Intellectual Virtues	Moral Virtues	Social Virtues	Emotional Virtues	Political Virtues
Intellectual capital	Leadership	Trust	Empathy	Justice
Visioning and	courage	Cooperation	Emotional	Organisational
foresight	Prudent	Social capital	intelligence	citizenship
Knowledge	stewardship	Humour	Emulation	behaviour
Innovation	of resources	Teamwork	Care	Fairness
Learning capacity	Honesty and	Loyalty	Appropriate	Principled conflict
	truth telling	Respect for	intimacy	management
	Promise keeping	diversity	Self-respect	Shared
	Determination		Resilience	empowerment
			Shared pride	Power abuse control

This raises questions about where the responsibility for wise and ethical research rests. IECs have a statutory responsibility for ensuring that research complies with an ethics framework, derived from internationally agreed statements of principle, which are principally about the treatment of subjects (through concern for, for example, informed consent, vulnerable populations and adverse consequences). This is the finely tuned deontological model at work. A question arising here is what if the rules or their application are inadequate, and if IECs can themselves take unethical action; for example, by preventing what might be very beneficial research from occurring simply because of inadequate rules that have not kept up with changes in research or in the world?

Flyvbjerg (2001) argues that wise research focuses first on the micro-practices in the research site with particular interest in questions of power, values, who benefits from the research, and why they are able to benefit. Extending this point to social research ethics, we argue that one can see ethicality in one light when viewed from the position of abstract rules (as IECs must tend to do), and another when seen from concrete and direct experience of micro-practices of research (as individual researchers tend to do).

Research institutions also have different values which may inform research ethics. From this perspective, this question is implicitly or explicitly answered in institutional mission statements. For example, historically there are certain areas of research into which institutions such as the University of Notre Dame and Brigham Young University will not venture because of the religious values upon which the institution is founded and sustained. More recently, however, institutions such as Cambridge, Oxford and University College London (UCL) are moving to a more explicitly, and pro-actively articulated, wisdom-based research initiatives, and in the case of UCL, a wisdom-focused research culture (Maxwell, 2009). That these initiatives exist, though still emergent, and in the main located in specific fields of research such as health and environment (the human and physical sciences, rather than the social sciences), is a sign of hope.

If wisdom has ethics at its core, and wise research is concerned with micro-practices before the abstract, then the deontological position of IECs with abstract, generalising rules are not necessarily or always disposed to wise decision making. Individual researchers, however, are closer to Flyvbjerg's conceptions of wise research, but may be limited in wise decision making by self-interest, which IECs can question. Invoking Foucault, Flyvbjerg (2001, p. 55) advocates that practically wise researchers must develop intellectual and social virtues in tandem. Foucault (1990), however, also says that research must produce new ways of thinking that are transformative or emancipatory. This also means that research is part of praxis, that is, putting new knowledge and theory in to everyday social practice. This Foucauldian ethics is anathema, in Flyvbjerg's (2001, p. 127) words, to the 'thought-police'. Institutions and laws cannot guarantee justice and ethicality because they can take on their own agendas, or simply become unreflexive arbiters of compliance with abstract rules without regard for particular circumstances. Genuine public debate that informs both socially reflexive researchers and IECs about the value and practices of research is what is most important.

Individual researchers have always made choices about the nature of the research they undertake; we all know colleagues who will decline to participate on ethical grounds in any research activity which can be seen to be supporting 'the military–industrial complex'. There are also those who anticipate that their research may not be approved by an IEC and do not pursue that line of research anymore. However, in the emerging political economy of research, there is some evidence of jurisdiction shopping, that is, taking research away from one institution to another, sometimes including to a new country where ethics clearance will be easier. Again, we highlight the importance of the reflexively wise researchers who makes wise decisions.

CONCLUSION

If the purpose of being ethical is to do that which is right and good, each of the traditional ethical frameworks (deontology, consequentialism and virtue) is problematic when it comes to social research.

Fostering habits of good character among researchers and their institutions – the aim of virtue ethics – is a necessary but insufficient basis on
which to build an ethical research infrastructure in a knowledge economy.
In a knowledge economy, research is, because of its scale, and the funds
committed by external stakeholders such as governments and philanthropists, increasingly pushed to be essentially consequentialist. Public and
private investment in research in both the sciences and the social sciences
must make a difference by way of patents, new drugs and new social
practices. However, historically, consequentialism in research has led to
unethical research practices; this in turn brought about regimes of ethics
approval through statutory bodies based on rules, duties and principles, all
of which derive, by one path or another, from the Nuremberg Code. Despite
these regimes, there are still debates among legislators, in IECs and in
academic journals about what is and is not acceptable conduct in research.

The relatively more contested research outcomes in the social sciences, as
discussed above, make the situation of ethics in social research in a
knowledge economy more complex. Is the solution, therefore, recognising
the inherent limitations of both virtue and consequentialism, to return to
Kant's Categorical Imperative, with its two principles of universalisability
and respect for person? Or is the solution to frame Kant's principles using
W.D. Ross's notion of prima facie duties?

Our answer is a twofold one. First, we point to practical wisdom's
executive function as the primary virtue, which is the virtue that integrates
appropriately the other virtues to meet the needs of specific situations.
Second, we point to institutional change in universities to create more
ethical spaces (Werhane, 2002). Importantly, our position is that for
practical wisdom to operate effectively in social science research ethics,
institutional change is needed. Why? Because practically wise individual
behaviour is becoming increasingly difficult to display in contemporary
research settings (cf. Schwartz & Sharpe, 2006), and it is important that
space for those who engage in the micro-practices of research and the
researched are given this space to produce wise research. Returning to the
prima facie duty to respect persons, current trends of research evaluation
based on objective metrics shift research away from a direct view of making
a difference to people to the more abstract realm of making a difference to
key managerial performance indicators. When the motivation to publish is
to count, then research motivation shifts from wanting to contribute to
making a better world to contributing to the performance of one's university
and one's own measurable performance. In this regime, ethicality is
compromised, despite the abstract measures' ostensible focus on impact or

quality. The distancing of research and researchers from people by abstract managerial evaluation is ethically corrosive and implies a desire for objectivism that is values-free. Yet ethicality and wisdom necessarily embrace values, and thus, wise research is sensitive to values.

It is interesting to consider that universities have existed for centuries making substantial contributions through the social sciences and humanities without the information generated by quantifying managerialism. This managerialism is a force that brings closure and distancing, competition and selfishness, and less space for wisdom. Social science and humanities research, above all others, should bring wisdom to research, and in doing so, should contribute not simply to knowledge but also to creating wise societies (Maxwell, 1984). A list of achievements of social research might include those in relation to charters of human rights, social welfare provisions, anti-discrimination legislation, child protection regimes and many other now taken for granted social democratic institutions and values. Each of these engenders values and ethics in their conceptualisations and applications. Moreover, there is wisdom in these products of social research that is fundamental to civilisation and wise societies; this wisdom is partly a result of the achievements of social research having partly a rules-based nature and partly because they incorporate values and practical dispositions of social practice. What sense is there then in reducing the institutional framework that produces these outcomes to something hostile to them? Wisdom, we argue, flourishes in spaces that are conducive to, and consonant with, wisdom, not in spaces that are antagonistic to it and to the historical goals of social research. We finish this chapter with Nicholas Maxwell's para-phrasing of Socrates.

> Socrates might be interpreted to be arguing along the following lines: 'There is something here, implicit in our lives in Athens, that is of immense desirability and value, of profound grandeur, significance and beauty. This is to be seen in the world around us, but above all in ourselves, in our souls and in our civilization – in our crafts, our art, sculpture, poetry, drama, philosophy, in our freedom, democracy and justice. There are, however, in our souls and civilization devastating flaws – war, tyranny, injustice, violence, almost psychopathic ambition, deception, vanity and self-deception, self-annihilation of the soul. Our task is to discover how to help let that which we glimpse ... to grow, to come progressively into existence throughout our shared life, our polis ... It is towards the accomplishment of this task that we need to devote our thinking, our rational inquiry and our education'. (Maxwell, 1984, p. 120)

If the potential of social research and the academy is our Athenian agora, our task is to discover how our wisdom, shared lives and polis can ensure that the potential is realised.

REFERENCES

Aristotle. (1908). *The works of Aristotle* (W. D. Ross, Trans.). Oxford: Clarendon.

Bauman, Z. (2000). *Liquid modernity*. Cambridge: Polity.

Bentham, J. (1823). *An introduction to the principles of morals and legislation*. London: W. Pickering & R. Wilson.

Bentham, J., & Bowring, J. (1843). *The works of Jeremy Bentham* (Vols. 1–11). Edinburgh: William Tait.

Black, F., & Scholes, F. (1973). The pricing of options and corporate liabilities. *Journal of Political Economy, 81*(3), 637–654.

Blass, T. (2004). *The man who shocked the world: The life and legacy Stanley Milgram*. New York, NY: Basic Books.

Calkins, M. J., & Werhane, P. H. (1998). Adam Smith, Aristotle and the virtues of commerce. *Journal of Value Inquiry, 32*(1), 43–60.

Côté, J. (1999). The fateful hoaxing of Margaret Mead: A historical analysis of her Samoan research. *Pacific Affairs, 72*(2), 308–310.

Côté, J. (2000). The implausibility of Freeman's hoaxing theory: An update. *Journal of Youth and Adolescence, 29*(5), 575–585.

Côté, J. (2005). The correspondence associated with Margaret Mead Samoan research: What does it really tell us? *Pacific Studies, 28*(3/4), 60–73.

De Vos, J. (2010). From Milgram to Zimbardo: The double birth of postwar psychology/psychologization. *History of the Human Sciences, 23*(5), 156–175.

DeRenzo, E., Silverman, H., Hoffmann, D., Schwartz, J., & Vinicky, J. (2001). Maryland's ethics committee legislation: A leading edge model or a step into the abyss? *HEC Forum, 13*(1), 49–58.

Engelbrecht, H.-J. (2007). The (un)happiness of knowledge and the knowledge of (un)happiness: Happiness research and policies for knowledge-based economies. *Prometheus, 25*(3), 243–266.

Flyvbjerg, B. (2001). *Making social science matter: Why social inquiry fails and how it can succeed again* (S. Sampson, Trans.). Cambridge: Cambridge University Press.

Foucault, M. (1990). *The history of sexuality, vol. 2: The use of pleasure* (R. Hurley, Trans.). New York: Vintage Books.

Freeman, D. (1983). *Margaret Mead and Samoa: The making and unmaking of an anthropological myth*. Cambridge, MA: Harvard University Press.

Glendon, M. A. (1991). *Rights talk: The impoverishment of political discourse*. New York, NY: The Free Press.

Herrera, C. D. (1997). A historical interpretation of deceptive experiments in American psychology. *History of the Human Sciences, 10*(1), 23–36.

Herrera, C. D. (2001). Ethics, deception, and 'those Milgram experiments'. *Journal of Applied Philosophy, 18*(3), 245–256.

Howells, J. (2001). The nature of innovation in services. In *OECD, Innovation and productivity in services* (pp. 55–80). Paris: Organisation for Economic Co-operation and Development.

Kant, I. (1895). *Fundamental principles of the metaphysic of ethics* (T. K. Abbott, Trans.). London: Longmans Green.

Knight, K. (2009). Review article: MacIntyre's progress. *Journal of Moral Philosophy, 6*(1), 115–126.

Lowenstein, R. (2000). *When genius failed: The rise and fall of long-term capital management*. New York, NY: Random House.

MacIntyre, A. (1984). *After virtue*. Notre Dame, IN: University of Notre Dame Press.

Martin, N. G. (1984). Margaret Mead, Derek Freeman, and behavior genetics. *Behavior Genetics, 14*(3), 319–321.

Marx, K., & McLellan, D. (1977). *Karl Marx: Selected writings*. Oxford: Oxford University Press.

Maxwell, N. (1984). *From knowledge to wisdom: A revolution in the aims and methods of science*. Oxford: Basil Blackwell.

Maxwell, N. (2009). Are universities undergoing an intellectual revolution. *Oxford Magazine, 290*, 13–16.

Mead, M. (1928). *Coming of age in Samoa: A psychological study of primitive youth for western civilisation*. New York, NY: William Morrow.

Merton, R. C. (1973). Theory of rational option pricing. *Bell Journal of Economics and Management Science* (The RAND Corporation), *4*(1), 141–183.

Miles, I. (2008). Knowledge services. In G. Hearn & D. Rooney (Eds.), *Knowledge policy: Challenges for the twenty first century* (pp. 11–27). Cheltenham: Edward Elgar.

Milgram, S. (1963). Behavioural study of obedience. *Journal of Abnormal and Social Psychology, 67*(4), 371–378.

Milgram, S. (1974). *Obedience to authority: An experimental view*. New York, NY: Harper & Row.

Miller, A. G. (1986). *The obedience experiments: A case study of controversy in social science*. New York, NY: Praeger.

Mintz, S. (1996). Aristotelian virtue and business ethics education. *Journal of Business Ethics, 15*(8), 827–838.

Morgenson, G., & Rosner, J. (2011). *Reckless endangerment: How outsized ambition, greed, and corruption led to economic Armageddon*. New York, NY: Times Books.

National Commission on the Causes of the Financial and Economic Crisis in the United States [FCIC]. (2011). *The financial crisis inquiry report*. Washington, DC: U.S. Government Printing Office.

National Institutes of Health (NIH). (n.d.). *Nuremberg declaration*. Retrieved from http://ohsr.od.nih.gov/guidelines/nuremberg.html Reprinted from *Trials of War Criminals before the Nuremberg Military Tribunals under Control Council Law* (no. 10, vol. 2, pp. 181–182). Washington, DC: U.S. Government Printing Office, 1949.

Nozick, R. (1974). *Anarchy, state and utopia*. Oxford: Blackwell.

Orans, M. (1996). *Not even wrong: Margaret Mead, Derek Freeman, and the Samoans*. Novato, CA: Chandler and Sharp.

Orans, M. (1999). Mead misrepresented. *Science, 283*, 1649–1650.

Organisation for Economic Co-operation and Development (OECD). (2007). *Glossary of statistical terms*. Retrieved from http://stats.oecd.org/glossary/

Petrick, J. A., Scherer, R. F., Brodzinski, J. D., Quinn, J. F., & Ainina, M. F. (1999). Global leadership skills and reputational capital: Intangible resources for sustainable competitive advantage in the 21st century. *Academy of Management Executive, 13*(1), 58–69.

Rawls, J. (1973). *A theory of justice*. London: Oxford University Press.

Rooney, D., & Mandeville, T. (1998). The knowing nation: A framework for public policy in a knowledge economy. *Prometheus, 16*(4), 453–467.

Rooney, D., McKenna, B., & Liesch, P. (2010). *Wisdom and management in the knowledge economy*. London: Routledge.

Ross, W. D. (1930). *The right and the good*. Oxford: Clarendon Press.

Schulz, K. (2010). *Being wrong: Adventures in the margin of error*. New York, NY: HarperCollins.

Schwartz, B., & Sharpe, K. E. (2006). Practical wisdom: Aristotle meets positive psychology. *Journal of Happiness Studies*, *7*(3), 377–395.

Sen, A. (2009). *The idea of justice*. Cambridge, MA: Harvard University Press.

Taleb, N. N. (2007). *The black swan: The impact of the highly improbable*. New York, NY: Random House.

United Nations. (n.d.) *Universal declaration of human rights 1948*. Retrieved from http://www.unhchr.ch/udhr/lang/eng.htm

Van Loon, J. (2005). Risk and knowledge. In D. Rooney, G. Hearn & A. Ninan (Eds.), *Handbook on the knowledge economy* (pp. 54–66). Cheltenham: Edward Elgar.

Werhane, P. H. (2002). Moral imagination and systems thinking. *Journal of Business Ethics*, *38*(1/2), 33–42.

Wilkinson, R., & Pickett, K. (2009). *The spirit level: Why greater equality makes societies stronger*. New York, NY: Bloomsbury Press.

World Medical Association (WMA). (n.d.). *WMA declaration of Helsinki – Ethical principles for medical research involving human subjects*. Retrieved from http://www.wma.net/en/30publications/10policies/b3/

PUBLIC SOCIOLOGY, CRITICAL SOCIOLOGY, AND THE SOCIOLOGICAL ENTERPRISE

Richard A. Courtney

ABSTRACT

Purpose – *The purpose of this chapter is to explore the differing ways in which emancipation is conceived by (Burawoy, 2004) four types of sociology: professional, public, critical and policy. The chapter argues that taken in isolation these sociologies generate issues in research that can only be resolved by reference to the activities of other branches of the sociological enterprise.*

Approach – *The chapter starts with a conflict of values in public sociological research, where the researcher is confronted with respondents whose 'voice' is characterised as racist.*

Findings – *The chapter argues that whilst public sociology attempts to provide voice to marginalised social groups it often makes arbitrary judgments over the palatability of certain voices, preferring voices sympathetic to the sociological enterprise over populist voices. The nuance here is illustrated as a tension between public and critical sociology that is often overlooked in the literature.*

Research implications – *The chapter argues that to successfully make sociological judgments to marshal between divergent voices, public*

Ethics in Social Research
Studies in Qualitative Methodology, Volume 12, 51–70
Copyright © 2012 by Emerald Group Publishing Limited
All rights of reproduction in any form reserved
ISSN: 1042-3192/doi:10.1108/S1042-3192(2012)0000012006

*sociology needs to re-discover its relationship with professional sociology,
in terms of its engagement with political normativity and uses of evidence.
Ultimately, for the sociological enterprise to be emancipatory it has to
have a functioning interdependence between its four main activities.*

Keywords: Public sociology; critical sociology; emancipation; civil
society; social research; class analysis

INTRODUCTION

During my PhD research on 'race', community and social class in Essex I
encountered many problems that whilst not being ethical concerns in a
bureaucratic sense became central ethical concerns in an epistemological
sense. The PhD explored the above themes in order to uncover and explore
the narratives of social change that existed in an area that had undergone
rapid transformations in its population and economic profiles. The research
was designed to be emancipatory in a loose sense as it sought to provide a
platform for the people affected by such change to articulate their voice;
a voice which was largely hidden and obscured from public view. This
generated a series of value conflicts that challenged many of the underlying
assumptions of sociology, especially in regards discourses on 'race', ethnicity
and social class. One such incident occurred whilst waiting in a post office
queue with one of my respondents. It was a very hot and busy afternoon in
June 2006, I was waiting in-line with Colin (pseudonym) for him to conduct
some personal business. I suspected that this was in fact a ruse for him to
demonstrate the legitimacy of his earlier commentary – where he advocated
the repatriation of all ethnic and racial minorities – of course Colin was
stumped to answer my 'repatriate back to where?' line of questioning.
Instead he felt compelled to demonstrate the social location from which he
was 'calling'. We were waiting for a long time for a number of admittedly
black and minority ethnic groups to conduct their business that in accordance
with Colin's discourse appeared to be the collection of various types of state
benefits. It took ages and admittedly the aforementioned 'customers' were
slow and I have to say rather annoying! Colin, felt my frustration at waiting
and exclaimed 'you see Rich, this is what I'm telling you, if none of those were
here poncing we'd be done by now'. I felt complicit in his racism, and at
face-value it was a stupid thing to say, because surely there is always going to
be someone ahead of you in a queue and it's sod's law that they'll display an

ineptitude that leaves you waiting for far longer than you would want to be on such a hot afternoon. That wasn't the reality to which Colin was referring, his statement was one indicative of a holism to which I felt no hitherto attachment. The 'we' in his statement wasn't us as individuals, but us as a group of white people; them were not legitimately pension aged first generation migrants and long-term contributors to British Society and Social Security, they were agents of a different and 'parasitic' group of ethnic others.

Colin's narration of the queue incident was one of war and struggle between what he viewed as legitimacy and illegitimacy, it was black vs. white. Despite his 'buts' and it's 'different now' I had no problem in referring to him as a hardened racist. Colin's vocalisation of racism was unique and was shared by only a few of my respondents and usually only in intimate situations; however, his sentiment was shared by many who sheltered in the secluded place from which Colin was calling – this self-elected 'silent majority'. From this point of view Colin was right and felt vindicated by the self-evident truth that the people in front of us were to put it bluntly holding up his business. Despite self-evidence I did not resent the folk in front of us for any holistic reasons, but simply because as individuals they were taking up my time! This problem became a central epistemological concern for my PhD and much of my post-doctoral work to date. It can be summarised by this question: am I sociologically justified to call Colin a racist and to find error in his characterisation of his social world, including what he saw as its major fault lines, namely immigration – despite the fact that I was conducting an ethnographic enquiry to give 'voice' to working class community.

This chapter is designed to explore the ethics of sociological research when viewed through the discourse on public sociology, popularised at the 2005 ASA conference by Michael Burawoy (Burawoy, 2004). Public sociology is a productive frame of reference for my research as it takes the challenges of public voice as a serious subject in and of themselves (Brewer, 2005). In this way, it provides a methodological means to open up a space for the emancipation of hidden, obscured and misunderstood voices that lay outside of mainstream public discourse. However, Colin also wanted emancipation, but from the discourses he saw this as discrimination against him and what he felt were his kind. Given that public sociology is funda-mentally wedded to ideas of emancipation, how then does it deal theoretically and methodologically with conflicts of values over what constitutes emancipation? The chapter argues that the concept of emancipation is crucial to public sociology, but that this is made problematic by the dual nature of emancipation – are we to consider it as an ideal promoting freedom to express oneself or an ideal to free people from the expressions of others. Overarching these questions is a question internal to sociology, which asks whether sociology should have a distinct moral voice of its own? To perform this task I'll look at the debates surrounding public sociology and its relationship to professional sociology. Then in order to explore more fully the problems of public sociology I'll discuss its relationship to critical sociology; arguing that this relationship needs to be more fully theorised in order to illustrate what and who is under critical scrutiny in research terms. I will then draw this discussion together with a demonstration of the way in which sociological responses to anti-social acts such as rioting generate arbitrariness. I'll conclude with a suggestion that the relationship between public and professional sociology should be seen as a choreographed division of labour as it is on this basis that sociology can articulate its own voice as a sociological enterprise.

BURAWOY'S CLASSIFICATION OF SOCIOLOGY

Burawoy classifies the sociological enterprise as consisting of four ideal types – that in reality are overlapping, but he reduces the core difference as one of a dualism between instrumentality and reflexivity. He argues that professional and policy sociology are distinctly instrumental and that public and critical sociologies are inherently reflexive (Burawoy, 2004, 2008). Before documenting the limitations of these four types, I will now briefly explain three types with reference to a few notable examples and I'll then explain critical sociology in the next section in order to intensify the argument. Professional sociology is characterised as methodologically and theoretically engaged and that these activities enable it to be a self-perpetuating body of distinct knowledge (Ghamari-Tabrizi, 2005). This self-perpetuation emanates from the fact that problems are identified internally – as a problem of theoretical explanation or methodological inconsistency. Functionalism and structural Marxism are good examples, as their ideas on society developed as a result of internal inconsistencies over cause and effect, structure and agency, economy and society, or other abstract dualisms. At moments in the perpetuation of professional sociology, ideas emerge from observations external to professional sociology leading to a counter-form of professional sociology that is often empirically driven. A good example here is the Affluent Worker Studies that was developed against the 'embourgoisiement thesis', popular with many neo-Marxists of the 1950s–1960s (Goldthorpe, 1969). This is where there was a recourse to the empirical in order to sustain professional sociology against Marxist hyperbole. It is important to note here that professional sociology remains professional on the basis of the authority of the knowledge that it produces. This is for two reasons, firstly because the objects of sociological knowledge are studied by no other area of scholarly enquiry and the knowledge they produce exists despite public opinion – so, for example economic inequalities exist and are observed and analysed by professional sociology because individuals in societies experience inequality indirectly (Marshall, Swift, & Roberts, 1997; Marshall et al., 1997). In this way, professional sociology provides detailed and analytical information that describes an overview of societal systems often obscured or invisible at the individual level. It is in this sense emancipatory because it liberates people from the constraints of their social location; allowing people to view society from an impersonal perspective that identifies their location and relationships to others directly (Tittle, 2004).

In reality, the boundaries between sociologies are never so precise and this is why Burawoy argues that professional sociology shares an instrumentality with policy sociology (Burawoy, 2004, 2005). Whilst policy sociology should be seen as no less theoretically and methodologically rigorous than professional sociology, it differs in that it is client-directed. So, problems emerge in external contexts and are internalised into sociological research in procedural ways. Health and education research are of course the strongest examples – with research agendas being rigidly dictated by the needs of government, think-tanks, and industry; however, there are examples of policy-driven community research, a recent one is Dench, Gavron, and Young's (2006) New East End. This research is policy driven albeit in a 'weaker' fashion as the policy recommendations emergent from them are less recognised by official policy directives. However, there are also good examples of syntheses between professional and policy sociology, Lin's (2001) 'Social Capital' is a notable example – where arguments internal to professional sociology are reconciled towards the demands of industrial and economic policy-making.

It is the weak recognition of some policy-driven research that makes the distinction between instrumental and reflexive sociologies meaningful. This is because the relative merits of policy recommendations are in effect normative issues that require reflection rather than instrumental application. public and critical sociology are in this way calling from very different corners of the room to professional and policy sociology. They therefore represent a 'concern' with the objects under study that is emotively involved through the promotion of advocacy. Burawoy argues that public sociology is the central component of the sociological enterprise on the basis of its subject matter. He claims that economics is the study of markets, politics is the study of government, and sociology is the study of civil society (Burawoy, 2008). At the outset this is a very classically liberal idea as the sociological enterprise is therefore governed by political principles of inclusivity and recognition. This is very similar to Wright Mills' (1959) idea of 'The Promise', where he argues that sociology makes private troubles, public issues – thus raising the recognition of issues such as domestic violence, homophobia, racism and economic exploitation. The goal of public sociology is to emancipate voices that are excluded from mainstream civil society by economics or politics (Burawoy, 2008). I will show later on that this goal becomes confused because of differences in the application of public sociology as either a liberal/procedural activity to pluralise voice for emancipation, or as a libertarian activity that emancipates ALL voices marginal or otherwise.

In its classically liberal form, public sociology socialises the private aspects of people's lives and opens up a space to engage private realms distanced or hidden from public view. As a consequence of this activity public sociology is brought into a closer dialogue with the activities of critical scholars. Inherent in this engagement are ideas of critique, emancipation, and accountability, spaces populated by critical sociology, which includes, Critical Race Studies, Critical Feminist and Citizenship Studies, Critical Management Studies, Critical Marketing Studies amongst many others. The next section will explore the nature of critical sociology in more depth in order to illustrate the tensions that arise with public sociology. This will question the construction of sociological normativity to enquire whether sociology can reasonably define what is right and wrong in these so-called liquid rhizomatic times of competing legitimacies in ideas and beliefs (Latour, 2005)?

PUBLIC SOCIOLOGY CONTRA CRITICAL SOCIOLOGY

The debate over the status of public sociology has developed largely as a tension with its putative 'other' that being professional sociology. However, this chapter will illustrate that there is an important tension between public sociology and critical sociology, which once resolved will enable a more productive relationship between public and professional sociologies. The main point is that public sociology cannot easily identify a convincing and rigorous empirical or normative reason why certain ideas should be regarded as legitimate and others should be seen as the stuff of ideology. This tension is emergent from its implicit engagement with critical sociology, because the latter is the body of knowledge upon which norms and values are critiqued. This moves beyond the realm of ideas and identifies social relations as the object of critique, as judgments can be reduced to judgments on the credibility of the people that express them, just as much as the ideas *sui generis* – therefore the opening example shows me to not just be critically engaging with Colin's ideas, but actually critiquing his reasons and intentions for holding them. One of the problems expressed from professional sociology is that public sociology is far too partisan and takes sides arbitrarily (Tittle, 2004). Beyond my own personal disdain for racial discrimination is there tangibility to my normative judgment of it, or am I simply being arbitrary and politically correct?

It is this predicament that professional sociology problematises in its disavowal of public sociology. Their concern is that in many instances this partisanship appears arbitrary and at its extremes legitimises what professional sociologists would see as errant and unreliable observations on the nature and order of social life. An example can be seen when public sociology supports the ideas and beliefs of sublimated groups (Katz-Fishman & Scott, 2005). There is certainly nothing politically errant in supporting sublimated groups to achieve recognition, but the point made against public sociology is that it treats their claims as true regardless of the arguments that question their reliability and extent. Public sociology therefore assumes that sublimated groups, seemingly by virtue of their position alone, see a world without ideological distortion. Of course ideology is the stuff of powerful interests, but this is an accusation directed at the authorial status of professional sociology too. A public sociology that attributes and legitimises voice without critique is libertarian rather than liberal. The danger to the integrity of sociology, as a generally liberal discipline, is that public sociology conducted as a libertarian ideal gives legitimacy to conspiracy theory! Why then would we regard leftist conspiracy theory as any more credible than the Nazi conspiracy theory on the Jewish diaspora, or Colin's popular conspiratorial discourse that blames 'foreigners' and liberal-minded elites for displacing the English white working classes?

The answer to this question, I believe is founded in a more sustained and analytic debate over the relationship between public sociology and critical sociology, especially in regard to the norms that follow from liberalism, libertarianism and authoritarianism. Taken at face-value public sociology could be used to give voice and thus legitimacy to any set of social values, be they racist, anti-racist, spiritualist or sceptical – this is a libertarian strategy rather than a liberal one on the basis that its goal is to emancipate voice in and of itself and regardless of its political hue and credibility of its evidence. This is because public sociology envisages emancipation to consist of principles that appeal to freedom of conscience, more than emancipation built from a scrutiny and critical engagement with various forms of evidence. The problem is that moral authority is not fully theorised – it is contingent on the opinions and prejudice of the researcher. The following section on critical sociology explores the opposite side of this relationship and demonstrates that critical sociology embodies a sense of authority that whilst it provides an answer to the dilemma as to whether someone's opinions are errant, is illiberal next to the liberal basis of sociology more generally.

CRITICAL SOCIOLOGY: EMANCIPATION
AND IDEOLOGY

Critical sociology is a reflexive form of research that is often seen as oppositional to 'traditional' research, which is regarded as positivistic in outlook (Harvey, 1990). Although, this is often a simplistic dualism of research paradigms it is useful as it helps to establish the 'essence' of critical research over the other forms of research that Burawoy (2005) characterises as public, professional and policy-driven. Critical social research consists of theory and research that is in some way critical of, or antagonistic toward, the status quo (Elder-Vass, 2011). The reason for this is twofold; firstly, it is related to organisations, structures and institutions; and secondly related to the politics of identity, representation and social texts. As will be explained, power is a central feature of both levels of reasoning as emancipation is considered to emerge from the unmasking of the power of ideology.

Materiality is more commonly a feature of critical realism, where the label 'critical' gains currency as it critiques the aspects of society and social organisation that facilitate the domination of individuals and/or social groups by powerful interests. Power is criticised in institutions/organisations as a means to hold them to account, because the individuals who are dominated are done so under unequal conditions – this is despite the organisation or institution being legitimate and valid, for example employment and schooling. Just because these are inevitable aspects of living in society, it doesn't follow that activities internal to their operations should be oppressive and exploitative to the individuals who populate them, regardless as to whether such factors are enshrined in the law of the land. Critical social research plays a public good in these respects as it examines the nature of 'normal' life in institutions and subjects it to analytic scrutiny (Alexander, 2003). This has been the case with many critical pieces of research in marginal, flexible and insecure employment and also critically engaged criminological studies; not to mention feminist research on the home, family life and sexuality. Whilst all but the ardent classical Marxist accept that 'some' kind of inequality is acceptable and even necessary in society, critical social research is used to explore the potential ill-legitimacy of inequality; central to this is the identification of power as an unequally distributed social resource, which holds the ability to be exploited – especially in contexts where there is little or no external scrutiny – see for instance in sex work (O'Connell-Davidson, 1998). Emancipation from the point of view of critical theorists is the liberation from oppressive structures through the unmasking of ideological power.

The second feature of critical research is an emphasis on the discursive nature of identity and the social texts that govern identities through discursive formations (Elder-Vass, 2011). This is a body of academic work that, following Foucault, grounds analyses of power in the instruments of governance that describe and constructs identities as objects of knowledge. Critical 'race' studies are a highly important aspect of this kind of critical work, because they deconstruct the 'scientific' racial discourses that have led to the creation of racial subjects (Banton, 1998). One influential example in this respect is the work of Frantz Fanon, when he famously identified racial discourses as a secondary form of colonialism, meaning that the subjects of slavery and colonialism were made to think of themselves through the eyes of white Europeans (Fanon, 1972). Other notable works in this genre are Said's Orientalism (2003), where he argues that the identity of non-western societies is a product of Western society's imagination of an oriental subject, rather than a reality congruent representation of social and political life of East of Europe. This post-structuralist thinking in terms of the power/knowledge that constructs identities opens up an emancipatory space for research to allow subjects to define themselves.

Central to both these strands of critical research is the concept of ideology, where it is argued that the ideas available in society are the ideas of the dominant. In this way the dominant ideas in society shape and define what can and cannot be said through discursive acts. Underwriting this theorisation of society is the idea of 'false consciousness', that is that a person may think of themselves in terms antagonistic with their own interests. This implies that power works against people's own interests and in the favour of the powerful. Critical research seeks to overturn ideologies and aims to construct new knowledge(s) that emancipate subjects from being defined by ideology. This is emancipatory in the extent to which it seeks to de-centre ideas of the human subject to reflect plurality and diversity of perspective and social conditions, and therefore liberalises the amount of ideas within society. However, crucial questions remain: what counts as ideology and from what basis can critical research be said to be 'outside' ideology? These are important considerations because just as religious authority dictates the interests of its subjects so too does critical theory and there is an inherent danger where this is regarded to be delusion and should be substituted by something that critical theorists are inclined to view as more 'real'. This assumes that knowledge outside of the critical canon is always flawed and people require correction by the authority of critical insight. Many scholars outside of critical research view this as errant and arbitrary, because despite their appeal to the material dynamics of society there is little to distinguish critical knowledge from conventional knowledge – it is a simple difference of opinion in terms of who holds power and the means by which it is exercised.

The example of Colin demonstrates this tension in the field of community research, because from Colin's point of view he is attributing a critical gaze upon his immediate social surroundings and there is no knowledge unique to the critical canon that decides that his racialised view of society should be replaced with something more amenable to liberal tastes. Colin saw his world view as a pragmatic materially grounded response to globalisation and migration, when questioned about this he argued that 'political correctness' was an ideology designed to re-programme him against what he felt was his better judgment and furthermore a means to deny him his freedom of conscience. Power for Colin was firmly in the hands of what he described as 'liberal elites'. The emancipatory project of critical research is to argue that people are delusional in their characterisations of self and society; this is something he vehemently argued against. The problem here is that despite recourse to notions of inequality and materialism critical research operationalises emancipation as a moral authority and as such is often highly illiberal and elitist in its prescriptions for society. Within this and due to the influence of the Frankfurt School is a bias where leftism is seen as normatively superior to right leaning populist thinking, with the latter viewed as surreptitious ideology and false consciousness.

This political bias in much sociological work may, as I'll show later, be justified on a wider basis, but at the point of a conflict over norms and values is arbitrary and is what many professional sociologists view as errant in public and critical sociology. The solution used by many public and critical sociologists is to frame the questions raised by Colin's voice as an issue pertaining to social class, not to cultural relations as the subject of scrutiny. There is a sense of expediency in this strategy, because by identifying social class as the subject around which narratives of self and society emerge, sociologists can explain racial discourse as an object rather than a subject – thus contradicting the often libertarian starting point of public sociology. In this way, many have turned critical insights into a means of emancipating white working class subjects from the discourses of shame and derogation encased in the trope of the 'Chav' (Brewis & Jack, 2010). In keeping with Colin, he then becomes a subject of study, whilst his discourse is articulated as an object of study. This is what enables sociologists to accept socially awkward voices without legitimising its politics. As will be shown in the next section this tactic raises the same questions, because on one hand it accepts autonomy, that is the legitimacy of voice, but rejects autonomy by drawing discursive boundaries over what aspects are seen as active and others seen as errant.

PUBLIC SOCIOLOGY: SOCIAL CLASS AND ANTI-CIVIL VOICE

Recent developments in the sociology of class can be viewed as forms of public sociology that attempt to re-frame the ideologies that classify the norms to which working class people are judged. In this way, the sociology of class is a good example of where public and critical sociology hold a common goal. It has therefore become a discourse by which narratives of public life and struggle are discussed within sociology – a good example is the 2005 special issue of *Sociology* devoted to a reappraisal of class analysis (Lawler, 2005). This section will outline some of these recent arguments and will use the above tension between critical and public sociology as a means to identify the internal issues that create external tensions with professional sociology. Skeggs' (1997) 'Formations of Class and Gender' and her ensuing paradigm in the sociology of class have been influential, as they have created a British articulation of Bourdieu's theory of distinction (Bennett et al., 2008). At the outset Bev Skeggs presents a libertarian understanding of social class in that she removes any sense of legitimacy to moral authority within society – this has the effect of liberalising ideas of taste, style and distinction (Skeggs, 2004). Central to Skeggs' argument is the idea that social class is reproduced through the relative values of distinction generated by different social groups, rather than a theory of economic class relations and formations. In and of itself this is very similar to Weber's classic argument about status. However, Skeggs' view is different in that it attempts to identify one set of values as more powerful than another set; and that this power relationship means that one or more sets of values are derogated by an authorial other associated with economically and politically ascendant status (Skeggs, 2005).

For Skeggs, there is an assumption that the basis of this power lies in the structural aspects of economic and political class. This argument has become a trope in which the discourses attached to the social derogation of working class people is discussed in terms of labelling; thus what were the lumpen-proletariat, the undeserving poor, or the underclass are now referred to with the moniker 'chav' (see Jones', 2011 popularisation of the critique of the 'chav' trope). So for Skeggs and many who use this methodology to understand class they are simply saying that social class is discursively constructed through the values attributed to lower social classes by 'middle class' values of aspiration, decency etc. – values that Skeggs labels and criticises as a neo-liberal entrepreneurial self project (Skeggs, 2004). She then claims that popular day-time television shows and other low-cost television sold with the USP of being 'reality television' are the apparatus through which middle class values police the values that working class subjects attribute to their leisure and lifestyle choices (Skeggs, 2005). This has led to a style of class analysis that seeks to recognise the 'voice' of the working classes outside the discourses within popular culture. This is libertarian on the basis that her class analysis emancipates people from the shackles of judgment by socially ascendant groups. In prescriptive terms, she is claiming that it is morally just for people to behave in the way they do and that class emancipation is about others not judging people for doing so, not a prescription that seeks to redistribute opportunities or resources. So all the classic prescriptive judgments of Liberal-Left British post-war professional sociology are de-centred in favour of a libertarian acceptance of people's right to cultural autonomy and hence their emancipation (Savage, 2010).

Much of the academic response to the riots across England in the summer of 2011 follow this discourse on working class people as a subaltern, who are assumed to be different to the pathologised views expressed in the media and popular opinion. It has been noted on academic blogging sites such as sociologyandthecuts.wordpress.org, that the political response to the riots as feckless and apolitical nihilism is a further attempt to pathologise working class people as 'chavs' with little or no sense of decency, virtue and personal responsibility. The academic response has been to treat negative opinions of individual rioters with suspicion as these opinions are seen to be tainted by liberal and conservative ideologies (Allen & Taylor, 2011). Despite the fact that there has been very little empirical research conducted on the riots thus far the academic comments seem to reflect statements of personal testimony as valid truths from which to make judgments as to the causes of the riots, and ultimately to define a master narrative that seeks to demonise those that publically demonise the rioters. This is emergent from an advocate position that refuses to criminalise the activities of rioters. Therefore, sociological responses have largely been to not defend the act of looting, but to defend the people who engaged in such activities – therefore giving credence to values that are anathema to ideas central to civil society, that is respect for public and private property. This is problematic in the same sense that Colin's narrative of racialised resentment is problematic. This is because it involves sociologists taking a partisan advocacy of one set of narratives over another, that is narratives of economic inactivity on behalf of the rioters over and above the voices of the victims of crime, which narrated the riots as born of a decline of civic being.

The public statements made by rioters and figures that endorsed the riots as political were diverse and contradictory. In Tottenham the discourse was about police brutality and discrimination, in other places it was a reaction to the perceived illegitimacies of MP's expenses, and in Manchester and Greater London it was about white communities losing out to migrant labour. It is in this way that contemporary sociologies of class are in effect performing the role of a public sociology, as they are attempting to recognise the voice of beleaguered communities in England's metropolitan centres. Given the levels of inequality in Britain as a whole and the impact of changes in the financing of public services there is a very real need for sociology to engage with communities faced by hardship, deprivation and poverty. However, appealing to the narratives of class and power found in statements made by these communities is problematic, because unless the researcher is willing to endorse everything that is voiced, it is arbitrary to explain and defend it as a process of social class, rather than a process of 'racial' group formation and resent; or a defence of justice against injustice moreover than an example of anti-civil intolerance of generalised inequality. In short, sociology cannot be selective in what aspects of 'voice' are seen as legitimate and what are seen as illegitimate and furthermore what concepts are subjects and what are objects. The public sociology of social class is then plagued with theoretical and normative problems that cannot be answered from within itself, but only with recourse to other branches of the sociological enterprise, simply because it cannot demonstrate why looting was a valid response to inequality, whereas holding a racialised and resentful view of ethnic' others is invalid. From a lay point of view, the rioters were acting in a 'class conscious' albeit anti-social fashion. This is something that satisfies critically engaged public sociologists who are keen to advocate on behalf of beleaguered individuals and communities. Also from a lay point of view Colin was right to say that if all migrants were removed he would have been able to use the post office quicker – this is self-evident on the basis that if there are fewer people in a queue you will get to the front quicker! These seem like completely different points, but from the point of view of assessing the palatability of public sociology they represent the same problem. This is because public sociology seeks to empower 'voice', but it is philosophically impotent in explaining the boundary between voice that attacks an abstract concept of 'property' with a voice that attacks ethnic others. In many of the areas of rioting in 2011 these discourses were intertwined, with people reacting against the property ownership of minority ethnic groups. The problem is that from what evidence or philosophy does sociology judge behaviour and the objects of its disdain without resorting to mere descriptive accounts?

In this vein, very few academic researchers, myself included, would want to legitimate and thus defend the validity of Colin's racist discourse as an outcome of a general imperative in research to penetrate the ethnographic content of class community. My research programme was however designed to allow Colin to express his 'voice'. The problem is that the boundaries between what we identify as class community/identity and racialised community is primarily a normative, not conceptual or material point; for if it was material then Colin is right in more than his own sense and if it was conceptual then what is the rationale for choosing one over the other? From a purely procedural point of view, a public sociology would recognise Colin's right to conceptualise the world as he sees fit – this happened to be along the fault lines of racial resentment – it would also recognise rioter's view that they were 'getting something back from society' as legitimate protest. There is a scholarly point to make here as a libertarian project public sociology is simply journalism – in that it makes no sustained effort to analyse Colin's statements in regards to other forms of sociological knowledge and empirical evidence. The ultimate point is therefore, to what forms of sociological knowledge and empirical evidence, which are multiple and diverse, do we subject Colin's narrative of social relations? The problem for sociology is from what normative base we accept the internal legitimacy of individual and community voice, without legitimising anti-civil divisiveness. Furthermore, what are the sociological norms that decide and judge what is a right and wrong way to conceptualise the structure of society? This is a point about the origins of sociological concepts, such as class or ethnicity; but as public sociology views legitimate knowledge as emergent from voice, then the efficacy of concepts constructed and employed through sociology is impossible to defend theoretically, empirically or normatively. These questions can be consolidated into a question as to the nature of sociological voice amongst 'other' voices and the basis of its own distinction. There was much of value in Colin's narrative on his social world, but it is the task of sociology to decide what parts were valid and what parts were to put it bluntly 'racist nonsense'. This tells us something about the authority which sociology has and should continue to exert in its influence over public policy and discourse, something that must be conducted consistently and evenly in a conceptually rigorous fashion.

The fact of the matter is that Colin's societal perspective and prescriptions for his emancipation were illiberal, as whilst they defended his right to freedom of consciousness and emancipation from ideological control they erected an authoritarian boundary between who could participate in this Jerusalem. His conceptual schema was drawn from emotional resentment not 'scientific' principles. The 'voices' drawn from rioters narratives suffered the same paradox, whilst rioting to challenge the status quo of property and affluence in order to empower themselves through the expropriation of consumer goods (i.e. to liberate themselves!) they erected an authoritarian boundary that deemed private and public property to be profane. This is again illiberal, because it uses anti-social force to secure emancipation and liberation for some over and above others as an outcome of an emotional basis of its conceptual articulation. Skeggs' (2004, 2005) analysis of the neo-liberal entrepreneurial self suffers the same disadvantages as it recognises voices labelled as 'chavs' through a libertarian ideal of cultural autonomy, whilst simultaneously applying an authoritarian disdain to identities that voice a neo-liberal ideal of self-hood – so on the one hand it is libertarian, but only on the basis of culturally annihilating other antagonistic forms of self through its analysis. If public sociology is to be regarded as a libertarian movement in social theory then sociologists have to accept the legitimacy of both these discourses on emancipation, because there is no warrant to prefer one form of expression over another. To make an assessment as to the validity of identities and voice they require analytical recourse and detachment to the capacities of other branches of the sociological enterprise.

CONCLUSION: THE VOICE OF THE SOCIOLOGICAL ENTERPRISE

It is worth recapping on the disjuncture between professional and public sociology in order to conclude. The argument against professional sociology on behalf of public sociology is that professional sociology social problems, social struggles and inequalities in an impersonal and indifferent manner, preferring to view them in an abstract way relative to sociological debates surrounding structure/agency, causality, function, methods etc. Public sociology also responds to the strategic client-centred view of social research promoted by policy-orientated researchers by emphasising advocacy over managerialism. In an attempt to provide a 'voice' for sublimated groups and identities public sociology struggles in maintaining a sense of moral authority over which truth claims made by various publics are valid – due to its outlying libertarian ideals. To put it simply this means that 'voice' constructs concepts as well as their meaning so the concepts are a priori. This applies to class equally as it applies to 'race' and ethnicity. It has been argued so far that the veracity of public sociology cannot really occur without a more explicit dialogue with critical sociology, which is the often-neglected aspect of Burawoy's four types. This is because critical sociology is the domain where norms, ideas and concepts are debated more extensively; however, the critical edge comes at a cost to the overall liberalism of sociology's enterprise, because critical research is often un-critical of its own assumptions, especially in their critique of ideology, which is the case when critical sociology is drawn into dialogue with public sociology. So to conclude, we're still no closer to asking the outlying question as to whether sociology can legitimately provide a critical analysis of Colin's racialised world view!

The answer to this problem is a more productive relationship between public and professional sociology. This is on the basis that professional sociology has developed two very important scholarly activities pertinent to the problems associated with public and critical sociology, namely an engagement with political theory via theories of citizenship and social justice and methodologies that marshal evidence. Both these activities inform the development of concepts. In this way, Burawoy is mistaken to see professional sociology as solely instrumental; though it does possess a less direct regard to the 'emotional' underpinnings of concepts in terms of their 'natural' status. The justification of this recourse can be found in the fact that it is through these scholarly traditions that sociology finds its academic meaning and voice, without which it is little more than journalism; projects that are professional in domains outside academe. Professional sociology works mainly as a project to develop constructions *of* sociological theory, rather than social theory, which can be characterised as discourses *about* theory.

Whilst critical sociology plays a purposeful role in criticising norms, values and the use of concepts it cannot with any validity construct them, because to what then is its critical purpose? As explored above, critical sociology ceases to become critical if it defines the concepts it uses since the boundaries between critical and conventional knowledge become obscure. As noted, this is a problem when critical sociology applies a concept like emancipation to field research – in that it ceases to be critical of the concept and often relies on critiquing public (mis)understandings of the concept. A much under-evaluated aspect of professional sociology is that it socialises concepts drawn from political theory and is therefore important because political theory is the scholarly tradition in which norms and values are discussed in rational terms to the ends of concept construction. A very good example of where professional sociology indulges an engagement in the discourses on normativity, the staple diet of the political theorist, is Marshall et al.'s (1997) *Against all Odds*. This book organises its sociological theorising of economic inequalities in relation to the normative principles of justice – in this way it demonstrates the potential paradoxes and inconsistencies that emerge through researchers' neglect of the political origins of their own staple conceptual diet! This example is further meaningful, because it draws its conclusions from a thorough investigation of 'evidence' – which as noted above is a second major force of professional sociology.

When considering the role evidence plays in sociological enquiry it is easy to fall into stale debates over the advantages of qualitative and quantitative methodologies; this chapter is not concerned with such an issue and regards these debates to be technical discussions internal to any sociological enquiry. What is being argued in this chapter is that evidence is taken seriously regardless of the methods of data capture, because it is through the investigation and scrutiny of evidence that the sociological enterprise truly argues for some variety of 'emancipation'. As Goldthorpe (2000) explains, after years of tension and dispute between quantitative and qualitative researchers as to the 'correct' social science method, an appeal to evidence is perhaps the commonly held standard regardless of perspective. He argues that there is in fact little philosophical difference between survey methods and ethnographies on the basis that both follow the same path in that there is one logic of inference, namely that theory follows evidence. There is therefore no tension between public and professional sociology beyond productive differences of perspective, but this only works if public sociology is conducted in a liberal rather than libertarian way, because the latter substitutes evidence with the legitimacy of voice as the basis of valid knowledge claims.

Let us return to Colin and his discourse and explore the potential sociological responses to his claims and the way in which they differently marshal the concept of emancipation. Firstly, conventional professional sociology would refute Colin's discourse as mere opinion based upon the claim that individual perspectives are inherently flawed – this disempowers voice, but often purposively so in order to sustain some wider sense of emancipation – in British sociology this has historically been to argue for the Welfare state and comprehensive education etc. (Savage, 2010). Public sociology has developed as an attempt to go beyond this disempowerment of voice in order to capture the emotional power of community voice to create a more civic sense of emancipation (Burawoy, 2005). However, some community voices are implicitly seen as more valid than others and worthy of emancipation, so Colin is still mistaken because his characterisation of society is in opposition with the wider values of most sociologists. In order to sustain this moral authority over the 'correct' way to characterise sociology it has been argued that public sociology engages with critical sociology – it strives towards the emancipation of voice by criticising the role of ideology in constructing people's worldviews – this is held to be emancipatory, but we can see that it still falls back onto a moral absolutism that more often than not regards populist thinking to be the outcome of errant ideology. It was explained with reference to the 2011 English riots that many (not all) sociologists find anti-social behaviour theoretically acceptable when it revolves around a particular worldview rooted in class oppression.

There are two routes out of this quagmire, one is to have a completely libertarian public sociology that accepts ALL voices as equal, by virtue of this would to include the voice of sociology, also. Therefore concepts inherent to the sociological enterprise would hold equal validity to those constructed by lay members of society – it was argued that this strategy ultimately de-professionalises sociology to the point where it can make no claims over and above the voices it represents. I want to argue that there is a second route that is sociologically more productive in that it includes the aims of both professional and public sociologies. The point of concession is that both activities have to humble themselves to the fact that they cannot replace each other's activities with any degree of validity, but they can work in a division of labour that also includes policy as an external activity and critical sociology as an internal activity. The concession for professional sociology is that it has to accept that the objects of its enquiry often fall outside of its 'professional' scope – the subject of sociology is ultimately public. However, public sociology needs to concede that it cannot chase emancipation as an immediate end of simply representing voice. It needs to be constantly critical and reflexive of its relationship to the sociological enterprise, which includes a study of its truth claims and normative foundations. Despite the fact that the subject of public sociology is outside the boundaries of conventional professional sociology there is still an imperative to appeal to wider professional principles, these are found within the domain of political theory and standards of evidence. The overall sociological enterprise is then one of a choreographed interdependence of specialisms. The reason why this is an imperative is because, for sociology to be truly emancipatory it must remain rigorous with a voice distinct from others, because a failure to ensure this is to fail the individuals and communities who should most benefit from the sociological enterprise. The answer to the opening conundrum is not then to surrender to voice, or to arbitrarily declassify some voices as mere ideology, but to actively construct bodies of knowledge based upon a range and diversity of evidence that challenge understandings of society antithetical and antagonistic to general liberal principles – through this sociology is the professional route to emancipation of the societies it seeks to know and understand. As a consequence, all sociology conducted in this arrangement can be considered professional.

REFERENCES

Alexander, J. (2003). *The meanings of social life: A cultural sociology*. Oxford: Oxford University Press.
Allen, K., & Taylor, Y. (2011). Retrieved from http://sociologyandthecuts.wordpress.com/2012/01/17/failed-femininities-and-troubled-mothers-gender-and-the-riots-by-kim-allen-and-yvette-taylor/
Banton, M. (1998). *Racial theories*. Cambridge, MA: Cambridge University Press.
Bennett, T., Savage, M., Silva, E., Warde, A., Gayo-Cal, M., & Wright D. (Eds.). (2008). *Class, culture, distinction*. London: Routledge.
Brewer, R. (2005). Response to Michael Buroway's commentary: "The critical turn to public sociology". *Critical Sociology, 31*(3), 353–359.
Brewis, J., & Jack, G. (2010). Consuming chavs: The ambiguous politics of gay chavinism. *Sociology, 44*(2), 1–18.
Burawoy, M. (2004). American sociological association presidential address: For public sociology. *The British Journal of Sociology, 56*(2), 259–294.

Burawoy, M. (2005). The critical turn to public sociology. *Critical Sociology, 31*(3), 313–326.

Burawoy, M. (2008). What is to be done? Theses on the degradation of social existence in a globalizing world. *Current Sociology, 56*(3), 351–359.

Dench, G., Gavron, K., & Young, M. (2006). *The new east end: Kinship, race, and conflict.* London: Profile.

Elder-Vass, D. (2011). The causal power of discourse. *Journal for the Theory of Social Behaviour, 41*(2), 143–160.

Fanon, F. (1972). *Black skins/white masks.* London: Paladin.

Ghamari-Tabrizi, B. (2005). Can Burawoy make everybody happy? Comments on public sociology. *Critical Sociology, 31*(3), 361–369.

Goldthorpe, J. H. (1969). *The affluent worker in the class structure.* London: Cambridge University Press.

Goldthorpe, J. H. (2000). *On sociology: Numbers, narratives, and the integration of research and theory.* Oxford: Oxford University Press.

Harvey, L. (1990). *Critical social research.* London: Unwin Hyman.

Jones, O. (2011). *Chavs: The demonisation of the working classes.* London: Verso.

Katz-Fishman, W., & Scott, J. (2005). Comments on Burawoy: A view from the bottom-up. *Critical Sociology, 31*(3), 371–374.

Latour, B. (2005). *Reassembling the social: An introduction to actor-network-theory.* Oxford: Oxford University Press.

Lawler, S. (2005). Introduction: Class, culture and identity. *Sociology, 39*(5), 797–806.

Lin, N. (2001). *Social capital: A theory of social structure and action.* Cambridge: Cambridge University Press.

Marshall, G., Swift, A., & Roberts, S. (1997). *Against the odds: Social class and social justice in industrial societies.* Oxford: Oxford University Press.

O'Connell-Davidson, J. (1998). *Prostitution, power and freedom.* Cambridge: Polity Press.

Said, E. (2003). *Orientalism.* London: Penguin.

Savage, M. (2010). *Identities and social change in Britain since 1940.* Oxford: Oxford University Press.

Skeggs, B. (1997). *Formations of class and gender.* London: Sage.

Skeggs, B. (2004). *Class, self, and culture.* London: Routledge.

Skeggs, B. (2005). The making of class through visualising moral subject formation. *Sociology, 39*(5), 965–982.

Tittle, C. R. (2004). The arrogance of public sociology. *Social Forces, 82*(4), 1639–1643.

Wright Mills, C. (1959). *The sociological imagination.* Oxford: Oxford University Press.

PART II
ENCOUNTERS

ETHICS AND SOCIAL CONFLICT: A FRAMEWORK FOR SOCIAL RESEARCH

Marco Marzano

ABSTRACT

Purpose – *To fill the gap between conflict theories and ethnographic methods. In fact, if one considers recent sociological production as a whole, one notes that, on the one hand, scholars belonging to the European Marxian and Weberian traditions have indeed centered their analytical interests on the theme of conflict and power, on the other hand they have studied them using the tools of macro-analysis and historical sociology, and therefore in more abstract and general terms. For their part, interactionists and ethnographers, especially American, have closely and efficaciously studied society at the elementary level of micro-interactions and everyday life; but they have often (with some felicitous exceptions) underestimated the weight and importance of conflicts and power.*

Findings – *The paper shows that the situation was different (better) in the 1950s and 1960s, and that recently, the field of conflict methodology (or critical ethnography) has been left almost entirely to brilliant investigative journalists. One of the causes of this has certainly been the spread, in recent decades, of an ethical regulation of research and of a deontological conception of the ethics of social research.*

Ethics in Social Research
Studies in Qualitative Methodology, Volume 12, 73–90
Copyright © 2012 by Emerald Group Publishing Limited
All rights of reproduction in any form reserved
ISSN: 1042-3192/doi:10.1108/S1042-3192(2012)0000012007

The paper calls for the discovery of a new ethical conception (utilitarian, ethics of responsibility) alternative to the dominant deontological approach and for the adoption, following the sociologist Jack Douglas, of an investigative method of social research. In the final part of the paper, some concrete research examples are provided and a final appeal for critical ethnography and the study of powerful organizations has been made.

Keywords: Social power; conflict methodology; conflict theories; fieldwork; research ethics; symbolic interactionism

Conflict theories have long occupied an important place in social and political theory. Their forerunners were the masters of European political realism, primarily Machiavelli (2005) and Hobbes (and the great Greek historian Thucydides, as their ideal progenitor). For Hobbes (2010), as well known, in the state of nature – that is, in the absence of political regulation – every man considers his fellows to be rivals and competitors in the quest for power, and the social world is dominated by mutual suspicion and a constant struggle to acquire resources. In a context of this kind, reason is predominantly used to calculate and select the best means to pursue one's interests, while the existence of religion – today we would say of political ideologies as well – is explained by a thirst for knowledge about how the universe works and its prime mover, but above all by the desire to reduce, or to eliminate, the insecurity and fear of the future that uncertain and precarious life on earth inevitably induces in its inhabitants. Also the pain felt at the misfortunes of others is, for Hobbes (2010), caused by the terror that those misfortunes may happen to oneself.

In more recent times, conflict theory (Collins, 1988) has found fruitful application in the Marxian and Weberian traditions, which sometimes overlap and interweave. Simplifying to the extreme, the main difference between the former and latter tradition is that, for Marx, conflict was essentially and primarily a clash between social classes, whilst for Weber it could occur in numerous contexts and dimensions, and therefore not only between classes but also, for instance, between status groups and parties, and in diverse and historically unpredictable patterns. Moreover, for Marx, conflict was a temporary condition of human history. It would inevitably dwindle away with its protagonists, the social classes. For Weber, by contrast, history did not have a final stage, a conclusive outcome, so that conflicts were not bound to disappear with the passage of time and the succession of historical eras.

I would say that the majority of contemporary conflict theorists now firmly side with Weber (Collins, 1988): that is, they have adopted a 'Verstehen' approach and 'agnostic' attitude in their study of the phenomenon, and they are prepared to consider conflict as a permanent (though often implicit) datum of social ontology, refusing to assign priority of one form of conflict over another, or to pronounce on the desirability of revolution or socialism.

We can take a further heuristic step forward by arguing that the analysis of conflicts can be profitably extended beyond confrontation/competition among human beings, among institutions or among both, to encompass the aporiae and contradictions of social life, the distances among what appears to be and what actually is, between rhetoric and reality – or better, among different versions of social reality, and again, between promises and intentions, on the one hand, and results on the other. Such analysis thus comes to coincide with a realistic – some might say cynical – political philosophy.

This cynicism is difficult to discern in the American interactionist tradition, in which the theme of conflict, and those closely connected concepts of power and dominance, have certainly not been of such central importance (Athens, 2007, 2009).[1] For Mead and Blumer, the routine of social life was made up of cooperation and trust, the capacity to empathize with others, and to contribute to the progress of society. Also those symbolic interactionists, like Strauss (1978), who devoted more thorough, and more profitable, study to organizational settings – those in which conflict is more likely and frequent – preferred to centre their conceptual apparatus on the notion of 'negotiation' rather than those of conflict and power. To cite a more recent example, the work of Weick (1990, 1993, 1995), the most sophisticated heir to the micro-sociological and psycho-social traditions (of symbolic interactionism, ethnomethodology and cognitivism) in the field of organization studies, is almost entirely unconcerned with conflict and power. The breakdowns in sensemaking which Weick blamed for many organizational disasters that he reconstructed (the Tenerife air disaster and that of Mann Gulch, to cite the two most notorious ones) exhibit in abundance (a) bounded rationality, (b) deficient learning, (c) lack of trust, (d) misfortune, (e) inadequate technologies, (f) the presence of unconscious factors and many other things besides. But no mention is made of conflicts, of differences in interests and perspectives, or of the struggle for power. In short, entirely absent in Weick is the Hobbesian *homo homini lupus* (man is a wolf to man), or the actor who, by resorting to violence and power, limits the actions of another: the authoritarian Leviathan.

The difficulty of interactionists in recognizing the role and weight of conflicts and power in social life is entirely consistent with the priority traditionally given by ethnographers – primarily anthropologists (in rejection of political and cultural colonialism) but also by sociologists – to the study of the weakest, most marginalized and 'voiceless' social groups, in an endeavour to ensure that their cultural practices also obtain dignity and social recognition. This ethically admirable undertaking, however, has led to an underestimation of the importance of also studying, in-depth and 'empirically', the 'strong' social groups – the powerful and victorious ones.

If one considers sociological production as a whole from this point of view, one notes that, on the one hand, scholars belonging to the European Marxian and Weberian traditions have indeed centred their analytical interests on the theme of conflict and power, but they have studied them (especially the Marxians) using the tools of macro-analysis and historical sociology, and therefore in more abstract and general terms. For their part, interactionists and ethnographers, especially American, have closely and efficaciously studied society at the elementary level of micro-interactions and everyday life; but they have often underestimated the weight and importance of conflicts and power.

Fortunately, there is no lack of felicitous exceptions to this pattern, especially in the 1950s and 1960s. Here I shall rapidly survey only some of the most important ones. I start with Erving Goffman's masterpiece, *Asylum*, which describes, with exceptional analytical density, the organizational mechanisms (violent even in the absence of physical coercion!) by which 'total institutions' seek to shape the identities and behaviours of their inmates.

In another context, some years previously, in typically interactionist terms and armed with experiences acquired directly from a year's work in a factory machine shop, Roy (1952, 1960) had radically overturned the image of the factory as a cooperative system governed by rationality and fairness. On the contrary, Roy described in detail the profound and constant conflicts – especially on definition of piecework rates – between workers and managers. The two groups ceaselessly deceived and challenged each other. The workers resorted to every means, to every subterfuge, to evade control by the managers over times, volumes and even the 'meaning' of production and work.

For example, the machine shop operatives were at least partly able to circumvent the rigid Taylorist discipline imposed on work times and methods by the management. They tied the discipline to the 'playful' and cheerfully competitive dimension of so-called 'making out'. Such entirely informal behaviour was not envisaged by any of the rules regulating routine work, but it made the latter more pleasant and acceptable for the machine shop operatives, without expressly challenging the power relations between workforce and management within and outside the factory.

In regard to organization and business studies focused on conflict and power, besides the works by Roy, mention must certainly be made of the impressive study by Melville Dalton, *Men Who Manage*. Based on rigorously covert participant observation, and using an array of investigative methods worthy of outright espionage, the book, published in 1959, furnishes a pitiless description of everyday life in a number of American industrial companies. With a wealth of data, and writing with a cool and clinical style attentive to every detail, Dalton depicts all events and social interactions that help in understanding the factory climate and the Hobbesian state of nature at the heart of industrial civilization. This is a *bellum omnium contra omnes* (a war of all against all), but in which, contrary to Hobbes' account, a Leviathan does not eventually arise to establish the political order contractually, and to resolve, with the force of its rule, the endless mini power wars that develop within factories. On the contrary, Dalton conceives the firm, the industrial organization, as the outcome – contingent, elusive and constantly changing – of all the legitimate and above all illegitimate stratagems, subterfuges, ruses and alliances that the members of the organization deploy to achieve their purposes. Of course, there are some general constraints, rules of the game and thresholds which cannot be breached lest the entire institution collapse. But there still remains ample space for individual and group action which produces an incessant struggle in which individuals or groups resort, in more or less uninhibited and blatant manner, to all their available resources in order to obtain results favourable to them.

According to Dalton, therefore, real power does not spring from formal organizational charts, but rather from the results of everyday struggles. These are not ideological conflicts; indeed, it is often discovered that those who should be fighting on opposing fronts (for instance managers and trade unionists) are secretly in alliance.

The map of power relations within the companies studied by Dalton was drawn by 'cliques', secret groups that acted for various ends: licit and illicit, moral and immoral. Dalton furnishes a detailed typology of them, ranging from cliques founded on the division of labour, through generational, ethnic, religious or political cliques, to 'random' ones consisting, for instance, of people who refrained from power games and productive activity and tried to spend as much time as possible between the bathrooms and the coffee machines. Each clique had a particular hierarchical structure, either more horizontal or more vertical, and similar to those of political parties. After all, as one of Dalton's informants told him: 'There is as much politics here in the plant as in Washington'.

Dalton's 'anthropological' conclusion is that people earned their livings from the organization but they were unwilling to do everything required of them and, especially when they were endowed with certain specific resources (intelligence but also charm, opportunism, the 'right' religion and so on), were able to turn their weaknesses into very concrete strengths.

In the past 50 years, few scholars of corporate life have followed the empirical path marked out by Dalton. But one who has done so is Robert Jackall with his book *Moral Mazes* (1989). The most striking novelty of Jackall's work with respect to Dalton's masterpiece consists, I believe, in the fact that, in the decades that elapsed between the two works, the idea circulated in the Western world that business must have an ethical dimension, that it must be conditioned by moral factors. On reading Jackall's book, however, one realizes that this was to a large extent mere hypocrisy and that little had changed in substance. Indeed, for the managers of the twentieth century, as for Machiavelli's Prince in the sixteenth, the presence of moral criteria in business choices was regarded as one of the most serious obstacles against the rapidity and efficiency of decision-making processes. For this reason, according to Jackall, when managers acted within their firms, they abandoned – and they invited their subordinates to do the same – every moral scruple, and primarily the political or religious principles that guided their actions externally to the firm in the family or the local community. The only acceptable moral criteria within the firm were those that served the interests of those in command, no matter whether these concerned conformism or nepotism. For these managers, the Protestant ethic of the American protocapitalists was only a faded image in the family photograph album and they appear rather similar to the bureaucrats described by Bauman (2000) in his *Modernity and the Holocaust*.

However, factories and organizations in general are not the only places where conflicts and power struggles have been narrated and described with close attention to 'ethnographic' detail. Equally excellent and striking results have been obtained in the field of community studies. This is, for instance, the case of the book, published for the first time in 1958, by Vidich and Bensman, *Small Town in Mass Societies*. The research on which the book was based came about accidentally, so to speak, as the unexpected result of Arthur Vidich's appointment as field director of an ambitious urban research project by the *Department of Child Development and Family Relations* of the University of Cornell, in New York State. To perform his duties, Vidich was required to move to Ithaca, the town subject to the research and which was close to Cornell. Vidich spent two and a half years in Ithaca, with the task not only of directing the collection of the large mass of encoded information envisaged by the project but also to immerse himself in the urban atmosphere, to observe at first hand and in detail the entire social and community life of the small town. Vidich performed this latter task so well that he discovered numerous aspects of life in Ithaca which clashed with the idealized and harmonious image that the local sponsors of the research so earnestly wanted and that the university research team dutifully reproduced in its final research report (Vidich & Bensman, 1968).

Vidich soon realized that he had acquired ethnographic material of great interest for a community study separate and distinct from the official project. He talked about this with his friend and colleague, Joseph Bensman, and the two of them set about drafting what would become *Small Town in Mass Societies*: a highly unflattering portrait of life in Springsdale (the fictitious name given to Ithaca). Vidich and Bensman described in detail, although they used pseudonyms, the composition and operation of the 'invisible government' which informally regulated the life of the town. They also treated many other themes rigorously excluded from official report: mechanisms of social exclusion, privileges, the closed and sectarian attitudes of certain protagonists of local life.

Publication of the book provoked scandal and indignation among many of Springsdale's residents. The most striking reaction occurred on the occasion of the traditional Fourth of July parade, when a float carrying a large-scale replica of the cover of the book was followed by a procession of the town's dignitaries described in the book, each of them wearing a mask bearing the pseudonym assigned by Vidich and Bensman in *Small Town*. 'But the payoff', one reads in a local newspaper report published some days later, 'was the final scene, a manure-spreader filled with very rich barnyard fertilizer, over which was bending an effigy of the "Author"'.

But it was not only residents of the town that reacted angrily to the revelations contained in *Small Town*; so too did many of Vidich's colleagues at Cornell University, and especially the already well-known William Foot Whyte,[2] who decided to organize, in the journal of which he was editor at the time, *Human Organization*, a broad critical debate on the alleged 'ethical sins' committed by the authors of *Small Town* in regard to the residents of Ithaca (Whyte, 1993).

The responses by Vidich and Bensman to their critics strike me as being of great interest still today. There is a fundamental difference, wrote the two sociologists, between financed or sponsored research and free, individual research. The former is obliged to furnish descriptions and interpretations of the social reality which satisfy the sponsors of the research, which encourage, and reassure them. It treats as pathologies, or more often glosses over or omits entirely, the negative and contradictory aspects of collective life: racism, discrimination, inequalities, conflicts and power struggles.

By contrast, independent research can, indeed must, according to Vidich and Bensman, pursue the goal of disinterested knowledge. It must, of course, reduce the harmful consequences for the people studied to a minimum, but it should not be paralysed by fear of their possible negative reactions.

After all, Vidich and Bensman continue resentment and hostility in the populations subject to organizational or community studies, especially if they circulate widely, are entirely predictable, even inevitable. This happened after publication of the Linds' *Middletown* and after that of Warner's *Yankee City*, as well as Selznick's book on the TVA (Selznick, 1949). In fact, the worse reactions, the most aggressive and indignant ones, are provoked when research is damaging to those who matter, the powerful. But, Vidich and Bensman aptly ask, should the interest of the latter in receiving a 'good press', in defending their image, coincide with that of the social sciences? Must sociologists become harmless, self-censoring, non-committal, only for fear that someone might be offended by what they say? Is it really necessary, we would say today, to be politically correct at the cost of conducting research that is banal, irrelevant and technically and methodologically inoffensive?

I shall return to these questions in the second part of the paper. For now I wish to conclude this brief review with a paradoxical, and in my opinion highly significant, curiosity: the editor of *Human Organization* in 1958 who was so unrestrained in his ethical condemnation of Vidich and Bensman was the same William Foot Whyte who, exactly 30 years later, was subject to a harsh attack by Marianne Boelen, who accused him, in an issue of the *Journal of Contemporary Ethnography* which has gone down in history, of having caused a large amount of moral damage to many of the protagonists of his masterpiece *Street Corner Society*, and principally to the celebrated Doc, for years Whyte's principal informant, accomplice. This was a 'boomerang' for Whyte which confirms, if nothing else, the difficulty of claiming – in ethnographic research which involves long 'cohabitations' and detailed narrations – some sort of moral superiority or virginity.

In any case, what is certain is that it is difficult to find in the more recent ethnographic literature examples similar to those that I have cited, studies that 'offend' like those by Goffman, Dalton, Vidich and Bensman. The field has been left almost entirely to brilliant investigative journalists like Barbara Ehrenreich (2011) or Roberto Saviano (2008).

One of the causes of the impoverishment of social research has certainly been the impressive spread, in recent decades, and especially in the United States where the social sciences are more firmly established, of the ethical regulation of research (Dingwall, 2008). A host of ethics committees has sprung up not only in universities, but also in public institutions (especially health care), to supervise the work of researchers, especially qualitative ones, and ensure that they do not violate the rights and dignity of the people subject to their research. The problem is that, as testified by the complaints of numerous researchers, the reasons why ethical committees block or require changes to a research project are not always clear and indisputable. It may happen, in fact, that, one of the reasons for 'censorship' of a research project is the desire not to expose the relative institution to the risk of being observed and severely criticized, or the fear, in the case of a university ethics committee, that publications by an employee of the university may expose it to legal problems.

Turning to the past, it comes to mind that, if Erving Goffman had been obliged to appear before the ethics committee of the St. Elisabeth psychiatric hospital in New York to illustrate and 'ethically justify' every phase of his research project on total institutions, we would probably not be able to read *Asylum* today, or at least those parts most directly based on Goffman's participant observation at the hospital. And perhaps Leon Festinger would lose his university post if he today published his 'scandalous' *When Prophecy Fails* (a memorable 'covert' observation of the activities of a small American millennialist sect waiting for the end of the world). And the list could continue (Festinger, Riecken, & Schachter, 1956; Goffman, 1961; Johnson, 1975).

In short, it has become extremely difficult to conduct empirical research from a conflictualist perspective without encountering numerous obstacles, the result being that even the many sociological analyses that adopt a critical gaze on Western capitalist society remain at the level of very generic abstraction.

What is to be done? How can we react to this cultural and political climate? Certainly not by ignoring the changes that it has produced. In other words, it is not possible to invoke, *sic et simpliciter*, the justifications adduced many years ago by Humphrey, Dalton or Vidich and Bensman for the conduct of covert research: the mere freedom of research, the right to pursue scientific knowledge as the principal goal. In this changed cultural context, it is necessary to take serious account of ethical issues.

From this point of view, put extremely briefly, the problem seems to consist especially in the fact that predominant in recent years has been a deontological conception of the ethics of social research, according to which the rightness of a certain human action can only be judged in relation to compliance with a rule (for example, the rule that makes informed consent mandatory). Everything that breaches a general and abstract moral rule is, from this point of view, inadmissible and immoral.

But the deontological approach to the ethics of social research is not the only one possible. There is at least one alternative, the utilitarian or consequentialist approach, which evaluates the moral goodness of the actions of human beings, and therefore also those of social researchers, according to their consequences in the social world. It is an approach that closely resembles the Weberian 'ethics of responsibility', as opposed to the absolute 'ethics of principles'. Those who choose the former, Weber wrote, are willing not only to accept responsibility for the consequences of their actions but also to admit that the good does not always derive from the good, and vice versa, that the bad does not always derive from the bad, in the sense that the choice of more morally suspect means (for instance, in our case, covert research) sometimes produces results better than those that ensue from the selection of less doubtful means.

This view of the relationship between means and ends is also that of the sociologist Jack Douglas who, in his *Investigative Social Research* – although without express mention of any particular ethical problem – proposes a conception of research work compatible with the ethics of responsibility and a utilitarian approach.

For Douglas, social life consists of moments of cooperation and (possibly fierce) conflict. If researchers are to understand the latter, they must admit that numerous people do not spontaneously tell the truth to those studying their behaviour except with regard to marginal, innocuous and often irrelevant aspects of their lives. They obfuscate because they have things to hide of which they are ashamed, or which they do not want to be made public; and also because they do not trust the researchers, suspecting that they may harm them or have ulterior motives. After all, Douglas writes with Hobbesian pessimism, suspicion and distrust are integral to everyday life 'society is a jungle and the animals that inhabit it are predators'. Anyone who behaves otherwise, whether a researcher or a social actor, is a simpleton destined for marginalization and defeat (Douglas, 1976).

For this reason, if researchers are to gain thorough understanding of social life, they must resort to investigative techniques like those used by many other social groups without being criminalized for it: the police, the military, industrial spies, social workers, tax inspectors and investigative journalists.

Investigation is not necessary solely to uncover the fictions or outright lies, which generally concern sex, power and money, and which everybody

– including Boy Scouts, Douglas specifies – may utter according to the situation. It is also necessary to get round their reticence ('Ah, I didn't tell you that because you didn't ask me'), and often ignorance (people very often truly do not know what happens within their organizations), or worse, self-deception.

Using an investigative method intelligently, especially by conducting direct participant observation, also makes it possible to understand the often taken-for-granted meanings that nobody thinks worth reporting, or to go beyond the impression of perfect rationality and order that those running organizations want to convey to those who observe them. If this method is not used, the researcher is compelled to remain at the surface, furnishing a version of the reality which reproduces the desires of the actors studied. In other words, I submit, the researcher ends up producing ideology or propaganda. Without investigation, Douglas declares, society is a banal object.

After all, and this is a crucial point, it is not the investigative researcher who has caused the conflict. It is the society, which is intrinsically conflictual and violent, that has done so. The researcher can either bring that conflict to the surface or leave it submerged, either show it or conceal it, either seek to explain it or ignore it. But it is certainly not the researcher who is responsible for having caused that conflict. Nor can it be said that s/he inflicts on the people being studied greater moral suffering than that perpetrated by other groups, such as police officers (who often resort to heavy-handed methods) or journalists (who have no qualms about destroying people's reputations). And if some untruth is necessary, especially at the beginning of the research, when researchers declare their intentions while trying to appear harmless, or when they present themselves as better than they really are by concealing some or other defect, this subterfuge is amply repaid by the results obtained in terms of knowledge and truth. Such knowledge and truth are useful for justifying falsehoods and are therefore also ethically unimpeachable. In fact, giving detailed and empirically 'dense' accounts of conflicts makes it possible not only to furnish a more realistic and accurate description of social life but also to increase its 'openness' and foster greater civic awareness – in other words, to improve the quality of public life.

I shall seek to back this statement with a concrete example taken from my research (Marzano, 2012). Some time ago I decided, within a broader project on Italian Catholicism, to study a religious movement formally affiliated with the Catholic Church: the *Cammino Neocatecumenale* (Neocatechumenal Way). This is one of the most powerful and widespread Catholic organizations in Italy, but to date it has also been one of the most mysterious and least studied.

For precisely this reason, I decided to approach the group and observe it from close at hand. As my first move, I contacted a parish priest in my city whom I knew to have ties with the *Cammino* and explained my intentions to him. He immediately suggested that I attend the 'catechesis for adults', which is the 'course' organized by the movement to recruit new adherents. The course consists in two and a half months of 'lessons' during which leaders of the organization, called 'catechists', furnish all the rudiments of the catechumenal theology to the participants, together with all the instructions necessary to conduct ordinary ritual activity appropriately (i.e. according to the dictates of the founder) and autonomously: from the mass to the *liturgia della parola* (liturgy of the word), from *convivenze* (gatherings) to group confessions. At the end of the 'course', and if a sufficient number of participants still remain, the group of 'students' (so to speak) becomes a 'community of the Way', or a full-fledged 'cell' of the movement.

For two and a half months, I attended all the catechesis meetings. The catechists, who were aware of the reason for my presence, asked me to be 'discreet', in the sense that they requested me not to reveal the true reason for my presence to the other participants. This proved to be an obstacle for my research. It hampered me not so much in gaining better knowledge about the movement (given that the people who I met on the course were almost all, like me, approaching the organization for the first time) as in investigating why they wanted to be neophytes, how they had been approached, the social strata from which they originated and their previous experiences of religion or political participation.

The catechists treated me courteously but very formally, with politeness but also with detachment and diffidence. This attitude may have been due, at least partly, to their having read a book of mine published a few years back and entitled *Cattolicesimo Magico* (Magical Catholicism), in which I reported the results of ethnographic research on pilgrims to the famous Marian site of Medjugorje, and on adherents of *Rinnovamento nello Spirito* (Renewal in Spirit), the largest charismatic organization of Italian Catholicism. It may well have been that if the catechists had read the book, they would not have appreciated the (critical) manner in which I had described those organizations, and they would not want to repeat the ingenuousness of the protagonists of *Cattolicesimo Magico*, who had warmly welcomed me and given me ample freedom to observe many aspects of community life. There may have been a further reason for their diffidence. I do not and cannot know what it was, but I suspect that is due to application of an extremely rigorous 'company policy' which required all members to maintain strict secrecy about the group's most sensitive activities.

At the end of the course, we all had dinner together at the home of two of the catechists. On that occasion, they willingly answered – but still with extreme formality and reserve – the many questions that had occurred to me concerning the organization, its doctrine and its practices. When I asked them for permission to observe the ritual moments of an already-formed community, they allowed me to attend a prayer meeting, a mid-weekly *liturgia della parola* of a community already established for some years. Although this was a useful experience, it was still largely insufficient for me to understand the essential characteristics of the organization's operation. I then asked for permission to watch the movement's well-known (and controversial) *scrutini* (scrutinies). These are particular rituals during which (as many suspect and as I also learned), at a certain point during the initiatory process, in parish-owned premises well-protected against prying eyes, each member of a certain community is 'tried' in the presence of the brethren and sisterhood, and if necessary rebuked and humiliated by the catechists. I received a cordial but firm refusal; the same refusal as forth-coming when I asked to witness at least one *convivenza*, that is, a weekend of prayer and communal living which, at regular intervals, all the members of a community are obliged to attend. Finally, I asked to interview Paolo, the head of a community who had attended my course as an observer, or better as a 'trainee catechist': a large man aged about 40 and the father of four children. He reacted to my request with a childish expression of dismay and hastened to tell me that I should first ask for permission from Giulio, his 'catechist': 'If he says yes, then I agree as well!', he told me. I let it drop. I had already understood that any such conversation would have been futile.

The best alternative way to gain thorough knowledge of the movement would obviously have been to become a 'true initiate' regularly attending the meetings of 'my' new-found community of the 'brothers' and 'sisters' who had taken the catechesis course with me. But this would have required a considerable sacrifice, considering that (a) it would have been very difficult to maintain my status as a simple observer, which would have been extremely embarrassing for me; (b) I would have learned the truth only little by little, given the extreme parsimony and caution with which the organization's secrets were gradually revealed to its members. For example, I would have had to wait at least two years before participating in my first *scrutinio*. In short, that approach was not practicable. In the meantime, however, I had discovered the existence of a number of websites on which former members of the *Cammino Neocatecumenale* posted dramatic testi-monies, detailed denunciations, and very precise allegations against the movement. An astonishing amount of stories and analyses were posted on the websites, but their reliability was obviously doubtful if I could not meet the posters in person.

I had almost decided to set my mind at rest and abandon the matter when a friend, on listening to my despondent account of my participation in the catechesis, told me that she knew a family of apostates. 'They'd certainly be willing to talk to you. But you'd have go and meet them in the deep south of Italy, because that's where they live!' I immediately asked her if these were 'normal' people: that is, if they were not neurotic, fanatical or mentally unbalanced. 'But they're normality personified! A normal family like so many others', she reassured me. 'They ended up in the movement by chance, and they have a story to tell that will certainly interest you'. She promised me that she would immediately try to contact them, and after a few days she called to give me her friend Aldo's address and telephone number.

Thus, somewhat by accident, the second part of my research began. A few weeks after our first telephone conversation, I travelled to the city where Aldo lived with his large family: his wife Patrizia and four children, two of them adults, who had also quit the *Cammino*. For many days, I interviewed them repeatedly, both separately and all together, in the living room of their home. I gathered a large amount of chilling details about daily life within the *Cammino*, about internal power struggles and rivalries, about the methods used by the neo-catechumenal leaders to gain the obedience of their followers or take possession of their money. And much more besides. The fact that the information came from members of the same family, but with such different ages and experiences, struck me as making it more reliable.

Aldo and Patrizia put me in contact with dozens of other former members of the organization, who added nuances and disquieting details to the overall picture. I then met further former militants in other but always informal ways.

After some months of work, I obtained an in-depth description of the organization which, on the one hand, contradicted what I had observed in the first part of the research, and on the other, was not only much more complex and detailed but also more thorough and convincing.

It is very likely that the activists and leaders of the *Cammino Neocatecumenale* are unenthusiastic about the imminent publication of my research data, given that these will demonstrate that, for numerous adherents, the movement has been a source of much suffering, numerous family tensions, and public and private pain, from which they have freed themselves by a long process of 'purification' and 'disintoxication'.

Nevertheless, it should be admitted that the presence of conflicting assessments of the organization has certainly not been invented by me. What

I have done is deliberately bring them to light, evidence them and set them out in a text.

It is likely, of course, that if I had been obliged to submit my project to the scrutiny of an ethics committee, the latter would have ordered me not to change my research strategy midway through the project and abruptly set off in search of the movement's apostates. Some members of the committee might have objected that, when the neo-catechumenalists had agreed to be observed, they had not known that I would also interview their adversaries, so that they did not have the possibility to refuse to be observed. My account would certainly have been impoverished, for it would have immediately appeared partisan, being based solely on the testimonies of former activists.

But, one may ask, on considering the overall result and from the point of view of the 'ethics of responsibility' or a consequentialist approach, cannot one say that the advantages for society and for the academic community deriving from the procedure that I followed outweigh the costs (substantially those of concealing from the first group the results of my work with the second)? Is it not beneficial for the scientific community to know, for example, that these new Catholic movements operate in a way sociologically very similar to that of numerous traditional sects (mainly Protestant)? And is it not equally beneficial for the public to know what may happen, and indeed has frequently done so, to a citizen and his family if it becomes caught up in the tentacles of an organization like the *Cammino Neocatecumenale*? Moreover, is it not beneficial to give a voice, concerning that phenomenon, to those who appear ready to defend the organization and to justify its practices, but also to the many others who are instead anxious to denounce the violence, manipulations and the injustices that they believe they have suffered (or have inflicted on others) during their militancy in the movement?

This decision to recount two such contrasting versions of the same social reality is the basis of my following analytical interpretation of the phenomenon. For me, in fact, the *Cammino Neocatecumenale* is an organization much more cohesive, welcoming and protective than the traditional Catholic parishes. Yet, on the other hand, it may prove to be a mental prison from which it is difficult to emerge unscathed.

A last observation concerns the ethical imperative to remove the veil of mystery from the everyday operations of particularly influential organizations. Whilst, in fact, all individuals, all human beings, deserve equal respect, the same cannot be said about some of the social groups to which they belong. It is difficult to deny that there are enormous differences of power, reputation, resources, and psychological and social vulnerability within society and organizations. An ethically aware micro-sociology of conflict cannot ignore these differences. And it must behave accordingly: protecting the weak' in all possible ways, but subjecting the 'strong' to constructive social criticism. Qualitative researchers have never held back in pursuit of the former objective, while they have been much more indecisive in pursuing the latter.

This has been partly due to the already-mentioned commitment of ethnography to giving voice to those who do not have it, to representing the reasons, motives and everyday lives of those on the margins of social life, restoring dignity and citizenship to them.

There is more than this, however. For it is difficult to deny that conducting research on 'strong institutions' is enormously more difficult. 'How easy it is not to do certain studies, not to ask certain questions, not to report one's findings; how easy to juggle the data and the analysis', wrote Douglas. Gaining transparent and straightforward access can often be already a major undertaking: strong institutions protect themselves better; they are more aware of the risks of opening their doors to social researchers; their legal offices are ready to take action against those who threaten their interests; many of their members have less need of celebrity, they are less interested in having someone to listen to them; and they carefully conceal the grey zones which proliferate within them.

In the drawers of my desk – I believe that I am not the only ethnographer in this situation – there are two research projects aborted or drastically cut back because of the obstacles raised by the management of the organizations concerned. I started the first project in the 1990s, at the time of my doctoral dissertation, when I decided to study, amongst others, the *Communion and Liberation* religious movement. I was placed in contact with the organization's press officer, whom I repeatedly asked for permission to attend meetings of the movement's 'community schools', that is the groups which it runs in every 'setting' (a school, university, workplace) in which it is present. My request was rejected, but the press officer told me that I could instead conduct interviews with the organization's senior officials, and that I would receive a copy of the works of don Giussani, the movement's founder, 'from which', he told me, 'you can easily deduce what our spiritual and cultural experience consists of'. Obviously, I made a virtue out of necessity. But there is no doubt that if I had been given ampler opportunity to observe the 'real' life of the movement, my research would have much richer with insight.

I fared even worse when I tried some time later to observe ethnographically the everyday activities of Publitalia, the advertising agency owned by the Berlusconi group, and from which had come many of middle-level and senior officials of the *Forza Italia* party headed by the famous tycoon. My intention was to understand how it was possible for a business culture, however strong and closely integrated, to generate a political party, and for what reasons so many Publitalia employees had decided to enter politics alongside their employer: had they mobilized spontaneously or had they been compelled to do so? Through a friend, I obtained an interview with a Publitalia executive, who received me a couple of times in his office and even invited me to a sumptuous company dinner with a final show put on by a television star. But he also told me that no thorough research on his organization would be possible. My presence in the offices would impede the work of the employees, and interviews with the latter were out of the question.

Therefore, with regret that I still feel today, I was forced to abandon the project. I asked myself what immoral act I would have committed, what ethical code I would have breached if had then used Dalton's method: that is, if I had arranged to have myself hired by the organization so that I could observe at first hand the workings of that very peculiar Italian firm. But this is an endeavour in which no one has ever succeeded and which still leaves so many aspects of the genesis in mystery – perhaps unique in the world – of a political party from a firm. But in an open society is it not permissible to reduce as much as possible the secrets and mysteries harboured by society and organizations?

This would be to shed light on the action of 'strong' institutions, of powerful organizations. It is this that I believe should be the intention of those who engage in critical ethnography: to bring out the grey zones of social life, the latter's overt and covert conflicts.

NOTES

1. David Maines (1977, 2000) takes a different view.
2. Whyte's *Street Corner Society*, with its celebrated methodological appendix, had been republished with great success a few years previously, in 1955.

REFERENCES

Athens, L. H. (2007). Radical interactionism: Going beyond mead. *Journal for the Theory of Social Behavior, 37*(2), 137–165.
Athens, L. H. (2009). The roots of "Radical interactionism". *Journal for the Theory of Social Behaviour, 39*(4), 388–414.

Bauman, Z. (2000). *Modernity and the holocaust*. Ithaca, NY: Cornell University Press.

Collins, R. (1988). *Theoretical sociology*. New York, NY: Harcourt Brace.

Dalton, M. (1959). *Men who manage*. New York, NY: Wiley.

Dingwall, R. (2008). The ethical case against ethical regulation in humanities and social science research. *Twenty-First Century Society: Journal of the Academy of Social Sciences*, *3*(1), 1–12.

Douglas, J. (1976). *Investigative social research: Individual and team field research*. Thousand Oaks, CA: Sage.

Ehrenreich, B. (2011). *Nickel and dimed: On (not) getting by in America*. New York: Picador.

Festinger, L. R., Riecken, H. W., & Schachter, S. (1956). *When prophecy fails*. Minneapolis, MN: University of Minnesota Press.

Goffman, E. (1961). *Asylums: Essays on the social situation of mental patients and other inmates*. New York, NY: Doubleday.

Hobbes, T. (2010). *Leviathan. Or the matter, forme, & power of a common-wealth ecclesiasticall and civill*. New Haven, CT: Yale University Press.

Jackall, R. (1989). *Moral mazes. The world of corporate managers*. Oxford: Oxford University Press.

Johnson, J. (1975). *Doing field research*. New York, NY: Free Press.

Machiavelli, N. (2005). *The prince*. Boston, MA: Bedford/St. Martin's.

Maines, D. R. (1977). Social organization and social structure in symbolic interactionist thought. *Annual Review of Sociology*, *3*, 235–259.

Maines, D. R. (2000). Some thoughts on the interactionist analysis of class stratification: A commentary. *Symbolic Interaction*, *23*, 253–258.

Marzano, M. (2012). *Quel che resta dei cattolici. Inchiesta sulla crisi della Chiesa italiana*. Milano: Feltrinelli.

Roy, D. F. (1952). Quota restriction and goldbricking in a machine shop. *American Journal of Sociology*, *57*(5), 427–442.

Roy, D. F. (1960). "Banana Time": Job satisfaction and informal interaction. *Human Organization*, *18*(4), 158–168.

Saviano, R. (2008). *Gomorrah: A personal journey into the violent international empire of Naples' organized crime system*. New York: Picador.

Selznick, P. (1949). *TVA and the grass roots. A study of politics and organizations*. Los Angeles, CA: University of California Press.

Strauss, A. L. (1978). *Negotiations: Varieties, contexts, processes, and social order*. San Francisco, CA: Jossey-Bass Inc.

Vidich, A. J., & Bensman, J. (1968). *Small town in mass society: Class, power and religion in a rural community*. Princeton, NJ: Princeton University Press.

Weick, K. E. (1990). The vulnerable system: An analysis of the tenerife air disaster. *Journal of Management*, *16*(3), 571–593.

Weick, K. E. (1993). The collapse of sensemaking in organizations: The mann gulch disaster. *Administrative Science Quarterly*, *38*(4), 628–652.

Weick, K. E. (1995). *Sensemaking in organizations*. Thousand Oaks, CA: Sage.

Whyte, W. F. (1993). *Street corner society: The social structure of an Italian slum*. Chicago, IL: University of Chicago Press.

THE POLITICS OF TELLING: BEYOND SIMILARITY AND DIFFERENCE IN THE INTERVIEW RELATIONSHIP

Michael Keenan

ABSTRACT

Purpose – *This chapter reflects on my research experiences as a heterosexual man interviewing gay clergy. The chapter focuses on the interviewer/interviewee relationship reflecting on the place of similarity and difference in the research interaction.*

Methodology/approach – *The chapter reflects on my experiences of undertaking feminist inspired qualitative interviews on sensitive issues.*

Findings – *The chapter argues for a move beyond a binary understanding of similarity and difference and illustrates interviews as dynamic interactions.*

Research limitations/implications – *It is hoped that the reflections presented will inform future research in sensitive areas and encourage an open, engaged and reactive approach to interviewing around sensitive topics.*

Keywords: Qualitative interviewing; sensitive research; interviewer/interviewee relationship; disclosure; difference; sexuality

Ethics in Social Research
Studies in Qualitative Methodology, Volume 12, 91–109
Copyright © 2012 by Emerald Group Publishing Limited
All rights of reproduction in any form reserved
ISSN: 1042-3192/doi:10.1108/S1042-3192(2012)0000012008

I'm straight. For a long time that didn't seem to need saying. Indeed due to the heteronormative nature of social life in the West, such lack of reflection is often expected (Jackson, 1999; Richardson, 1996). However, my decision to focus my attention on researching the lives of gay men was a moment when the importance of 'straightness' came to the fore. Indeed, when discussing my research interests and intentions with others my 'gayness' was taken for granted, rather than my 'straightness' not being an issue. This is rather an interesting perspective for a straight researcher to have their gayness presumed when professionally reflecting on the effects of the presumption of heterosexuality on gay lives. Thus from the very inception of my research it was clear to me that I was an embodied presence in the process, I was more than just being an interviewer who asks questions. My embodiment was an issue. I was different, but different in a way that can be invisible in interaction. Therefore I faced the questions – Do I hide? Do I tell? Does it matter?

Doing face-to-face research requires reflection on such issues whether one takes the view that interviews require a structured approach with minimal involvement of the interviewer (Buckingham & Saunders, 2004) or a view that interviews are co-creations in which the interviewer is a partner (Myers & Newman, 2007; Plummer, 1995). In the first, one must be concerned with interview bias, while in the second one must be reflexively aware and reflective on influence, dynamic and the part one plays. Researchers of minority sexual identities, ethnic minority experience, disability studies and other vulnerable populations have closely identified with the aims of feminist research, and more specifically ideas associated with standpoint epistemology, which requires experience to be at the base of an enquiry (Harding, 1987). This requirement for experience is often seen to emphasise similarity or even sameness between the interviewer and the interviewee. Thus similarity/sameness is recommended in terms of the identities or experiences of interviewers (Oakley, 1981; Riessman, 1987). This issue comes even more strongly to the fore when research concerns intimate or silenced issues. Here a sense of shared experience and outlook is often seen to be central to good research (Liamputtong, 2007).

Thus, I am wrong (at least in terms of my sexuality)! I am an outsider attempting to look through the opaque window of a life experience which is often hidden from view. Although many secular gay lives are becoming increasingly present and spoken, the lives of gay clergy often remain closeted and unspoken. Knowledge of gay clergymen's sexuality can be a dangerous knowledge as being known can lead to difficult personal and professional consequences. Therefore, any research which requires gay clergy to make themselves known qualifies as sensitive, and the possible consequences highlight the vulnerabilities of the population. Seeing myself as a sensitive researcher, I find myself wanting to agree with much of the arguments within feminist methodology around connection, rapport and sameness. However, not only do I not share the same sexual story as my respondents, I also (as mentioned above) previously understood my own story as not really a story at all. Therefore, although in undertaking the research I was myself unfolding my sexual story, understanding its emergence and making sense of my decisions, this remained a very different experience to that of my respondents. Thus, I found myself in the position of connecting with standpoint epistemology, but lacking the standpoint (Janack, 1997). However, as much as my difference was clear it was not complete. Neither I nor my respondents were fully represented by sexual identity; rather this was a piece of a rather complex whole. The research focused on lives including sexuality, religious identity and workplace identity. Thus, a variety of issues and identities were at play in interactions.

This chapter is a reflection on my experiences as a self-defined heterosexual man interviewing self-defining gay and homosexual men within a research project on the lives of gay men in the Anglican clergy. It is part description, part reflection, part argument for the importance of difference, part argument for the importance of similarity and part defence of practice. It is also at its centre an attempt to question what a relevant standpoint is and to emphasise the dynamic and changeable nature of the interview interaction.

The chapter begins by reflecting on existing discussions of qualitative interviewing and the interview process before turning to issues of connection and disclosure in the interview setting. Following from this the focus shifts to episodes from my own research experiences. The chapter presents a number of occasions which highlight the complex, changing and unpredictable nature of the interview interaction and emphasises the importance of care and awareness over telling and avoiding essentialising identities. Throughout, the chapter emphasises the importance of creativity, action and reaction in the interview process.

UNDERSTANDING THE INTERVIEW INTERACTION

Interviews, whatever their nature are a form of talk, a form of communication and a form of interaction (Roulston, 2010), they involve the asking and the answering of questions. When focused on sensitive issues it seems clear that the embodied researcher will have an effect on the interaction. Plummer theorises this interaction in terms of interaction between the teller and the coaxer (Plummer, 1995). The coaxer coaxes the narrative in a particular way and without such coaxing the narrative may never be told, or may be told in an entirely different way.

Rubin and Rubin (2005, p. 4) refer to the qualitative interview as an extended conversation in which the interviewer 'guides a conversational partner in an extended discussion', thus both parties are present and active, and the resulting product emerges from interaction and interconnection. On similar lines Douglas (1985) discusses the need for creativity in interviewing, highlighting the interviewer as an active agent in the interaction. He illustrates that interviews, like human life, are unpredictable, and we must take into account the situation and the context in which knowledge is created. Thus, the interview is a 'situation' which impacts upon the very knowledge it elicits. With this in mind it is important to reflect on influences on and episodes in interviews, particularly as Liamputtong (2007) suggests, when reflecting on how we as researchers impact upon interviews on what are considered to be sensitive issues. Therefore, it is necessary to reflexively consider our and our interviewees' positions, locations and experiences, to consider possible areas of difference and similarity, of clash and connection, in order to reflect on the possible impact of such experiences.

THEORISING DIFFERENCE AND SIMILARITY

The work of Stanley and Wise (1983) and guidance on the undertaking of sensitive research (Dickson-Swift, James, & Liamputtong, 2008; Liamputtong, 2007) is seen to emphasise similarity of experience as key to accessing information. Similarity is seen to enable connection, to suggest understanding and to allow for the greater flow of information. Liamputtong (2007), for example reflects on a variety of research projects where similarity is seen to have enabled research, and difference is seen to have curtailed or negatively affected the research process. Here the focus is generally on 'seen' or visible similarity or difference, for example in terms of gender or skin colour. However, others have questioned such views. Carter (2004) for example discusses that his white maleness did not negatively affect his interactions with black women, and others have argued that difference can be positive in interview interactions. Song and Parker (1995), for example emphasise that difference may lead to creativity or a fresh perspective. Similarly, overreliance on similarity or overgeneralising of experience can raise concerns. Devault (1990) (cited in Luff, 1999) when reflecting on the process of being a woman interviewing women discusses 'filling in from experience'. This is problematic for a number of reasons, but most clearly because filling in from experience suggests that experiences are not only similar but interchangeable and thus negates the differences which may be equally present – essentialising, in this case, what it is to be woman.

Others reflect on the shortcomings of a binary understanding of similarity and difference and have emphasised the complex nature of human inter-actions (specifically qualitative interviews). Edwards (1990), reflecting on being a white woman interviewing black women, emphasises how she experienced both similarity and difference with regard to her research respondents. This allows, she argues, for recognition of specific issues of black womanhood, as well as reflections on similarity of experience between black and white women. Similarly, although Heaphy, Weeks, and Donovan (1998) emphasised the benefits of shared experience in the research process, for example through their decision to disclose their gay and lesbian identities to gay, lesbian and bisexual respondents being understood to have led to respondents being 'very willing, and eager to tell their stories' (Heaphy et al., 1998, p. 456). They also recognise the complexity of interactions and highlight that similarity (e.g. coming out to respondents) may be outweighed by other personal differences or may risk overgeneralisation. They write

There is, however, a danger in overemphasizing these commonalities. While respondents and researchers may share identities in terms of gender and sexuality, other differences, such as those relating to class, nationality, and ethnicity can be at play in the research situation. (Heaphy et al., 1998, p. 456)

Therefore, reflections on connection must go beyond the headlines of interviewer/interviewee identity to examine more fully the dynamics of what is a fluid and changeable process. Here moments of interaction can be as important as components of interaction. For example in reflecting on his interviews with male-for-male Internet escorts, Walby (2010) reflects on the moments when he was asked 'are you gay?' this Walby suggested both sexualised him as researcher, illustrating his active presence in the interaction, and also 'momentarily flips over established researcher–respondent roles' (Walby, 2010, p. 649). The word 'momentarily' is important here. These occurrences may have had an influence over the entirety of the interview, may have been overtaken by a later revelation or occurrence or may have made no difference to the interview/ee. Thus, I suggest our focus should be on moments rather than overarching identifications.

The above discussions illustrate the complexity of the interview inter-action and the very real possibility of the co-existence of similarity and difference in such interactions. However, Heaphy, Weeks and Donovan's focus on disclosure also adds a need for reflection in terms of the possible invisibility of areas of similarity and difference. It is to this issue we now turn.

TO TELL OR NOT TO TELL

Hand in hand with an emphasis on similarity within the literature on undertaking sensitive research is an emphasis on telling. Such guidance argues that sensitive researchers should self-disclose in the interview interaction. This is particularly the case for researchers working on sensitive issues who feel that their own experiences or less visible identities may impact positively on the research process. Again Liamputtong (2007) provides us with some examples of the types of disclosure being referred to, she includes experiences of abuse, divorce and sexual identity. Such disclosures are understood to emphasise shared understandings, or an aware empathy, which are seen to minimise misunderstanding. Again however, such emphasis on similarity risks overgeneralising, or essentialising the experience, constructing 'the' divorce experience, or 'the' gay experience, rather than illustrating an understanding of the diversity in such experiences.

Therefore, it is important to remember that such discussions of disclosure of similarity are only one possible aspect of self-disclosure by the researcher. Indeed, where Liamputtong suggests that disclosure is 'essentially important' (2007, p. 72), and Douglas (1985) suggests that disclosure is an intrinsic part of a creative interview, this disclosure can be understood more widely as an openness which emphasises the reciprocal nature of the research process, rather than the vocalising of a particular identity or experience. Thus, one could argue disclosure may not be obviously connected to the aims of the research undertaken; rather it might be a general openness, or a willingness to provide general, seemingly unrelated details about personal life. Interviews are fluid and dynamic, therefore interviews focused on lives are likely to cover all kinds of experiences and it is likely, as Heaphy et al. (1998) suggest that different identities will come to the fore at different times. Thus, in interviews based around sexuality issues of ethnicity, age, class, gender and work may come to the fore. Therefore, although it is clear that in terms of sexuality I am an 'outsider' looking in, this is not a death knell to connection or rapport. The discussions above illustrate that although my difference may be a challenge to accessing depth, it may also be a quality that allows me fresh perspective on the respondents' lives. Further, taking on the understanding of interviews as changing interactions, some moments in interviews will illustrate connection while others will emphasise distance. Some of these moments will be fleeting, whilst others will have more lasting consequences. The remainder of this chapter reflects on my own research experience including a number of moments of interaction and what they say about the interview process.

THE RESEARCH BACKGROUND

The research experiences upon which the majority of this chapter are based were undertaken as part of an ESRC funded doctoral study (award number PTA-0390-2003-01724) which explored the identity negotiations of gay male Anglican clergy and specifically focused on sexual, religious and work identities (see Keenan, 2008, 2009, 2012). The aims of the research were to (1) explore the identity creation, negotiation and presentation of gay male Anglican clergy, and (2) to explore the interplay of tradition and innovation, or structure and agency within this identity work. The research undertook a multi-stage approach to the research in order to access breadth and depth, and to explore the life-changing and the everyday. Thus, the research included a questionnaire ($n = 29$), interview ($n = 14$), reflective diary ($n = 10$) and a second interview based on the diary ($n = 9$).

In terms of the need for sensitivity, the desire to explore both the significant 'big' moments and more mundane day-to-day events meant that the research aimed to access both moments which could be professionally and personally threatening to report, or emotionally challenging to recount; and also very personal details which may not be easily told. Further, it was not just in its subject that the research could be challenging, but also the research asked for commitment from respondents who could be asked to take part in up to four separate stages. Though the focus of the research is likely to connect with respondents and encourage participation, there is still a real requirement for connection between researcher and researched in order to encourage sustained participation, and to allow for depth of information to be accessed. I was therefore acutely aware of my place in the research dynamic and my need to encourage trust and develop rapport.

The men who took part in the interview stage of the research were aged between 30 and 70 years and had served various lengths of time in the ministry at the time of the research (from 2 years as head of parish, to over 30 years). All of the clergy who were interviewed were involved in Parish ministry at the time of the research, and the sample included various levels of authority including vicars, rectors, rural deans and canons. The clergy had varying relationship statuses; some were single, others in committed same-sex relationships and some in heterosexual marriages. Some were open about their sexualities with their congregations while others were closeted and felt likely to remain so. For a number of reasons respondents varied in the level of sexual activity they engaged in, some felt geographically removed from possibilities to explore their sexuality, while others specifically limited themselves due to their profession. The respondents' churchmanship included Evangelical and Anglo-Catholic approaches, and their geographical position ranged from rural village to city centre.

A final important point is that although sexuality is indeed central to this research the focus crosses a number of boundaries and engaged with individuals' lives in terms of their sexuality, their religion and their profession. Such interactions illustrate not only the negotiations required in the interconnection of lifeworlds but also the changing roles and identity areas which would come to the fore at differing times in the interview process.

The following discussions include a mixture of conversations which occurred on first or second meetings with my respondents. These episodes are presented to illustrate the fluid nature of the interview interaction. The episodes blur the insider/outsider binary and question what relevant standpoints are present. In totality they raise the importance of openness, awareness, reflexivity and reactivity in the research process. Particularly, I hope these reflections illustrate the need for an active and reactive researcher who is attentive and places effort on allowing interviews to develop according to their progression, keeping in mind the key focus of sensitive interviewing, that being to allow stories to be told.

PERSONAL BACKGROUND

In order to fully reflect on the issues of similarity and difference and the need for disclosure it is important not only to discuss the research, but also who I am. To fully reflect on my insider/outsider status I need to first discuss how I felt such issues were important with regard to my own biography.

At the time of the research I self-defined as heterosexual and was in a committed long-term heterosexual relationship. I was in my mid to late twenties and was a full-time PhD student. In terms of my background, I am originally from Northern Ireland and at the time of the research still had a recognisable accent. I come from a religious family, and my father was a minister in the Presbyterian Church, thus I was a 'clergy kid', which is itself a population of interest to the sociology of religion (Guest, 2010). I would also say I was at the time of the study quite shy and reserved, generally not being particularly good with new people (thus once again illustrating myself as being potentially unsuitable for the job!).

Initial interviews proceeded after the potential interviewee had completed a questionnaire and also following phone and email contact, second interviews occurred after respondents had already taken part in the three preceding research stages. Time was put aside at the beginning of each interview for an informal discussion and some coffee. I decided that I would disclose information about myself when asked in the interview or informal discussion, rather than as a required precursor to the interview. This was partly due to feeling that such a focus on my own life and experience may jar with the running of the interview itself, and also due to concerns of essentialising aspects of the clergy's identities (Hennessy, 1993).

The following examples reflect specific interactions which occurred during the fieldwork. The experiences are not presented as illustrative of an entire interview interaction but rather as specific moments when the interviewer/ interviewee dynamic changed.

MULTIPLE CONNECTIONS – EXPERIENCES OF DIFFERENCE AND SIMILARITY IN THE INTERVIEW INTERACTION

Experiencing Difference

My commitment to openness in the research process meant that although I did not set out with the express intention to disclose particular aspects of my identity or experiences, I also did not want to hide them. I thus entered interview interactions with the desire to be open and present as an embodied agent within the interactions, and to answer questions which were asked. This meant that the majority of clergy interviewed learnt of my sexual identity before or during the interview. Others showed no interest in this aspect of my identity but were keen to know why I was so interested in the clergy (an issue to which we will return). With regard to knowledge of my sexuality, this did not lead to any specific experiences of negativity within interactions. Of course, any concerns may have remained unspoken, and there was one occasion in which this seems to have been the case, and the interviewer/interviewee dynamic was changed permanently.

Following a lively, interesting and telling interview I walked back to the train station with my respondent. After swapping further anecdotes and ideas about the research he turned to me and asked 'so are you one of us'? My response was always in such situations to answer honestly while emphasising a desire for the recognition of gay clergy. My response was taken well and we left each other at the train station in seemingly good spirits. However, following this initial meeting I attempted to reach this respondent through a variety of avenues of communication, never managing to make contact.

Of course there may be many reasons for non-response. In the interview the clergyman in question emphasised that he had experienced very negative treatment when his sexuality had been suspected, and spoke of his intention to be more open. He also emphasised how busy his life was, and his thoughts about leaving the clergy. Therefore, there may be many reasons why this respondent did not take any further part in the research; however, in the moment above I felt very clearly a sense of difference, which retrospectively I suspect had a lasting effect on the respondent's engagement with the research.

However, although this above experience emphasised the possible negatives of sexual difference in the research, some welcomed my heterosexuality as illustrating that the experiences of gay clergy were being taken seriously outside of the gay press and community. On one occasion when a respondent was driving me to the train station we got talking about my sexuality, and the concern I and colleagues had had regarding the possible negative consequences of 'speaking it'. The respondent said for him it was the opposite and he was very pleased to be taking part in something which would exist outside the 'gay ghetto'. Here then difference was a specific positive to the research, not just illustrating a viewpoint that was valued, but also a bridging of previously experienced boundaries of acceptable locations for such discussions.

On other occasions my difference was a key reason I was able to access detail. One interviewee took time to describe the geography of saunas he had visited emphasising he was doing so because I 'wouldn't know'. Similarly, one respondent while talking about a relationship pointed to a ring on his little finger saying that he had now decided to wear it. Seeing my confusion he began to discuss how the ring could be a sign of gay identity and he had chosen to wear it to mark this relationship. This was also a public symbol and a risk, which he gained meaning from. Therefore, my difference offered access to details which would otherwise have been lost. This detail was key to understanding one of the little rebellions that this respondent undertook within his public life, and the discussion of the sauna above developed into a discussion which emphasised the anonymity and the separation from the everyday that the sauna gave to the respondent, feelings that were key to his identity as a sexually active gay man.

Difference was not just experienced in terms of sexuality. Being in my mid-twenties at the time of the research I was significantly younger than my respondents, by sometimes over 40 years. For some this was surprising enough to comment on, for example 'I didn't expect you to be so young' and at times may have contributed to difficult initial interactions. Perhaps most interviews begin tentatively however there was a clear sense of initial wariness with some of the older respondents which although perhaps not solely due to age, definitely included age as a contributing factor.

There were also moments when age difference contributed positively to interactions. One respondent only started to talk about his painful memories of school and the unfairness of segregated education when he felt I was too young to remember it for myself. This was a clear example of a moment where the respondent felt there would be a shared knowledge between himself and an older researcher which may have led to something remaining unsaid, or being 'filled in from experience'.

Finally, difference was also present in terms of self-presentation, for example some respondents reflected on their clothing choice for the interview. One stated while taking off his ministerial collar, that he had worn it so I could recognise him, but he wanted to take it off before the interview as he felt it would mark a distance. Others similarly reflected on their clothing choice emphasising that there was perhaps a safety in wearing 'uniform' as it marked their role, whereas not wearing it allowed access to the individual. Such respondents perhaps felt that through their presentations they would be able to have some control over the running of the interview. For example wearing 'uniform' was seen to increase the likelihood that the interview would focus on the professional rather than the personal. Thus, there was a sense of being able to mould and control. Therefore, difference was at times chosen or rejected knowingly by the respondents in terms of taking an active part in controlling, or at least influencing the interview content.

In general, these episodes illustrate the dynamics of the interview around issues of difference. Difference was a source for concern when undertaking the interview, and was an issue which did arise on a few occasions. However, it arose positively as often as negatively. My difference in terms of age, and sexuality allowed access to discussions and information which may not have otherwise been discussed.

Experiencing Similarity

Experiences of connection or similarity within the interviews were often around issues of church life. When disclosed, my experiences as a 'clergy kid' were referred to by respondents when discussing their own experiences of living a life so connected to the Church, with some suggesting 'but it must have been worse for you'. An example of the kind of issue emerges from an interview based on a diary entry, reflecting on the entry I asked a question about the vicarage as a home:

> Ah, that's the big [partner] issue that is, because he goes absolutely berserk if the vicarage is used for anything, and has a real problem with this. I probably don't see it as my home in perhaps quite the same way, because I invite people from the parish in, and you know that's fine. But strangely enough I don't really have a thing about possessions either, which quite surprised me because I always thought I did, and yet I never really cared if they come in and use the kitchen, or sit on the furniture, or find things in a drawer or whatever, that doesn't bother me. Whereas actually my partner doesn't like that at all. Whether that's because it's my job and so my house as it were, and he is the person who has had to make it his house, which means perhaps the invasion is much more personal. That is quite an interesting thing that you have picked up on that. If you want us to fall out that's the issue to mention. (George Diary Interview)

His point, 'it is interesting you pick up on that' relates directly to my own experiences of living in a Church-owned house and the issues that I felt arose from this. Of course such similarity was far from sameness as mine was a different perspective on a similar situation. However, my 'clergy kid' status meant I became of interest to respondents as they were of interest to me.

My accent also led to specific reflections on similarity. Particularly in terms of the presence of religion in childhood. For example one respondent said;

> I suppose a bit like Northern Ireland you can't get away from religion if you are brought up there. Religion, especially [Christian denomination] is all around you. [Christian denomination] in its various manifestations. (Daniel Interview)

This similarity, of living in a part of the UK with strong religious presence, became a strong area of connection in this interview and my background was referred to on a number of occasions. However, on this occasion looking back at the transcript I do wonder if I could have learnt more about the specific issues he is referring to if I was not believed to have shared similar ones. Have I 'filled in from experience'?

Similarity, as with difference, was experienced as both a positive and a negative in the research process. On these occasions my similarity may have allowed for the development of rapport but may also at times have meant that detail was lost. This chapter now goes on to reflect other areas and issues where the interviewer/interviewee dynamic were changed within the research, which move us beyond discussions of similarity and difference in identification and experience.

INTERVIEWER/INTERVIEWEE INTERACTION: BEYOND SIMILARITY AND DIFFERENCE

My awareness of 'moments' of positivity and negativity in interviews was not limited to direct experience of similarity or difference in experience or identity. There were also a number of occasions where other issues or episodes had obvious effect. The following examples illustrate how interviewee responses, difficult first impressions and unexpected occurrences can affect interview dynamics.

The Challenges of Interviewee Responses

Qualitative interviewing relies on shared understandings of the language used. At times terms and phrases can be translated in ways we do not expect possibly leading to unexpected information being presented and expected information being lost. Sometimes such responses are intentional and sometimes unintentional. On one occasion this challenge was particularly clear in the research. During an initial interview I asked a respondent if he was currently sexually active. He replied:

> No. Well it depends what you mean, it depends what active and practicing means. I know that much of my ministry I'm aware of sexuality being within it in a positive way. So in many of your contacts and relationships when they get beyond superficiality there is a sexuality element in them isn't there? [When] you are visiting there is a sexuality going on because they relate to me differently than they do to my colleague who is a woman. So we relate all the time with that sexuality don't we? And I know throughout my ministry I have been able to relate to men I think far more warmly. ... If your being true to yourself then you are active all the time aren't you? (Rupert Interview)

In the first instance this quotation quickly answers the question as expected, however there is a clear sense of the transformation of the question from one about involvement in sex acts, to one which focuses on the presence of sexual identity in the everyday. The quotation highlights the power of respondents to mould and influence the questioning process. By interpreting the question the respondent offers information which was not directly requested. This information highlights the continuing and important place of his sexuality even on occasions when he is not active sexually. Thus perhaps underlining the respondent's desire to be seen and recognised as a gay man within the interview, and within his own self-reflections. Following this question I asked whether the respondent still visited pubs and clubs, he responded saying he did 'out of duty' and went on to emphasise how as a clergyman he was able to offer support to people who needed it in gay-friendly locations. Again this illustrates a desire to remove the focus from an active sexual or social sexuality towards a personally understood one which perhaps emphasises what the respondent understood to be acceptable in the eyes of outsiders, and may illustrate his desire to avoid contributing what he sees as bad information (i.e. that focused on physical sexual acts) to the research project. My feelings that the respondent wanted to move away from such questioning led to a moment of discomfort and caused me to redirect the interview, thus details may have been lost.

This interaction illustrates a moment in the interview where the respondent took control intentionally or unintentionally and became guider of the inter-view. The episode connects with Walby's (2010) reflections on moments when the interview relationship changes, it also illustrates the dynamic position of power in the interview process, and the need for the interviewer to be constantly actively reading and reacting to the situation of the interaction.

Challenging First Impressions

Another issue which is rarely discussed in literature on interviewing and sensitive research which can have a key effect on the interaction of an interview is connected to personal chemistry and first impressions. Feminist methodology focuses on connection, and on the development of a warm relationship between interviewer and interviewee. Indeed Yow (1997) reflects on whether she negatively impacts upon the interview and her reporting of it asking 'Do I like them too much?' However, little has been written about the issues and effects of dislike. Of course reflections on extreme difference exist and have relevance. Smyth and Mitchell (2008) have explored issues raised by studying a population one finds it hard to empathise with; Blee (1998) reflects on her dislike for the white supremacists she interviews; Luff (1999) discusses times in interviews when political differences were clear; and Christine Horrocks (King & Horrocks, 2010) has reflected on the need to silence personal opinions when interviewing individuals with alternative world views. In terms of discomfort, feelings of personal danger have been discussed (Jamieson, 2000) as have threats of violence and actual violence (Huff, 1997). However very little is mentioned in the literature in terms of how to cope with personality clash, bad first impressions between interviewer and interviewee or simply not liking someone very much (in fact the gap is so wide it makes me question whether I am just not a very nice person!).

I have on occasion entered houses or interview situations where I feel uncomfortable, and I have met individuals I dislike initially. It is an interesting ethical question to reflect on what the responsible interviewer should do on such occasions. Firstly, it is quite likely that the feeling is mutual and this will have a definite effect on the research process. Understanding interviews as co-creations means allowing stories to be told while understanding our own personalities, reflections, actions and responses are a very present aspect of the interaction. Therefore dislike will influence the research process. The question is whether the responsible interviewer accepts this and leaves as soon as possible recognising the negativity they may bring to the interaction. With regard to my argument above I feel this is not the case. As sensitive researchers we are not only sensitive, but also aware of our duty to our respondents. If an individual has offered their time and their willingness to talk, we owe it to them to engage with that interaction. Plus as reactive and empathetic researchers we should be able to engage in an interaction and find areas of empathy and connection.

In the research under discussion I reflected upon the initial interview I had undertaken with a respondent, I was aware of discussions feeling unnatural and uncomfortable, part of the reason for such reflection was due to my reaction to the interviewee and a sense of uncertainty about who he was. This concern and an initial negative reaction to the individual had a strong negative influence over the beginning of the interview. However as a focused and active interviewer I was able to tune into the respondent's story and find areas of connection and empathy. The interview progressed and we both seemed to settle in to the interview.

On other occasions I was aware of less significant clashes occurring with regard to specific viewpoints, for example personally clashing with conservative opinion on women's ordination or pre-marital heterosexual sex. This connects with the reflections of Heaphy et al. (1998) on the fluidity of the interview. It is not just some research projects which will proceed better than others, nor specific interviews, but rather within interviews themselves there will be periods of ease and depth, and periods of difficulty and lack of insight. The reflective interviewer needs to be aware not just of how they are perceived initially but also how the interview progresses and how interview dynamics change within the interview itself. Kvale (2007) suggests an understanding of the interviewer as traveller who goes on a journey with the interviewee. One might extend this to emphasise that the terrain on such a journey is diverse. At times mountainous at other times easy going, while negotiating challenges it is likely partners may feel less connected, however with focus and effort it is possible to regain that connection. Thus, as researchers we must be consistently reflecting on an interview and the dynamic relationship involved, in order to make the best of each diverse interview, and episode within each interview.

Unexpected Challenges

Finally, returning to the discussions of Douglas (1985) concerning creativity in the interview process, there were a number of occasions where flexibility or responding to the unexpected had a clear influence on the running of an interview during the research. One particular occasion occurred during an interview which though progressing effectively had no clear spark of connection between myself as interviewer and the interviewee.

During the course of the interview we became aware of some odd sounds in the house. We continued with the interview but finally the noises were becoming disruptive. A bird had got stuck in the respondent's chimney. Together we managed to free the bird, and in doing so our guards were lowered through this very real shared experience. This sense of connection continued into our further interactions and offered a real sense of shared experience which benefitted the research interaction.

Oakley (1981) reflects upon her willingness to be involved in the lives of her respondents in order to be open and flexible to their needs. Though the above is a very specific example, here too we can see that flexibility and the willingness to leave the script, or to get one's hands dirty can benefit the research interview and develop the rapport in the interviewer/interviewee relationship. Indeed when we met for a second time it was clear both I and the respondent had very clear memories of our time together and joked about our rescue effort before the start of the second interview. Here the development of rapport came specifically through something which was unexpected and unplanned. Of course I am not suggesting that interviewers take a stock of birds to every interview, but rather that they be open to opportunity and respond to need. For example on occasions I stayed in specific rooms, so as to avoid meeting visitors. I accepted all offered hospitality and ate with respondents on a number of occasions. Such small acts of connection can have huge impact, and allow for greater understanding. For example one respondent with whom I developed a close connection, influenced by my efforts to travel to meet him and our sharing of time and food made mention of the fact that despite his nerves and concern about the interview he had experienced it as a very positive thing.

The examples above highlight the dynamic and changeable nature of the interviewer/interviewee relationship. These examples are not presented as illustrative of interviews but rather as illustrative of events where power dynamics or relationships changed. Thus, rapport, acceptance and the free flow of information are elusive issues which can ebb and flow throughout an interview. The most expected and the most unexpected issues can affect the interview process and we as researchers must be ready and willing to move with events, or react to difficulties through embracing the interviews dynamic nature in order to do the best by our work and the interviewees who offer so much and take such risks.

CONCLUSIONS

This chapter has reflected on the interview process with specific focus on the interviewer/interviewee relationship. The chapter has emphasised the dynamic nature of the interview, and the variety of issues which may have an effect on the interview process. The chapter has attempted to question the concept of insider/outsider in the research process, and also raise issues with expected 'relevant' experiences. Through focusing on my experiences of similarity and difference, and the variety of possible influences of the interviewer/interviewee relationship I hope I have gone some way to emphasising that the 'how' is at least equal to the 'who'. The following quotation from Janack (1997) raises a similar point

> We also need, however, a rough story about the kinds of epistemic virtues we want in our researchers ... we want people who care passionately and who recognise the impact of the effects of knowledge production on human lives. We also want people who listen sensitively and sincerely to other divergent perspectives and who can try to work creatively with the disruption that differences can create. (Janack, 1997, pp. 136–137)

My argument is that there are no definites in complex interactions like qualitative interviews. What is important is that the interviewer is reflective and aware of their active presence in the interview interaction. The interviewer must be active and reactive, open and accommodating. In short, willing to listen and focused on the unveiling of respondents' narratives. We must move beyond binary reflections on similarity and difference and work towards a more complex and inclusive understanding of active and reactive interconnection in the co-creation of interview narratives.

REFERENCES

Blee, K. (1998). White knuckle research: Emotional dynamics in fieldwork with racist activists. *Qualitative Sociology, 21*(4), 381–399.

Buckingham, A., & Saunders, P. (2004). *The survey methods workbook*. Cambridge: Polity Press.

Carter, J. (2004). Research note: Reflections on interviewing across the ethnic divide. *Social Research Methodology, 7*(4), 345–353.

Dickson-Swift, V., James, E., & Liamputtong, P. (2008). *Undertaking sensitive research in the health and social sciences: Managing boundaries, emotions and risks*. Cambridge: Cambridge University Press.

Douglas, J. (1985). *Creative interviewing*. London: Sage.

Edwards, R. (1990). Connecting method and epistemology: A white woman interviewing black women. *Women's Studies International Forum, 13*(5), 477–490.

Guest, M. (2010). Socialisation and spiritual capital: What difference to clergy families make? In S. Collins-Mayo & P. Dandelion (Eds.), *Religion and youth*. Farnham: Ashgate.

Harding, S. (1987). *Feminism and methodology*. Bloomington, IN: Indiana University Press.

Heaphy, B., Weeks, J., & Donovan, C. (1998). 'That's like my life': Researching stories of non-heterosexual relationships. *Sexualities, 1*(4), 453–470.

Hennessy, R. (1993). *Materialist feminism and the politics of discourse*. London: Routledge.

Huff, J. (1997). The sexual harassment of researchers by research subjects: Lessons from the field. In M. Schwartz (Ed.), *Researching sexual violence against women: Methodological and personal perspectives*. Thousand Oaks, CA: Sage.

Jackson, S. (1999). *Heterosexuality in question*. London: Sage.

Jamieson, J. (2000). Negotiating danger in fieldwork on crime: A researcher's tale. In G. Lee-Treweek & S. Linkogle (Eds.), *Danger in the field: Risk and ethics in social research*. London: Routledge.

Janack, M. (1997). Standpoint epistemology without the "standpoint"?: An examination of epistemic privilege and epistemic authority. *Hypatia, 12*(2), 125–139.

Keenan, M. (2008). Freedom in chains: Religion as enabler and constraint in the lives of gay male Anglican clergy. In A. Day (Ed.), *Religion and the individual*. Aldershot: Ashgate.

Keenan, M. (2009). The gift (?) that dare not speak its name'. In S. Hunt (Ed.), *Contemporary christianity and LGBT sexualities*. Farnham: Ashgate.

Keenan, M. (2012). Separating Church and God: An exploration of gay clergymen's negotiations with institutional Church. In S. Hunt & A. Yip (Eds.), *The Ashgate research companion on sexuality and religion*. Farnham: Ashgate.

King, N., & Horrocks, C. (2010). *Interviews in qualitative research*. London: Sage.

Kvale, S. (2007). *Doing interviews*. London: Sage.

Liamputtong, P. (2007). *Researching the vulnerable.* London: Sage.

Luff, D. (1999). Dialogue across the divides: 'Moments of rapport' and power in feminist research with anti-feminist women. *Sociology, 33*(4), 687–703.

Myers, M., & Newman, M. (2007). The qualitative interview in IS research: Examining the craft. *Information and Organisation, 17*(1), 2–26.

Oakley, A. (1981). Interviewing women: A contradiction in terms. In H. Roberts (Ed.), *Doing Feminist Research* (pp. 30–61). London: Routledge and Kegan Paul.

Plummer, K. (1995). *Telling sexual stories: Power, change and social worlds.* London: Routledge.

Richardson, D. (1996). *Theorizing heterosexuality: Telling it straight.* Buckingham: Open University Press.

Riessman, C. K. (1987). When gender is not enough. *Gender & Society, 1*(2), 172–207.

Roulston, K. (2010). *Reflective interviewing: A guide to theory and practice.* London: Sage.

Rubin, H., & Rubin, I. (2005). *Qualitative interviewing: The art of hearing data.* London: Sage.

Smyth, L., & Mitchell, C. (2008). Researching conservative groups: Rapport and understanding across moral and political boundaries. *International Journal of Social Research Methodology, 11*(5), 441–452.

Song, M., & Parker, D. (1995). Commonality, difference and the dynamics of disclosure in in-depth interviewing. *Sociology, 29*(2), 241–256.

Stanley, L., & Wise, S. (1983). *Breaking out: Feminist consciousness and feminist research.* London: Routledge and Kegan Paul.

Walby, K. (2010). Interviews as encounters: Issues of sexuality and reflexivity when men interview men about commercial same sex relations. *Qualitative Research, 10*(6), 639–657.

Yow, V. (1997). "Do I like them too much?": Effects of the oral history interview on the interviewer and vice-versa. *Oral History Review, 24*(1), 55–79.

TRUST, COERCION AND CARE: RESEARCHING MARGINALISED GROUPS

Andrew Wilson and Philip Hodgson

ABSTRACT

Purpose – *To consider the possibility that research ethics committee perceptions of risk is tainted by their social distance from marginalised social groups and their lack of familiarity with carrying out fieldwork with criminally involved individuals. And to reflect on the potential for the negative perceptions create a vicious cycle by corroding trust and creating an over-reliance on a rigid interpretation of the ethical guidelines leading to tighter restrictions on researcher conduct.*

Methodology/approach – *Drawing on our experience of carrying out longitudinal research with a group of hard to reach drug using offenders the chapter uses case studies to offer a reflexive account of the practical problems raised by the research.*

Findings – *It provides examples of the way the ethical boundaries can be stretched and broken by the circumstances of the research. This arises, in part, from the tension of maintaining a trustful relationship with the participant or taking action that is in their interest and abiding by the ethical guidelines. The vicious cycle could be broken by changing the*

Ethics in Social Research
Studies in Qualitative Methodology, Volume 12, 111–128
Copyright © 2012 by Emerald Group Publishing Limited
ISSN: 1042-3192/doi:10.1108/S1042-3192(2012)0000012009

approach to ethical procedures by placing the care of the participants at the heart of the process and by giving due weight to their social circumstances. An ethics of care approach would shift the way researcher obligation to the participants and the project is conceptualised.

Originality/value of paper – *The paper makes a valuable contribution to the debate about the negative impact of bureaucratic procedures on academic research among marginalised groups.*

Keywords: Trust; research ethics committees; ethics of care; marginalised groups; cold calling

This chapter draws on our experience of carrying out longitudinal research with a group of hard to reach drug-dependent offenders. The process of tracking individuals who were mainly living in unstable, temporary, accommodation or had given a false address when they were first interviewed, raised a number of ethical and procedural concerns about researching marginalised groups. These relate to three main issues, trust, coercion and care. The first of them, trust, is an essential ingredient of the research process though there is little agreement over its precise quality. The section looks at the way trust is affected by a combination of research experience and confidence in the self-efficacy of the researcher on the one hand and the stereotypical social constructs that inform research ethics committee (REC) deliberations on the other. This dichotomy is further confused by the response of the REC to proposed research on marginalised groups such as those making up the subjects of this study. So the participants, the opiate and/or crack cocaine users caught up in the criminal justice system, can appear as threats likely to compromise researcher safety while also being constructed as vulnerable subjects needed to be protected through vigilant application of the ethical guidelines. When combined the two extremes produce a disincentive to research on such 'risky' groups through unreasonable demands to regulate the research or to protect the researcher from imagined threats. The use of ethical guidelines to protect research subjects is questioned in the section on coercion and care through the use of two case studies. These cases help to give some context to the issue around incentive payments to drug-dependent respondents and the potential for emotional harm of repeated calls at the homes of the unresponsive research subjects. This context setting is then used as a critique of REC consequentialist interpretation of the ethical guidelines which appears to be an inappropriate way to regulate conduct among groups whose conduct is likely to challenge conventional expectations. Finally, we consider whether adopting an ethics of care approach to the moral problems and ethical consideration of the REC would help to foster a greater willingness to allow for flexibility in procedures.

The research was initiated by the British Home Office to evaluate the outcome of drug testing in the criminal justice system under provisions set out in the Criminal Justice and Court Services Act 2000. A key element of the evaluation consisted of a longitudinal study of respondents recruited at the police custody suites after testing positive for use of opiates or cocaine following their arrest for a 'trigger' offence-acquisitive crime or Class A drugs offences (Matrix & NACRO, 2004; Wilson & Hodgson, 2012). The evaluation was dependent on producing a reliable response rate from three follow up interviews taking place at 3, 6 and 12 months following the initial interview. The methodology initially adopted at the main research site (Nottingham) required participants to attend the project office (based in a Housing Office), in the city centre, but with the level of attrition being above 70% action to boost response rates was required. This included reducing the number of follow up interviews to two (four and nine months), and appointing a researcher, one of the authors of this chapter (Wilson).

RISK, SAFETY AND TRUST

Wilson's main role was to follow up leads and track down respondents in the community by calling unannounced (cold calling) at the last known address of the respondent. Preparatory work included checking the Electoral Register for occupancy patterns at the address, searching through telephone directories and looking at satellite images of the neighbour-hood to help identify possible problems ahead. The next stage moved to the field and involved reading the available visual cues (garden, condition of the house, the windows, décor) when approaching the address for signs of occupancy and risk. Emphasis was placed by Wilson in presenting himself in a non-threatening demeanour which, should the participant be at the address, would reassure that he was not a debt collector or the authorities. In many respects this captures both the need to manage the presentation of self as benign while at the same time exercising caution and also displaying an air of openness and confidence. Trust is the key to the encounter, no matter how fragile its basis, the first meeting provides a fleeting opportunity for the two people to assess each other. Official perceptions of the research process tend to see these encounters from a researcher perspective rather than recognising that establishing trust is a mutual process.

The case study below is not typical of the encounters but it does give some indication of respondent perspective and the need to deal with an unfolding situation. It also presents an excellent example of the way using another person's perception of risk and acting on bad reputation can taint the process, though in this case it was avoided. During the course of a previous project (Wilson, May, Warburton, Lupton, & Turnbull, 2002) the researcher befriended the pharmacist who dispensed to dependent drug users local to many of the participants in the study. When asked to check the list of respondents the pharmacist only knew one person. Pointing to Don (not his real name) on the list he said 'This is a bad man. He carries a knife and he has been a lot of trouble. You should avoid this man'. Within minutes of leaving the pharmacy the researcher received a telephone call from Don in response to a message left at his mother's home address. It was the end of the day, dark and Don wanted to meet opposite a pub close to the pharmacy.

A tall man in his mid-to-late 20s with a black-eye walked towards me, I said Don? He replied 'no – who are you'. I blurted out an apology and muttered something about research. A few minutes later someone the same age, wearing a red bandana and walking with the swagger, appeared from the same direction. Don gave the appearance of someone who could look after himself. I asked where he wanted to do the interview, he suggested my car. The interview progressed well, though it was clear that Don was on edge. He 'eyeballed' (stared a challenge) at any passing car driven by someone who may have a 'street' connection. In the course of the interview he told me he was on bail for robbing a 'punter' of one of the girls (prostitutes) under his protection. It was not the first time. He had been charged with robbing 'clients' at knife point twice before but had been found not guilty after the prosecution witnesses failed to turn up. A memorable comment in his interview offered a counter to the image of a man in control. It came in responses to a question asking if he had experienced any problems as a result of his drug use. There was an air of resignation in his reply. Without hesitation, but delivered slowly as if reflecting on the problems he said 'anyone who's been using this shit for 9 years tells you they haven't had problems is lying'. He went on to say how he was under pressure from his long term girlfriend to get off the drugs, he wanted to get off them, he was going to start doing something. But it was also clear he was caught up in it all. At this point the person who had checked me out appeared at the passenger side of the car. Don asked if he could get in and wait. I agreed. A few minutes later two girls appeared who also waited in the car. At the end of the interview I gave them all a lift to a house a few streets away. Don asked me to wait. A few minutes later he appeared with a range of goods (laptop, camera, car stereo) that he was looking to sell. I declined and left.

Contrary to the image of a violent crack addict the man interviewed appeared weak, vulnerable and desperate only to change his lifestyle. It was clear that Don was a very capable individual caught up in a cycle that he recognised as destructive. He established, in the course of the interview, that the researcher had a good understanding of his situation and was prepared to take him at face value. The researcher's recognition and willingness to accommodate Don's anxiety about the interview (the fear he may be arrested) was the basis for establishing a rapport and from that, trust. In this case the process was aided by the fact that Wilson could draw on personal experience of involvement in the extremes of a drug using subculture (Wilson, 2007) to introduce a level of 'knowing' or mutual recognition (Lyng, 2005, p. 4) into the interaction. The confessional aspect of the interaction played an important role in establishing trust – to the point where Don was at ease offering stolen goods. From a researcher point of view the offer provided useful information about drug-related activities that went beyond the detail provided in the questionnaire but it also posed a challenge to the 'ethical' status of the researcher. The British Society of Criminology ethical guidelines are open to interpretation about the right course of action in situations like this, and there is no general legal obligation to report an offence unless it relates to physical or sexual abuse of children or vulnerable adults and for offences relating to the prevention of terrorism.

The encounter illustrates the way an experienced or confident researcher will gamble on their ability to win someone over. An absence of the factors that hold back a reasonable person from entering a risky situation may simply reflect the 'blind faith' born of naiveté. Venkatesh's (2008) account of the way he wandered into a tough housing project at the height of the crack epidemic in Chicago with a questionnaire appears to offer a good example of naiveté. The fact that plans for a study of drug dealing in Washington at around the same time had to be cut back because concerns about researcher safety (Maxfield & Babbie, 2010, p. 55) illustrate the problem of appearing to be left with a choice between risk taking on the one hand or retreat on the other. The perception of the risks, as noted earlier, is biased towards the negative when the interpretation lacks appreciation of the cultural context and knowledge of the personal attributes of the researcher. While this is not an issue for many of research projects that appear before the REC it is significant handicap for fieldwork-based projects among marginalised groups or other situations where the interpretation of risk is likely to be skewed by negative portrayal of the subject population. The irony of this lack of appreciation is the very groups most in need of the research that can provoke awareness of ill thought out policies can be further isolated by the risk-adverse decisions of the REC.

At the time of writing this chapter news that Marie Colvin, the *Sunday Times* foreign correspondent, had been killed while reporting on the conflict in Syria put the issues of risk and trust in perspective. Her death not only provides graphic illustration of the risks taken by correspondents in war zones, but also serves to make a link between the academic and the journalistic. For most academics the world of research is far removed from the chaos of the war zone where a good or bad decision can be a matter of survival. For a small minority of academic researchers, however, the presence of risk to personal safety will be as familiar as the need to think quickly to avoid a threatening or problematic situation. Moreover, many of the researchers who place themselves in risky situations would identify with Colvin's passion, motives and optimism that highlighting a problem is the first step towards a solution. These emotional motives for research go against notions of research as a 'detached' and 'objective' enterprise that some observers may regard to distinguish the academic from the journalist. Yet many of the inspirational publications emanating from the Chicago School in the first half of the 1900s were supervised or influenced by the journalistic principles advocated by Robert Park whose notion of the 'super-reporter' involved commitment to getting close to the subject with an analytic intent (Deegan, 1990). Park also understood that producing 'news' that was more accurate and detached than regular journalistic reporting was important, and that the production of 'facts' about people's lives was with an understanding that the process was an 'effective reformer' (Park in Thompson, 2005, p. viii). There is little doubt that Colvin would have agreed with Park's statement and his claim that reform can only be achieved by first hand study of the situation (Park in Thompson, 2005, p. vii) so it can provide insight into 'what is actually going on rather than what, on the surface of things, merely seems to be going on' (Park in Thompson, 2005, p. ix).

The difficulty is that when we see the problems from afar the justification for the anthropologist or correspondent to engage people in their natural settings has an intuitive appeal that is missing from the familiar local problems. As we mentioned earlier, the low income, poorer, deprived, high crime, marginalised, troubled or 'no go' areas appear as symbols of trouble that make them well known by reputation. This mixture of familiarity with all the negative aspects of marginalised neighbourhoods and the risk-averse regulatory system can create a less favourable environment for proposals researching the local encountered by projects studying more distant cultural settings with less litigious legal process. It could be argued that research that is 'out of sight' is 'out of mind' if we conceive sight and mind as all the factors that appear less precious to the REC when they are applied to far off situations and peoples who do not appear to share our values. The research in distant lands (both physical and cultural distance) conjures up images of benevolence, charity, discovery, excitement and romance with the researcher, or war correspondent, appearing as a noble or heroic figure. The death and destruction of war, whatever the complexities, present an accessible narrative and image of the good (the victims) and the bad (the perpetrator). It is difficult to draw the same kind of emotional support for research among criminals and drug users, groups that are identified as the bad guys. Research among such groups often appears questionable, or even an attempt to put offenders before victims and side with the subordinate group (Becker, 1967). Activity seen as heroic when conducted by the war correspondent is likely to be regarded as risky, reckless or just plain stupid when carried out by a researcher on a high crime estate. Of course, that does not mean we do not think the same about the work of correspondents like Colvin or researchers like Bourgois, but when we arrive at the conclusion that we 'wouldn't do that' it is with an awareness that we are singularly ill-equipped to do 'it': ill equipped by virtue of our cultural background, experience, preparedness to take risks and all of the many other factors that would make us both naïve and fearful.

MANAGING TRUST

So far we have argued that confidence in the research is likely to be strained by the distance between the knowledge and experience of the members of the REC and that of the researcher responsible for delivery of the project. In many cases there is an intermediary between the REC and the researcher, whether the grant holder or someone else with responsibility for managing the project. The manager has the difficult task of juggling the conflicting demands of responsibility for the health and safety of the researcher and effective delivery of the project. Hodgson's managerial role for the drug testing provides a good example of the dilemma posed the demands, as his account here illustrates.

> The idea of employing a researcher to track down participants in the community was greeted with scepticism by the research team, partly because of anxiety that they may be called on to adopt the same proactive method should it prove successful. From a management perspective the lack of response from many of the research subjects, along with the demands of the research commissioners for a rigorous sample, made the approach worth taking. With the method, however, came the pressure of creating and adopting a robust strategy to ensure the safety of the researcher. From the offset there were difficulties implementing the strategy as the researcher found the policy over-bureaucratic. On reflection this initial tension may have been exacerbated by a lack of confidence stemming from my own inexperience of responsibility for research safety.

This inexperience certainly introduced pressure to 'cover my own back' by following the 'deterrence–based' (Shapiro, Sheppard, & Cheraskin, 1992) procedures promoted by senior management. Within a relatively short time the manager/researcher relationship developed a level of confidence and 'knowledge-based trust' through a mixture of formal supervision sessions and informal discussions of the scenarios encountered in the field. The trust in our relationship finally developed into one of 'identification-based' where there was empathy and understanding between the parties of the other's intentions (Shapiro et al., 1992). This development of 'trust' was crucial as despite the identified risks of conducting research within the field it was soon evident that 'cold calling' worked. Consequently, given the pressure to reduce attrition the likelihood of removing this aspect of the research on the grounds of 'risk to the researcher' rescinded. Indeed any conversations that mentioned health and safety and risk issues were responded to with the comment: 'He knows what he is doing'.

As with the researcher/participant relationship, there is point in the relationship where 'the leap of faith interacts with reason, routine and reflexivity in trust' (Möllering, 2006, p. 198). In this case, the conversations about the various scenarios encountered in the field helped to re-calibrate perceptions of risk through both recognition of the capabilities of the researcher and the responses of the participants. This process is far removed from the remoteness of the REC and its reliance on the deterrence-based trust promoted in rigid interpretation of formal procedures. This rigidity sets up potential for conflict or unacknowledged shortcuts, as Venkatesh (2008) did by not keeping his PhD supervisor fully informed of his activities. The danger is that over-regulation will undermine confidence in the procedural justice of the process making it appear remote and out of touch thereby increasing the likelihood that information will be withheld or toned down to gain approval.

CONSENT, COERCION AND CARE

We now want to turn to the issue of informed consent and coercion. There were two ways that coercion related to the evaluation; the first was around the issue of incentive payments to individuals whose drug use made them vulnerable to the pressure of an offer of payment that may be accepted to obtain drugs. The second related to informed consent and the process of 'chasing up' respondents for follow up interview. The two examples drawn on raise a number of issues that could be seen as unethical from a REC perspective. We challenge that view on the basis that the REC process does not give enough weight to issues from the perspective of the participant.

The first case study raises issues around the coercive influence of the incentive payment to drug users. Payments were first noted to raise a question mark over the notion of informed consent during the recruitment and first interview stage of the project. Part of the reason for this stemmed from the problems faced in the early stages of the evaluation (Hodgson, Parker, & Seddon, 2006). This caused the commissioners of the research to criticise the relatively low recruitment of participants into the evaluation. Consequently, researchers became less 'precious' regarding how they were introduced to the 'detainees'. Initially, they were introduced as 'Home Office researchers' and were then offered a brief overview of what participation in the research entailed. Towards the end of the pilot, the most effective method of recruitment was found (albeit not encouraged) to be for the custody suite staff to make a more direct proposition: 'Do you want to earn a tenner?' and if the response was positive then the researcher would then explain what this entailed. The pressure of wanting to increase the numbers of research participants far exceeded the necessity of a 'correct introduction'. As one researcher said, 'I don't care who they think I am as long as they agree to be interviewed!' This attitude was justified in that once they had agreed to participate the researcher would then offer an overview of the research and ask the arrestee to sign a 'participant consent form'. Most of the arrestees appeared uninterested in who we actually were or which agency we were from or what the research was about. They mainly seemed to have two concerns – how long the interview was expected to take and when they would receive their 'tenner'.[1]

The strain on consent was particularly acute for dependent drug users whose agreement to participate appeared to be driven by the appeal of 'easy' money to buy drugs. There were certainly cases in this study where the agreement to participate was primarily motivated by a trade-off between deferring release from the police station and ability to buy drugs with the payment. The reaction of a respondent who impatiently repeated throughout the interview, 'Do I have to do this ... I just need the "fuckin" tenner' may be an extreme example but it gives some indication of the influence of the payment. In such cases where the participant appeared agitated and impatient with the time the interview was taking the researcher was require to determine whether this was a sign of reluctance or simply a strategy to speed up the process. That said another explanation could be that the interviewee had just produced a positive drug test and was suffering drug withdrawal symptoms – something the research team members were not trained to deal with. In most cases, where the research team encountered individuals who wanted a 'quick interview' they obliged as they themselves were being judged upon the quantity of interviews they completed and as such quick completions satisfied both parties.

If impatience had been read as an indication of reluctance and 'constrained' consent than we would be left facing the legitimate question, should the rejected participant ask it, why they were being denied the opportunity to take part? This applies no matter how the justification to participate is constructed – though in the case of intravenous drug users (IDU) it is difficult to escape the negative construction of action being motivated by need. While some individuals may be driven by personal need (we may question the need for what) previous research has produced contact with individuals, both drug users and dealers, who have had altruistic motives for giving up their time and, in one case, refusing the payment (Lupton, Wilson, May, Warburton, Turnbull, 2002). The following case study offers an example of someone who captures the moral dilemma of payments. This is a strange case because it involves someone whose drug use was supported by her 'sex work' so, given the relatively high earning potential; the £15 payment did not appear a significant inducement. As the extract suggests, the payment appeared to offer a short-term solution to the withdrawal problems the respondent was experiencing at the time.

> The semi-detached council house located about five miles from the city centre, the address Jenny gave to the project, showed signs of occupancy. Looking through the net curtains of the living room window next to the front door I could see ornaments and some furnishings and one of the upstairs windows was slightly open. There was no sense, however, that Jenny was home at the time of the call. This was the same for the next three calls, the last one confirming that the house was used as 'signing on' or 'accommodation' address, after looking through the kitchen window, I noticed the house did not have a cooker. A neighbour confirmed that the Jenny lived at the house, but that she wasn't around very often. He implied that this was related to her involvement in the sex trade without openly stating as much.
>
> On that third call I wedged a piece of paper in the front door to give some indication of the level of occupancy. On several subsequent calls over a three week period the paper remained in place. Each time I called I left a note, which became less formal with each visit, with my contact details so Jenny could call to withdraw from the research or call me to make an appointment.
>
> Enquiries at a needle exchange pharmacy in a red light area close to the city centre confirmed that Jenny was engaged in prostitution. A telephone call to the prostitutes outreach service confirmed that someone fitting the description of the person we were looking for was an infrequent user of the service – the outreach worker agreed to pass on a message about the research. Further confirmation that this was the person we were looking for came when interviewing a respondent engaged in the sex trade (a pimp) who knew Jenny – it later transpired that his accomplice tried to recruit the respondent as his 'worker'.

After eleven calls Jenny called to arrange an interview. There was no good reason why she did not call to make an appointment, though it may have been related to her infrequent calls at her contact address. It may also have been related to her income and addiction. When she did call to participate in the interview she was anxious to make sure that I would turn up and that she would be paid £15 for the interview. As the interview progressed it was clear that she was agitated by her need to secure drugs. There was little doubt that Jenny's need for drugs was the primary motive for participating in the follow up interview.

The ethical issues and benefits of payment to research subjects, in particular, drug users has been considered in detail elsewhere (Seddon, 2005). It is worth noting that there is little distinction made when considering payment to different types of research subject (that is, active participants (for instance in medical trials) compared with the type of passive participants (Wilson, 2011) that are most likely to be the subjects of social research), though this is clearly an important variance. The most notable difference, however, for payment of drug users is that the idea of payment appears morally unacceptable to many people. The researchers observed these negative attitudes among some of the custody suite staff (Hodgson et al., 2006; Seddon, 2005). This became a problem for the project after one of them informed the local newspaper about incentive payments and this report was given national attention through the *Daily Mail* in an article with the headline *Shopping vouchers given to criminals: Muggers and thieves rewarded if they agree to be interviewed for research*. The appeal to public sentiment about drug users played on the belief that consent was being bought when there is little evidence to support this assumption. As Seddon (2005) pointed out, the reasons for participating were varied with only a small minority, most likely the most marginalised participants most likely to be missed by the research, that were 'enticed' by the payments. As suggested earlier, if this issue is framed within the language of marginalisation, stripped on the idea of reward for wrong-doing, or a payment that will (it is assumed) be used to buy drugs, the benefits become more calculable as the red mist of the damaging emotional response dissolves.

The reasoning around payment to drug users is dominated by a stigmatised view of drug users (Seddon, 2011) that frames the issues within a moralistic narrative, one that slides to an easy denial of the rights of the drug user to participate on grounds that would be seen as unreasonable if applied to populations outside a criminal justice setting. As Seddon (2005) noted the same critical question about negative health-related choices, as may be applied to the person buying cigarettes or alcohol with their payment, are not applied. The notion of drug use as being driven by the compulsion of addiction rather than placing the activity with a range of choices that include a level of coherence and control by the user dominates. Essentially, we do not have the evidence to be able to make assumptions about the motives of IDUs to participate in research. Of course, there is no reason to believe that a drug user is any different from other paid participants: incentives are designed to encourage a trade-off between loss of time and personal gain – to facilitate the good will to participate. If we assume the worst, that payment was the primary reason to participate, how does this alter the value of consent? This is not someone being exploited in the same way as risking the status of their health through payment in return for testing the performance of a new drug. The notion of duress used to consider participation in these cases is based on a fanciful myth conjured up by oversensitive observers who have little direct experience of drug use or even research among drug users in the community.

Now we turn to the question of whether the repeated attempts to engage the participants could be regarded as coercive by drawing on another example from the drug testing evaluation. This was one of a number of cases where more than five calls were made before contact was established with the participant.

John did not live at the contact address he gave when first interviewed, which turned out to be the home of his brother. He assured me that he would pass on the message, a note giving details that a researcher had called to ask if still wanted to help with our 'lifestyles' research. When I called again I was assured that the message had been passed on but there was no clear answer to the question of whether John was prepared to be interviewed or if he wanted to withdraw from the research. Soon after the second house call the project managed to find out John's current address, a small mid-terraced house, by cross referencing with police records. I received no reply to my first call at the address but an open upstairs window suggested someone may be at home. The next three calls offered evidence that the house was occupied – such as the once open window being closed, curtains open or closed between visits. After four or five calls at the house there was a notable change, with the front door showing signs of having been forced open by a heavy object, such as a police battered ram (there was no sign of shoe marks). On almost all of the other calls at the house I gained a strong impression that there was someone at home when I called so that my role was to present the opportunity for John to make contact (whether to be interviewed or to decline further participation in the research) by presenting a friendly persona through posted notes and encouraging comments spoken through the closed door. The tone and content of the messages become less formal over the weeks of calling at the house to try gain a response. Shortly after receiving a message from John's brother saying that John was no longer interested in taking part in the research I heard that he was intensive care after being attacked in his home with a baseball bat. This helped to make sense of the damaged door, but it transpired that the beating he received was not the cause of his admission to hospital: his stay in the intensive care unit began with a burst stomach ulcer.

In the absence of concrete evidence that John wanted to withdraw from the research I continued to call at his home address, but now asking only for confirmation that he was no longer interested in participating in the research, though also offering to meet at time and place of his choosing. Eventually, after making more than twelve calls at his home over a three week period, John phoned me on my mobile phone offering to meet up in the city centre. We met at a café where we sat outside. His hands were shaking and he appeared to be in a poor emotion state. He was desperate for help. This state of mind, brought about by the hospital admission and the prognosis that (I took this to mean, if he continued his drinking alcohol) he only had a six month life-expectancy. He was receiving treatment at the time of the interview, though he recognised that this was not addressing his inability to stop drinking. John confirmed that he had been at home many of the times I called at his home but that he had been too drunk and/or too ashamed to answer the door.

The case brings the question of informed consent to the forefront, though we also want to use John's plight to show how the ethical constraints risk failing subjects of research by not paying enough attention to a 'duty' of care to the participants. By virtue of the fact that the project did not give specific detail of an intention to track the participants and call at their home address the 'cold calling' was unethical. This interpretation of the guidelines, however, makes no allowance for the fact that the unplanned resort to cold calling only came about because of poor participant response including many invitation letters returned to the project as undeliverable because the addressee moved on. While it can be argued that non-response 'should be interpreted as passive refusal' (Tyrer, Seivewright, Ferguson, & Johnson, 2003; p. 238) the project adopted the view that the participant remained 'active' until we had information to the contrary. This approached was supported by Tyrer et al. after adopting similar methods to maintain contact with the unresponsive 46% of subjects in a study of neurotic disorder. They concluded that 'cold calling' in follow up studies may be justified if there is reason to believe in advance that the population being studied is likely to respond poorly to correspondence and other conventional means of communication' (Tyrer et al., 2003, p. 241).

Cold calling at the homes of respondents as the case studies imply was frustrating and time-consuming process that required a high level of commitment and determination by the researcher. What may be seen as a virtue for the project, however, could be seen as harassment by observers or those directly affected. While we can only speculate on whether the project would have questioned the practice of cold calling had the respondents been drawn from law-abiding citizens, it is clear that the marginal status of the participants also signalled that they were drawn from groups who are more likely to miss a hospital appointment (Mitchell & Selmes, 2007, p. 426). In the case of John it is impossible to make any meaningful statement about his state of mind at the time of the calls. If he was disturbed by the 'cold calls' there were clear lines of communication for him to use to stop them: a note was left on each visit stressing the telephone numbers to call to cancel involvement in the research. There was no overt pressure on respondents to participate. We can, however, say something meaningful about the state of mind of the researcher. In cases like this where it appeared that someone was home but reluctant to open the door he was respectful of this decision and was mindful of the fact that it was for a good reason: whether relating to health or fear of arrest. After seeing the damage to the door the calls became enthused by concern for the health and safety of the participant – hence the call to John's brother to find out if he was okay. When John eventually responded he commented that he was embarrassed about his failure to answer the door because at the time he was too intoxicated. Although, his desire to meet in the city centre suggests that he may also have been uncomfortable with the state of his home.

We argued earlier in the chapter that stigmatised perceptions of risk and danger have unduly influenced research ethic committee (REC) deliberations to make a vulnerable and needy population appear as dangerous and threatening. The moral reasoning of the REC is premised on a consequentialist application of the rules governing researcher conduct without giving enough consideration to the possibility that this interpretation may have negative unintended consequences. As Noddings pointed out, when moving to consider a moral question from the 'rights and justice' approach the person 'moves immediately to abstraction where its thinking can take place clearly and logically in isolation from the complicating factors of particular persons, places, circumstances'. When considered from an ethics of care position, however, consideration of the moral issue 'moves to concretization where its feelings can be modified by the introduction of facts, the feelings of others, and personal histories' (Noddings cited in Browning, Cole, & Coultrap-McQuin, 1992). Researchers who engage people on the margins of society would recognise the need for a more reflexive approach to interpreting the moral problems thrown up during the course of their work. Openness to this begins with seeing research subjects as people to be understood. This may appear simplistic but it is a prescription that requires a leap of faith for those who only know marginalised groups through their (mis)representation in the media and the opinions of professionals. Reliance on a stigmatised image of poorer neighbourhoods creates the double burden of perceiving the residents as vulnerable and in need of professional protection while also dangerous and to be avoided.

While there is some reality to the negative image through the somewhat obvious increase in risk of victimization from 'living in a high crime area' (Miethe & Meier, 1994, p. 47) we know that these risks are not spread evenly throughout these (likely) inner-city neighbourhoods. The long history of these areas being regarded as physically dangerous places that respectable people avoid means that the 'socially disorganised and disorderly nature of inner-city life have become embedded' (Walklate, 2000, p. 50) and reinforced through stigmatised representation (Gourlay, 2007; Mckenzie, 2010). So an area that is seen as fertile ground for research from the perspective of the criminologists raises a series of concerns when viewed from a distance – not simply the distance between the university campus but the more crucial social distance cultivated from a combination of class and academic sensibilities.

These sensibilities are particularly unhelpful when researching criminally active marginalised groups whose perceived threat is more likely to mask the deficit of care and resources. But the hyper-sensitivity to researcher risk and demands of the RECs are creating a climate of research apartheid where the lives of the marginalised remain hidden. While some academics may be in denial about the significance of these developments others may use the problem of 'threat' or 'access' as justification for their inability to treat 'unemployed, drug-addicted, violent criminals with the respect and humanity that ethnographic methods require for meaningful dialogue' (Bourgois, 1996, p. 249). There are undoubtedly many barriers to research among people living in deprived areas but these problems tend to stem from the exaggeration of incidents in the media, misconceptions about conduct, the negative portrayal of 'high crime' communities as lacking/ empathy and engagement, and the risk averse decisions of the authorities managing neighbourhoods. Innes (2004) offers a useful way of understanding how the presentation of crime, specifically, the media focus on violent crime, impacts perception of risk. His concept of signal crimes explains how 'people interpret and define particular criminal incidents as indicators about a range of dangers that exist in contemporary society'. Set against the backdrop of the 'ambient insecurity' (Bauman, 1998, p. 122) that has been seen as a feature of late modernity (Giddens, 1991) with the heightened sense of risk (Beck, 1992) the portrayal and interpretation of crime has provided a potent image danger.

It is easy, however, to allow the relatively recent developments around the construction of risk and the codification of ethical procedures to appear as barriers to an enterprise that has struggled to overcome the practical difficulties of researching criminally active individuals. At the extreme this is illustrated by Polsky's (1967, p. 115) critique of criminology's failure to engage 'unreformed serious criminals in their natural environment'. Surveying the then contemporary criminological textbooks he commented that instead of encouraging field research most of them actively discourage it by offering a justification for 'copping' out. There is little doubt that carrying out the type of research Polsky suggests (with active criminals) is extremely difficult, but there are examples that show that risk taking brings the reward of valuable knowledge (Bourgois, 1996; Polsky, 1967). The institutionalisation of REC has added a significant motive to 'cop out' by developing an ethical 'iron cage' (Wilson, 2011) that restricts innovation, drains enthusiasm, and encourages a form of research self-censorship through avoidance of confrontation with the professionals assessing projects that they do not fully understand or appreciate.

CONCLUSION

The centrality of trust to each juncture of the research process makes the quality of fabric, the basis of the trusting relationship, an ingredient that can strengthen or undermine a project. While this statement may hold a general truth for all research it gains in significance when applied to social research among marginalised groups, in particular the type of stigmatised groups considered in this chapter. As we have discussed above, the social and cultural distance between members of the REC and the marginalised research subjects erodes REC confidence in being able to predict how the researcher may respond to any of the many threatening situations that may occur. The risks are real and researchers have added to the perception of this reality by recalling their exploits on the margins of society (Lee-Treweek & Linkogle, 2000; Lyng, 2005). Like the foreign correspondent there are a range of motives for entering the field but they tend to share the same identifying with the underdog ethos that Becker described in 1967 and Colvin paid for with her life. There is also a common appreciation that whatever the risks it is more likely that field research will throw up moral dilemmas that can involve tough choices to arrive at the 'right' decision. Getting there, balancing the pros and cons of action or inaction, invariably involves a compromise of some sort. Where this involves 'bending' the ethical guidelines the process is likely to be easier if ethical clearance has come at the cost of compromising the research or incorporating restrictive practices. The perception that the REC is 'out of touch' or that it 'lacks appreciation' is likely to provide a means of neutralising the moral bind. Indeed, it could reasonably be argued that restricting research on stigmatised groups is discriminatory and unethical because it allows the consequences of social policy to remain hidden or stigmatised.

We would like to end with a prescription for good practice based on two sets of guiding principles. One is using an understanding of moral responsibility based on an ethics of care to help REC to move away from a bureaucratic interpretation of the guidelines. The second is to base REC decision making on the principles of procedural justice (Tyler, 1990, pp. 6–7). The principle here is that people are more likely to respect and comply with a decision if they feel that they have been listened to and that their argument was taken into account by those arriving at a judgment (even where it is unfavourable). For this to work it would require the REC to open up a forum where the research could be discussed in detail – that is, enough detail for the REC to develop a genuine understanding of the issues, and get to know the researcher and/or the manager of the project. This process may help to instil confidence in the researcher, moderate negative perception of the research subjects and by doing so help to close trust gap.

NOTE

1. The issues raised by the employment of contract researchers is discussed in more detail elsewhere (Wilson & Hodgson, 2012).

REFERENCES

Bauman, Z. (1998). *Globalization: The human consequences*. Cambridge: Polity.

Beck, U. (1992). *Risk society: Towards a new modernity*. London: Sage.

Becker, H. S. (1967). Whose side are we on? *Social Problems, 14*(3), 239–247.

Bourgois, P. (1996). Confronting Anthropology, education, and inner-city apartheid. *American Anthropologist, 98*(2), 249–258.

Browning, E., Cole, E. B., & Coultrap-McQuin, S. M. (1992). *Explorations in feminist ethics: Theory and practice*. Bloomington, IN: Indiana University Press.

Deegan, M. J. (1990). *Jane Addams and the men of the Chicago school, 1892–1918*. New Brunswick, NJ: Transaction Books.

Giddens, A. (1991). *The consequences of modernity*. Cambridge: Polity.

Gourlay, G. (2007). *'It's got a bad name and it sticks…' Approaching stigma as a distinct focus of neighbourhood regeneration initiatives*. Paper presented at the Vital City, Glasgow.

Hodgson, P., Parker, A., & Seddon, T. (2006). Doing drugs research in the criminal justice system: Some notes from the field. *Addiction Research & Theory, 14*(3), 253–264.

Innes, M. (2004). Crime as a signal, crime as a memory. *Journal for Crime, Conflict and the Media, 1*(2), 15–22.

Lee-Treweek, G., & Linkogle, S. (2000). *Danger in the field: Risk and ethics in social research*. London: Routledge.

Lupton, R., Wilson, A., May, T., Warburton, H., & Turnbull, P. J. (2002). *A rock and a hard place: Drug markets in deprived areas.* Home Office Research Study 240. London: The Home Office.

Lyng, S. (2005). Edgework and the risk-taking experience. In S. Lyng (Ed.), *Edgework: The sociology of risk-taking.* London: Routledge.

Matrix & NACRO. (2004). *Evaluation of drug testing in the criminal justice system.* London: Home Office.

Maxfield, M. G., & Babbie, E. R. (2010). *Research methods for criminal justice and criminology.* Belmont, CA: Cengage Learning.

Mckenzie, L. (2010). *Being looked down on: Fear of stigma and its impact upon the participation in local services by working-class mothers.* Nottingham: University of Nottingham.

Miethe, T. D., & Meier, R. F. (1994). *Crime and its social context: Toward an integrated theory of offenders, victims, and situations.* Albany, NY: State University of New York Press.

Mitchell, A. J., & Selmes, T. (2007). Why don't patients attend their appointments? Maintaining engagement with psychiatric services. *Advances in Psychiatric Treatment, 13*(6), 423–434.

Möllering, G. (2006). *Trust: Reason, routine, reflexivity.* Oxford: Elsevier.

Polsky, N. (1967). *Hustlers, beats, and others.* New Brunswick: Transaction.

Seddon, T. (2005). Paying drug users to take part in research: Justice, human rights and business perspectives on the use of incentive payments. *Addiction Research & Theory, 13*(2), 101–109.

Seddon, T. (2011). What is a problem drug user? *Addiction Research & Theory, 19*(4), 334–343.

Shapiro, D., Sheppard, B., & Cheraskin, L. (1992). Business on a handshake. *Negotiation Journal, 8*(4), 365–377.

Thompson, K. (2005). *The early sociology of race and ethnicity: Race and culture.* London: Routledge.

Tyrer, P., Seivewright, H., Ferguson, B., & Johnson, T. (2003). "Cold calling" in psychiatric follow up studies: Is it justified? *Journal of Medical Ethics, 29*(4), 238–242. doi:10.1136/jme.29.4.238.

Tyler, T. R. (1990). *Why people obey the law.* New Haven, CT: Yale University Press.

Venkatesh, S. (2008). *Gang leader for a day.* New York, NY: Penguin Press.

Walklate, S. (2000). Trust and the problem of community in the inner city. In T. Hope & R. Sparks (Eds.), *Crime, risk, and insecurity: Law and order in everyday life and political discourse.* London: Routledge.

Wilson, A. (2007). *Northern Soul: Music, drugs and subcultural identity.* Cullompton: Willan.

Wilson, A. (2011). Research ethics and the iron cage of bureaucratic rationality. *Addiction Research & Theory, 19*(5), 391–393.

Wilson, A., & Hodgson, P. (2012). Elusive evidence: Hard to reach drug users and the missing values in drug policy decision making. *Howard Journal of Criminal Justice.*

Wilson, A., May, T., Warburton, H., Lupton, R., & Turnbull, P. J. (2002). *Heroin and crack cocaine markets in deprived areas: Seven local case studies.* London: Centre for the Analysis of Social Exclusion, London School of Economics and Political Science.

IMPROVISATION, ETHICAL HEURISTICS AND THE DIALOGICAL REALITY OF ETHICS IN THE FIELD

Mark Edwards and Sam Hillyard

ABSTRACT

Purpose – *This chapter builds on our personal experiences of researching primary schools. The chapter begins by discussing some important subjective accounts of conducting qualitative research, and the unavoidable (often unexpected) dilemmas that confront researchers whilst 'in the field'. This provides the backdrop against which our own experiences of conducting research will be considered.*

Methodology/approach – *Whilst it is vital and necessary for researchers to abide by the relevant code(s) of ethical conduct, the authors argue that the contingent nature of qualitative research necessitates a degree of personal ethical discretion. The ethical frameworks of bodies such as the British Educational Research Association and the British Sociological Association are prima facie generalised, and cannot cover all ethical potentialities. Ethically sensitive researchers not only will be vigilant in adhering to the guiding framework, but will also be acutely aware of the situated nature of many ethical issues.*

Ethics in Social Research
Studies in Qualitative Methodology, Volume 12, 129–148
Copyright © 2012 by Emerald Group Publishing Limited
ISSN: 1042-3192/doi:10.1108/S1042-3192(2012)0000012010

Findings – *Researchers can never be fully prepared for the ethical issues they will confront in the field. However, the authors believe that if researchers share the eccentricities of their empirical experiences with others in their field, then researchers can be better prepared for the ethical challenges awaiting them. As such, this chapter draws upon our own fieldwork experiences in a rural village school in Norfolk and in a series of suburban/rural primary schools in North East England. The chapter does not offer a series of recommendations, but rather an exploration of the practical lessons that the authors have taken from the field.*

Keywords: Situational ethics; educational research; primary school; reflectivity; case study

INTRODUCTION

The chapter stemmed from a conversation regarding the ethical issues that both authors confronted when conducting research in primary schools. Reflecting on our individual experiences in rural and suburban schools, we found that some ethical issues commonly faced by researchers are not widely discussed in standard methods textbooks. As a result, we felt it important to examine some of the issues we encountered whilst conducting our individual research projects in primary school contexts. Following the tradition set by Whyte's (1993 [1943]) *Street Corner Society* and Liebow's (1967) *Tally's Corner*, what follows is less a 'how to' methods guide than a reflective, 'confessional tale' of our research experiences, with a specific focus on the ethical issues that arose. Whilst introductory methods textbooks remain an important resource for social researchers, there is a danger in such texts to present normative guidelines of an unproblematic research process. Whilst the 'messy' nature of social research is increasingly acknowledged (Law, 2004), often the empirical work one *plans* to do is transformed by a wealth of unforeseen circumstances that arise 'in the field'. The chapter will begin by introducing the two research projects that provide the material to be discussed throughout. Attention will then go on to consider some contributions to the tradition of reflective research accounts before the importance of what we have termed a situated ethics, and a situated ethical account of how we faced and responded to such circumstances is discussed. The main part of the chapter will therefore explore the unique ethical issues that surfaced whilst conducting our own research projects – and how we addressed them at the time and now again in reflection.

Edwards' doctoral research was an evaluation of the impact of School Sport Partnerships (SSPs) in primary schools in North East England. The core element of the case-based study consists of interviews with teaching staff. The purpose of the interviews was to understand what individual schools believed the impact of SSPs to be. Gaining the views of teaching staff was considered the most effective way in which an overall assessment of the SSP's impact on the school could be made. Three schools with divergent characteristics (relative to the sample population) were selected so as to include a range of contexts and outcomes. One of the case study schools, with over 250 pupils, is located in a deprived[1] ex-mining town. The second had a pupil body of around 150 children and was positioned in a small affluent village on the outskirts of a mid-size town. The final school had fewer than 50 pupils and was situated in a relatively isolated rural area with an above average level of affluence. Certain characteristics of each school varied significantly – the size of the pupil body and staff force, rural/urban location, Ofsted inspectorate grading, location vis-à-vis the school's SSP, and the relative affluence of the locality and the process of conducting research in the three schools also differed significantly.

Hillyard's research[2] was a case study of a primary within the context of its rural village – challenging to what degree the school could be argued to be 'at the heart of the village'. The village was in north Norfolk, the East of England, with a population of circa 600. The village, in addition to its school, had a pub, a shop and Post Office and a Church of England church. It was located approximately five miles from the nearest market town and around an hour's drive from the nearest city (Norwich). The school role was circa 50 pupils, arranged into three classes. The fieldwork in the village involved three periods of residence, in September, Easter and early summer and the research methods drew on those within an ethnographic research tradition. It is the issues we encountered whilst conducting research in these schools that provides part of the material to be discussed in this chapter.

THE IMPORTANCE OF SUBJECTIVE RESEARCH ACCOUNTS

The seminal works of Whyte (1993) and Liebow (1967) are as celebrated for the reflective accounts of the research process as for their important theoretical contribution. Both authors provide a candid and insightful commentary on their ethnographic work, which locates the respective studies in a rich contextual framework. For Whyte (1993, p. 279), a lengthy narrative was necessary as he believed his contemporaries placed the discussion of methods 'entirely on a logical–intellectual basis' – an observation that retains much of its significance 60 years on. Whyte (1993, p. 279) contends that such reticence results in a failure to identify the important effect that researchers have upon the observed; he argues that a 'real explanation' of how the research played out necessitates 'a rather personal account' of the empirical process. Indeed, without such a subjective account of Whyte's research, readers would be ignorant of the extraordinary extent to which he immersed himself into one Italian family, and the impact that this level of submergence ultimately had upon his research. In *Tally's Corner*, Liebow (1967) also provides a fascinating insight into the research process, shedding some light on the ethical issues that arose as a result of his relationship with one respondent, Tally. After selecting a research site on the suggestion that it would be 'a good place to get [his] feet wet', Liebow demonstrates how one's research plans can be transformed as a result of unforeseen circumstances. As he reflects, 'I went so deep that I was completely submerged and my plan to do three or four separate studies, each with its own neat, clean boundaries, dropped forever out of sight' (Liebow, 1967, pp. 236–237). The actual path Liebow's research took was fashioned 'almost without [his] being aware of it' (Liebow, 1967, p. 237). Liebow found himself acting as a leader for some of his delinquent associates and, in one particular situation, acting as a spokesman in an extradition hearing. Similarly, Whyte (1993) found himself fronting a protest march on City Hall; standing up for members of the local Italian community who he had come to know intimately.

Liebow's account of how the research changed due to the unique situation in which he found himself supports the central contention of this chapter – no amount of organisation in advance can fully prepare researchers for the idiosyncrasies of the research site and the negotiations that must be made throughout the empirical process. The style in which Whyte and Liebow present their reflective accounts can be seen as catalysts for a trend towards more subjective insights into social research. It is not the content alone that prompted interest, but the style in which both reported on their research – more literary, perhaps essayistic, than academic; descriptive, engaging and humorous. A number of edited collections providing similar accounts were published from the 1970s onwards (e.g. Bell & Encel, 1978; Bell & Newby, 1976; Bell & Roberts, 1984; Burgess, 1984), and several collections specifically relating to educational research were also produced (Burgess, 1985, 1989; Walford, 1991). Indeed, to the extent that some reflective commentaries could be argued to have exceeded the length of some original research monographs! It is beyond the scope of this chapter to review the findings of these texts, other than to note that this is now a valued addition to the qualitative research canon.

At the heart of this movement, personified by such edited collections and this volume, is a belief that 'accounts of doing sociological [and educational] research are *at least* as valuable [...] as the exhortations to be found in the much more common textbooks on methodology' (Bell & Newby, 1976, p. 9). For a thorough account of the research process, authors should reflect on both the theoretical *and* subjective aspects of their work, so as to provide a broad, reflexive account. The predilection towards the former at the expense of the latter systematically evades important information about the research process. Walford (1991, p. 1) produces a damming critique of the conventional – 'careful, objective, step-by-step' – model of the empirical process. He argues that such traditional methods of teaching and reporting on research methods contribute to 'a myth of objectivity', leading to a situation whereby:

> Most social science and educational research methods textbooks have abstracted the researcher from the process of research in the same way as have natural science textbooks. The social dimension of research is omitted and the process is presented as a cold analytic practice where any novice researcher can follow set recipes and obtain predetermined results. (Walford, 1991, p. 2)

The emphasis on objectivity leads to what Burgess (1984, p. 1) terms a 'conspiracy of silence'. At the expense of striving towards objectivity, research often fails to adequately discuss the subjective, emotive and personal nature of the process. Many issues that are confronted in the field are, therefore, bypassed in the write-up and the opportunity for the dissemination of practical experience and advice is significantly reduced. The result is that researchers fail to learn from the experience of others and, for novice researchers in particular, enter the field with a naive (but justified) belief that their research will 'work itself out' as it does in methods textbooks. The myth of simply 'going forth into the field and doing likewise' as the early, great anthropologist instructed their students is no longer sufficient. A specific element of the process which is often skimmed over and treated more like an obligatory chore in the publication or research grant approval process than an insightful, constructive and important component, are that ethical considerations often overlap with the subjective realities of conducting fieldwork. The chapter now moves on to discuss examples of subjective ethical accounts, but defines these broadly: as situations or contexts in which the researcher sensed significant implications for the fieldwork were at stake. It also takes a steer from Delamont's (2009) confessional account – and concern – that her fieldwork was not 'getting at' the very processes with which she sought to engage. It attends to recent moves within the research community to appreciate the embodied and emotive nature of doing fieldwork (Coffey, 1999; Wolcott, 2010) and the potential dilemmas being in the field unwittingly and wittingly entails. As Wolcott's (2010) account almost ruefully discusses in relation to his own fieldwork conduct, what feels appropriate in the course of the data collection may warrant justification later.

SITUATIONAL ETHICS

The reflexive turn in ethnographic and qualitative research has drawn attention to ethical issues in social and educational research. The majority of methods textbooks now include a section, if not a chapter dedicated to the subject – whereas once such issues were buried, as Thomas and Znaniecki's (1958 [1919]) now famous 'methodological note' testifies, in the appendices.[3] Ethical statements – such as the British Educational Research Association's [BERA] (2004) and British Sociological Association's [BSA] (2002) ethical guidelines – are general principles, to be applied to all research conducted within the respective field. Of course, it would be beyond the scope of such a framework to attempt to cover *all* ethical potentialities. The BSA's *Statement of Ethical Practice* goes further than BERA's in acknowledging this situated character of ethical considerations, for example; 'The statement is not exhaustive but summarises basic principles for ethical practice by sociologists. Departures from the principles should be the result of deliberation and not ignorance' (BSA, 2002, p. 1). This statement implies that, *as far as possible*, researchers should abide by the stated principles, but in circumstances in which they become questionable, sensitivity and knowledge should guide the researcher.

Generalised frameworks, of which the BERA and BSA codes are examples, are of great importance, and few would refute their necessity; they provide researchers with 'an essential shared framework and reference point for checking the integrity and consistency of [their] actions' (Simons, 2000, p. 53). As the above quotation from the BSA code implies, though, such frameworks do not cover all eventualities and, as such, an additional form of ethical guidelines is needed. What is required is a situated ethics that takes into consideration local and specific practices. A situated ethics, by its nature, cannot be universalised and therefore no framework can theorise such an ethical code (Simons & Usher, 2000). Yet one way in which researchers can learn of, and reflect upon, ethical potentialities is through reading about the issues faced by others. A candid documentary of ethical problems, such is our ambition here, can raise the awareness of other researchers as to potential issues they may encounter. This chapter hopes to add to the existing repertoire of knowledge by highlighting ethical issues that may confront researchers, specifically in primary school contexts.

It should be noted that, combined, general codes and past research should be used as *guidelines* only, for ethical issues cannot be solved sufficiently in abstract or theoretical terms (Figueroa, 2000). The decisions that are taken should be firmly situated in the context in which they emerge. The actions one makes when confronted with an ethical dilemma must conform to ethical guidelines and ideally be informed by past research. Ultimately, however, decisions should be made responsively, with a thoughtful and reflective approach (Figueroa, 2000; Glen, 2000). As Wellington (2000) has suggested, one of the most frequent exercises researchers engage in is compromise.

THE IMPACT OF RESEARCHERS IN THE EDUCATIONAL SETTING

Prior to engaging in any empirical work researchers should be confident that the project's potential benefits outweigh any infringement on the research subjects. Expressed another way, the researcher should be able to leave the field reasonably confident in the knowledge that their presence has had no deleterious effect – akin to a 'countryside code' for fieldwork. Much qualitative research in schools necessitates children and/or teaching staff being observed within, or having to be absent from, the classroom setting. Be it through interviews with teachers, focus groups with children, observation of lessons, or any other method, the presence of researchers inevitably alters the educational – and fieldwork – setting. The legitimacy of any research that detracted from children's education would be highly questionable. This is not to pretend or deny that the presence of a fieldworker will have some kind of impact. Three significant ways in which a researcher can affect the normal operation of a school are by: (a) affecting the behaviour of staff and pupils, (b) detracting from the time teachers or pupils spend in, or preparing for, classroom activities and (c) becoming a logistical problem or a hindrance on the school's finite resources. It is the responsibility of the researcher to develop and adapt their own situational ethical code to ensure any potential infringement – witting or otherwise – is kept to an appropriate level.

In relation to affecting staff and pupils, overt observation is known to impact upon the behaviour of research subjects, the so-called 'Hawthorne Effect'. In schools, for example, teachers may adapt their teaching style or 'impression-manage' in the presence of an observer, or children might behave uncharacteristically so as to impress (or unimpress). It is impossible to determine the extent to which researchers affect those being observed because it is problematic to predict what 'the behaviour would have been like if it hadn't been observed' (Robson, 2002, p. 311). However, our own research suggests the researcher's presence does affect participants' behaviour, to the extent that even the possibility of a researcher's presence may risk or threaten access.

In Edwards' observation of physical education (PE) lessons specifically, it frequently appeared as though children and teaching staff altered their behaviour to project a 'front-staged' image of themselves. The purpose of the lesson observation was to monitor the total length of lessons, the duration for which children were engaged in physical activity, to record the lesson content, and to assess the motivational climate (competitive or task based) that was facilitated (see Solomon, 1996 on motivational climates). Therefore, it differed from the more generic ethnographic task, simply to see what was occurring in that context. Teachers were told that no notes were being made on their pedagogical approach or the structure of the lesson – in short, they were assured that no judgments were being made about their teaching, Ofsted-style. Staff were also asked to tell the children of the researcher's purpose, so that they understood there was no affiliation to a sports team or any other body interested in assessing their behaviour or performance. In most instances the class teacher would say that Edwards was conducting research for Durham University, based around what happens in PE lessons and how long they last. The children *were* told, in every lesson, that their behaviour or performance was not being assessed. Despite these measures, some teachers appeared to adapt their teaching style to influence Edwards' perception. In numerous lessons staff members would look to the observer for a reaction when a new activity began, or when particular announcements were made towards, or by the pupils. Regardless of the teacher's pronouncements that children were *not* being assessed by the observer, it appeared as though some pupils still attempted to impress with their talents (presumably believing the observer was a scout for a sport club) – despite the sensitivity on the researcher's behalf to the lesson being observed. In order to adapt to this unexpected situation, Edwards found himself having to direct attention away from those most eager to demonstrate their skills. After identifying this phenomenon, the importance attached to the children understanding the researcher's role was further stressed to teachers.

Whilst it is impossible to prove that the observed lessons would have progressed in a different manner if they were not being observed, the researcher's presence appeared to alter particular aspects or dynamics of the lesson. Again, whether this was a positive or negative affect is also difficult to ascertain. Whilst teachers looked in the direction of the researcher when they began new tasks, or disciplined/complimented pupils, it was the children who appeared to adapt their behaviour most significantly. Children would go to extra lengths to ensure their input was seen by Edwards; in particular, those (mostly male students) whose skills and technique appeared more developed than their peers would stand within close proximity of, and regularly glance towards the observer while executing tasks. This example demonstrates how the researcher's presence impacted upon the lesson; both on the teaching of, and the motivational climate within (Solomon, 1996). Given that both teachers and students were aware of the genuine research goals, but decided to reinterpret these, there was little more that could have been done to avoid such outcomes each lesson was observed, literally, from the 'side-lines', and due to the small size of most facilities I decided that moving position during the lesson would draw more attention to my presence.

The most obvious and unambiguous way that qualitative researchers affect schools is through the demands they make on research participants. For Edwards and Hillyard the greatest demand they placed on the schools' resources was the time taken up by interviews with teaching staff and pupils. All of Edwards' interviews were conducted within school time, thus meaning that teachers had to leave their class, or sacrifice their free time/lesson preparation, for the interview to take place. In one case a supply teacher was hired to cover the absence of staff, whereas in others the children were supervised by teaching assistants. Hillyard also interviewed groups of pupils during the school day, hence removing them briefly from their lessons. It is vital that such demands on respondents' time are fully justified by research that is able to make good or effective use of such opportunities. In the unexpected case of the supply teacher being hired to cover staff absence, Edwards ensured that the school was financially reimbursed to reduce the burden on resources.[4] Researchers should also be mindful of the sheer logistical demands their research can place on schools; accommodating researchers and allowing them to observe lessons, view confidential data, interview teachers or whatever else their project demands, can be time-consuming to arrange. With the gatekeeper often being a senior staff member, with their own significant administrative and organisational commitments, this inevitably places an additional pressure on their workload.

In the Norfolk context, the concentrated periods of fieldwork placed pressure on 'getting into' the school and making good progress by facilitating a rapport and making good opportunities for further fieldwork. Prior to arriving in Norfolk, access had been negotiated via letter and follow up telephone calls with the head teacher and the school manager. Like Edwards, several schools were approached before a positive response was secured. Therefore, there was undeniably a concern to consolidate this preliminary contact and further engender a working relationship within the school once we had met face-to-face. As Edwards described, initial meetings with members of staff were arranged or liaised by the gatekeeper – the head teacher – in a semi formal way. Such interviews, whilst useful for famili-arising the researcher with the school and its staff were however conducted briefly, in semi-public areas of the school (such as the reception foyer seating area) and hence limited in the rich kind of insight into the school Hillyard was keen to gain. In such a small school, it was possible to speak with all key members of staff within a short time frame, but it was not until she returned after the Christmas period, and again in the summer, that Hillyard came to understand some of the pressures and tensions the school was experiencing. Like Edwards, she had a sense that much was going on, but had little opportunity or access in the early stages to observe or to explore. Whilst opportunistic in negotiating access to lessons, school files and information, the pace could not be forced and entailed the repeated negotiation of access via different heads and class teachers. The continuity of contact with the school manager was also vital to maintaining a dialogue and the oppor-tunity to spend a great deal of time in the school.

Ironically, in the case of Hillyard's fieldwork in Norfolk (and she remains unclear to what degree this impacted upon her access), it was the school facing difficult circumstances that led to a greater insight. This arguably improved Hillyard's ability to demonstrate appreciation, sympathy and sensitivity towards their circumstances. As Rojek (2007) notes, 'traditional British values are slippery abstractions [...] Often it is only when these ideals are infringed or violated that they become a cause célèbre' (Rojek 2007, p. 11). In this instance, the school changed their head teacher again (there were three different heads during the course of my fieldwork); hosted an

Ofsted inspection at short-notice and both of their core, permanent members of teaching staff experienced significant illnesses. It seemed that every time Hillyard returned to the school for another period of fieldwork, or spoke with staff via telephone, that another challenge had arrived. By the end of the fieldwork, with a new head appointed and staff recovered or new appointments made, combined with an improved Ofsted inspection result, the year had been tumultuous. Yet by understanding this context, Hillyard was able to ask questions that demonstrated insider knowledge of their circumstances and hence to celebrate their successes, albeit as an outsider. This involved the renegotiation of fieldwork relationships with gatekeepers, such as the new head teachers.

The knowledge of an insider also brought with it responsibilities. As Hillyard became privy to some points of conflict between staff, the surrounding community and also former employees, I had effectively come to know more of the school's history and its past role in the village than many residents or school staff. I had also come to see a variety of points of view, not all of which were supportive of the pupils, school or community. This included overhearing a racist discussion of newcomers in the village pub one evening (Hillyard promptly left); accusations of bullying in the school (which she explored but considered unsupported by her fieldwork) and several allegations of embezzlement and fraud. As we have attempted to acknowledge, our concern was exploratory and non-interventionist. It is, as Payne (1996) argues, a misnomer that fieldwork will only involve meeting nice people and pleasant experiences. Hillyard did not expect to encounter such a variety of opinion in such a sleepy rural setting, but it demonstrated that fieldwork retains an important capacity to shock and surprise (Delamont, 2002).

This section has attempted to show through our own fieldwork that regardless of access or arrangements secured in advance, the realities of being in a school impacted upon the quality of data we were able to gather. It also highlights some of the logistical difficulties encountered in the field, and highlights the necessity of dealing with such issues in a situated manner. The situational 'issues' that confronted both researchers warranted immediate responses, in the absence of a prescriptive ethical framework, and in an appropriate manner. All researchers will inevitably differ in how they respond to unexpected occurrences, and it would be futile to expect researchers to manage their response directly in accordance with – what may be a situationally inappropriate – ethical code. Researchers must apply their knowledge of ethical frameworks in a sensitive, but largely *ad hoc* way in order to satisfy the issues confronting them.

WHY TRUST SOCIAL RESEARCHERS? THE 'INNOCENT FIELDWORKER'[5] IN LITIGIOUS TIMES

On the first day observing PE lessons in one pilot school, Edwards found himself in an uncomfortable and ethically challenging situation. Prior to the lesson beginning he was invited to wait in the classroom whilst the year one children got ready for a PE lesson. After sitting in the corner finalising the observation schedule, Edwards looked up to find the whole class in the middle of changing into their PE kits. Children were partially dressed (at best), walking about innocently in their underwear whilst they stumbled around putting their PE kits and footwear on. Being immediately struck by the degree of exposure to the children, he vacated the room, telling the teacher that he would wait outside. Sitting in the corridor waiting for the children to emerge for their lesson the severity of the situation was considered. The researcher had been in the school for an hour at most, had no prior knowledge of any teachers, and the school had only received a basic explanatory letter from him. A Criminal Records Bureau (CRB) certificate had been provided, but no further investigations were made. A series of questions ran through Edwards' mind; What if a person with ulterior motives had been granted such a degree of trust? How would parents react if their child told them a man was watching them get changed? What if another teacher had walked past and reported the researcher's presence in such a setting to the head teacher? The possible outcomes of any of these scenarios could have severely damaged the research project and reputation of the researcher, particularly in such litigious times for adults researching young children (Pole, 2007). Fortunately, none of these potentialities occurred on this occasion.

The school had consented to lesson observation, and the teacher evidently felt it acceptable to allow the researcher to be present whilst the children undressed. Ethically and morally, however, Edwards was uncomfortable with the situation and thus decided to remove himself from the classroom. This, he decided, was the obvious action to take. Should the teacher have been told that the researcher felt it inappropriate to be in attendance for such a situation? Or should the incident have been reported to the head teacher (to avoid the same thing happening in future)? In this instance the decision taken was not to say anything as it may have reflected badly on the teacher in question, the senior academic who had negotiated access for the research, and may possibly had even damaged links between the university and school. This is not to say that the safety and well-being of the children was not considered. There appear to have been several reasons that help explain the high level of trust received, and thus influenced the decision not to voice concerns. Being attached to a reputable university may have increased the level of trust, as possibly would the credentials of, and close links to the school that the academic staff member who negotiated access had. The age and appearance (a young, white, middle-class student) also may have given a positive image to teaching staff, that was interpreted as being 'trustworthy'. This is not to excuse the degree of freedom that was so quickly given to the relatively new outsider, but it does help explain the reasoning behind the apparent indifference of staff. It contrasts with Hillyard's experience in Norfolk, where attending the village pre-school, she was asked to leave her mobile phone (which contained a camera) in the secured staff room and was closely supervised in her contact with the children until confirmation of her CRB check arrived.[6]

A second issue that relates to trust is the different level of rigour with which schools conduct initial security checks of researchers. Visitors to schools must produce a CRB certificate on entry if they are spending any sustained period of time in the school and in contact with the children. Whilst a recent CRB was viewed in each school, the formality of the procedure varied widely. In one school Edwards was asked to provide photographic evidence so that the CRB certificate could be cross-referenced to ensure its legitimacy. The documents were then photocopied for reference. In another school (not case study) no request was made to view a CRB certificate. The CRB was viewed only at the researcher's (insistent) suggestion. It was glanced over by a teacher and then quickly handed back. All schools had a signing-in process but, again, only one asked for proof of identity. As researchers are often unsupervised in schools (or find themselves present within dubious situations – as discussed above), the onus is upon the ethically minded researcher to present the appropriate documentation, regardless of whether it is asked for, in the interests of good practice.

A further issue relates to gaining access. In two of the three case study schools that Edwards visited, the gatekeepers (head teachers) had PhDs in Education. Both of these gatekeepers were notably more accommodating than any other school that was visited ($n = 8$), with both allowing the researcher to interview staff, observe lessons and analyse PE files, as well as going to extra lengths to accommodate the researcher's needs. On several occasions these teachers empathised with the difficulty PhD students face when accessing primary schools and offered as much assistance as required. Whether or not this is a general issue would be interesting to know, although much research avoids mention of such issues. The implications of such a trend could impact significantly upon the reliability and representativeness of research in schools. If only a minority of schools frequently grant researchers access, this is also ethically problematic as pupils within these schools may have their education disproportionately affected by observation, or class teachers being absent from classrooms for research purposes. Indeed, in selecting her fieldwork site for her PhD fieldwork, Hillyard was steered away from approaching several local schools, which had already participated in university projects. Similarly to Edwards, the continued access into the Norfolk school was further eased by the new head teacher's son having attended Durham University.

An acknowledgment of the role that a subliminal-Old Boy Network plays in conducting field research itself risks ethical question marks being raised. The cross-permeation of business, political and social networks by the elite is long-acknowledged (Scott, 1992). Instances where professional networks impacted upon our fieldwork were discovered *during* fieldwork, and did not alter our research's trajectories or aims. Nevertheless, it further supports our argument that the situations researchers are confronted with vary widely, and in a way that contains ethical implications for the data that it is, or is not possible to collect. In some instances they are made good by networks, in others there is a need to withdraw or be pro-active in managing the circumstances in which you may find yourself.

DEGREES OF FREEDOM AND 'STAGE MANAGEMENT'

Head teachers often play a pivotal role in granting access to researchers in primary schools. As mentioned above, the likelihood of gaining access can be improved via several strategies – a referral from a mutual associate or even being an Old Boy (former pupil) yourself, such as when Hillyard once conducted research at her former primary school. When a head teacher – or any other gatekeeper – grants access to a school site, whilst they may be in a key position within the institution, it does not – and should not be taken to imply – that the individual staff members are consenting. The head teacher is merely allowing a researcher into the school; it is, theoretically, the decision of the teachers themselves as to whether they want to participate and engage with the research. When allowed into a school, however, it is difficult for researchers to establish the degree of freedom that teachers or pupils have in consenting to participate in research. That is, researchers may not be privy to the kind of conversation that preceded the research, or the manner in which the research was introduced or presented to the institution's members.

In both Edwards' and Hillyard's research, it was head teachers who granted initial access. It was they, also, who arranged for the interviews to take place with teaching staff (albeit in the first instance in the case of Hillyard). Edwards, for example, was told to arrive at school for a particular time to interview X number of teachers. This is clearly a more practical method than approaching each member of staff individually given the relatively limited time Edwards anticipated spending in the field. However, there remains the degree to which class teachers and those in the schools were given a free opportunity to opt out of the research. In accordance with BERA and BSA ethical codes, all respondents were briefed on the research and asked to sign an informed consent form in Edwards' research. Edwards found at least two respondents were dissatisfied with taking part in the research; although the individuals 'agreed' to be interviewed and gave informed consent, it was clear that they would rather not partake. As a result of their subsequent reticence, the interviews were short and the interviewees apathetic – a form of resistance from participation in itself. Similarly, in the early days of her fieldwork, Hillyard was very much a passing visitor-in-school and initial rapport with staff stood in the way of the more detailed and confidential conversations-with-a-purpose that unfolded across the year. Our point here is that these stages of negotiation or 'buy-in' for participants is key. Our concern was that participants may consent to be interviewed, but not in a situation in which they are completely at-ease. The institutional hierarchy of all schools and the relative power of the head teacher must be acknowledged, and it may or may not be possible to broker a more sustained relationship across the fieldwork or in order to allay participants' concerns and then generate a richer insight into that social setting. In the case of Edwards' fieldwork, he retained a sense that there was much more to 'unlock' in that social setting than his research had accessed. For Hillyard, the unfortunate co-incidence of a series of unforeseeable circumstances was to some degree eased by the background of the new head teacher and also the possibilities that extended periods spent in the field permit.

A further problem relating to the relationship between class teacher and head teacher concerns a certain degree of 'stage management' that can take place. When speaking to teachers in one school it became clear that they had been provided with information reminding (or telling) them to mention particular physical activities that the school had offered. When a teacher was asked to see the day's interview schedule there was, written on the

opposite side – and clearly not intended for the researcher's viewing – the
following handwritten notes:

Wide range offered.

Cheer leading – multi sports

Link with other experts/agencies – dancemats

– cheerleading
– tennis
– rugby
– hockey
– karate
– table tennis

This invites an interpretation that respondents were given a clear 'steer' by
a senior staff member as to what information to discuss during the
interviews. The staff member who made this list had thought about possible
lines of questioning, and in order to provide the researcher with a positive
impression of the school, then wrote down some prompts or potential
answers. This of course challenged the very validity of the research and its
ability to answer its core questions about SSPs. Little can be done to reduce
the chances of such occurrences as *all* interviewees, in most social research,
can be briefed by a superior prior to being interviewed, and of course in
schooling contexts, a great deal of preparation or staging is arranged prior
to formal evaluations, such as Ofsted inspections (Jeffrey & Woods, 1998).
In this particular case of Edwards' research, the 'briefing' bears little impact
on the overall findings, as it merely summarised the activities on offer within
the school. What was of more concern to Edwards was the degree of
freedom with which teachers could offer their own experience and interpretation of the initiative.

One of the challenges Hillyard faced was to attempt to get behind the
'front-stage' presentation of the school, in order to understand its relationship with the local community. Unlike positivistic research, there is rarely a
clear-cut hypothesis to confirm or reject during fieldwork, or a moment
where a clear sense of having become an 'insider' is gained. It is only a
blurred and indistinct sense that you have become part of an accustomed
'daily round' of the school day – a familiar figure who is included in events,

rather than a visiting researcher who is wheeled out before a class or assembly and formally introduced. It also, akin to Liebow's (1967) reflection on coming to care about the community he was researching, includes a sense of when to withdraw from the research setting and when to be sensitive about questioning. For example, during the Norfolk fieldwork, I was trawling through the school's early logs (a series of substantial volumes) and working in a small room outside the staff room after school hours. The school had just appointed its new head and I knew how important this was for the future of the school, as several people had questioned its viability and even whether the post would attract a field of suitably qualified applicants. The new head was visiting that afternoon and met the temporary head in the staff room. The school was by then empty and I was concerned not to hamper their conversation by continuing to work in a room within earshot. I therefore made my excuses, suggesting I hadn't the stamina of head teacher-types for working late (which invited a joke about university-types) and then left. I still was able to complete my review of the logs before leaving the field. Therefore, at times, exercising discretion becomes more appropriate than further data collection.

We have attempted to offer a few examples from our own time spent in primary schools as a means to raise some issues for further thought. Whilst we acknowledge that fieldwork preparation cannot anticipate every eventuality, we were still struck by the diversity of freedoms and opportunities that our case study schools and research sites permitted. Not all can be explained by the different characteristics of the researchers themselves, but it does seem to suggest that much responsibility must be taken on by individual researchers: both in their own interests of safety and also discretion and respect for the research site and social actors they will spend time with. Ironically, this includes being provided with too much access to unsupervised settings as well as being sensitive towards why respondents may be inhibited or less forthcoming in their engagement with the research.

CONCLUSION

This chapter has sought to demonstrate, via reference to our separate experiences of conducting research in primary schools, that researchers need to employ an ethical sensitivity that is responsive to the situations by which they are (often unexpectedly) confronted. We suggest that, in addition to adherence to wider ethical codes, researchers have no choice but to be reflective and adaptive. This 'situational ethics' is vital for, and perhaps unavoidable in, conducting ethical sound research. We hope that the various examples discussed above will aid readers in contemplating the kinds of situational issues that may emerge in their own research.

All fieldwork involves feeling uncomfortable and out-of-place at times, as the strange becomes familiar to you (Delamont, 2002). But the ethics of this become more serious and can hold greater implication when you also feel you are being steered towards a particular definition of the situation or receiving only 'half the picture'. There are also moments, as we have shown, when you may be shocked and unsettled by what you encounter. Some instances may threaten your professional standing and it is vital to be prepared – or at least mindful – as best you can. At other times, it is more apt to exercise discretion. In the interests of professional conduct, not all one hears will be appropriate for publication (less for fear of libel, as Bell and Newby (1976) reported). Qualitative research involves encountering opinion and 'gossip', but how this features warrants both careful reflection and careful use. In a similar respect, not all that one sees whilst conducting research – particularly in the presence of vulnerable persons – should be 'seen'. Researchers must use their disciplinary training, understanding of ethical codes and personal discretion to ensure that they act appropriately, even if this means the cessation (albeit temporarily) of their work.

We therefore follow with interest the arguments made by others in this volume as to the appropriate role for an ethical public ethnography, where intervention is embedded and an impact agenda championed.

NOTES

1. The relative deprivation/affluence of the schools' localities was determined by the assertions made in the most recent Ofsted inspection of the school (for further information see http://schoolsfinder.direct.gov.uk/).

2. ESRC research grant no. RES-000-22-3412.

3. The note was important in the impact it had upon fieldwork good practice (a landmark reflective piece). Nevertheless, if was placed in the appendices rather than embedded in the main research monograph volumes.

4. A cheque for just under £90 was written for the school, coming from Edwards' Researcher Training Support Grant.

5. After Barley (1986) *The Innocent Anthropologist.*

6. The timing of the fieldwork coincided with the Vanessa George's Plymouth playgroup abuse breaking into the UK news. The careful management of Hillyard's participation at the playground by the group's co-ordindator protected both researcher and the children in that first instance.

REFERENCES

Barley, N. (1986). *The innocent anthropologist*. London: Penguin.

Bell, C., & Encel, S. (Eds.). (1978). *Inside the Whale: Ten personal accounts of social research*. Oxford: Pergamon.

Bell, C., & Newby, H. (Eds.). (1976). *Doing sociological research*. London: George Allen and Unwin.

Bell, C., & Roberts, H. (Eds.). (1984). *Social researching: Politics, problems, practice*. London: Routledge and Kegan Paul.

British Educational Research Association [BERA]. (2004). *Revised ethical guidelines for educational research*. London, UK: BERA.

British Sociological Association [BSA]. (2002). *Statement of ethical practice for the British Sociological Association*. Durham, UK: BSA.

Burgess, R. (Ed.). (1984). *The research process in educational settings: Ten case studies*. Sussex: The Falmer Press.

Burgess, R. (Ed.). (1985). *Field methods in the study of education*. Lewes: The Falmer Press.

Burgess, R. (Ed.). (1989). *The ethics of educational research*. Lewes: The Falmer Press.

Coffey, A. (1999). *The ethnographic self*. London: Routledge.

Delamont, S. (2002). *Fieldwork in educational settings* (2nd ed). London: The Falmer Press.

Delamont, S. (2009). The only honest thing. *Ethnography and Education, 4*(1), 51–64.

Figueroa, P. (2000). Researching education and racialization: Virtue or validity. In H. Simons & R. Usher (Eds.), *Situated ethics in educational research* (pp. 82–100). London: RoutledgeFalmer.

Glen, S. (2000). The dark side of purity or the virtues of double-mindedness. In H. Simons & R. Usher (Eds.), *Situated ethics in educational research* (pp. 12–21). London: RoutledgeFalmer.

Jeffrey, R., & Woods, P. (1998). *Testing teachers: The effect of school inspections on primary teachers*. London: The Falmer Press.

Law, J. (2004). *After method: Mess in social science research*. London: Routledge.

Liebow, E. (1967). *Tally's Corner*. Boston: Little, Brown and Company.

Payne, G. (1996). Imagining the community: Some reflections on the community study as a method. In E. Stina Lyon & J. Busfield (Eds.), *Methodological imaginations* (pp. 17–33). Basingstoke: Macmillan.

Pole, C. (2007). Researching children and fashion: An embodied ethnography. *Childhood, 14*(1), 67–84.

Robson, C. (2002). *Real world research*. Oxford: Blackwell.

Rojek, C. (2007). *Brit-myth: Who do the British think they are?* London: Reaktion.

Scott, J. (1992). The old boy network. In A. GIddens (Ed.), *Human societies: Introductory reader in sociology* (pp. 87–93). Cambridge: Polity.

Simons, H. (2000). Damned if you do, damned if you don't: Ethical and political dilemmas in evaluation. In H. Simons & R. Usher (Eds.), *Situated ethics in educational research* (pp. 39–55). London: RoutledgeFalmer.

Simons, H., & Usher, R. (2000). Introduction: Ethics in the practice of research. In H. Simons & R. Usher (Eds.), *Situated ethics in educational research* (pp. 1–11). London: RoutledgeFalmer.

Solomon, M. (1996). Impact of motivational climate on students' behaviours and perceptions in a physical education setting. *Journal of Educational Psychology, 88*(4), 731–738.

Thomas, W. I., & Znaniecki, F. (1958 [1919]). *The Polish peasant in Europe and America.* New York, NY: Dover.
Walford, G. (Ed.). (1991). *Doing educational research.* London: Routledge.
Wellington, J. (2000). *Educational research: Contemporary issues and political approaches.* London: Continuum.
Whyte, W. F. (1993 [1943]). *Street corner society: The social structure of an Italian Slum.* London: University of Chicago Press.
Wolcott, H. F. (2010). *Ethnography lessons: A primer.* Walnut Creek, CA: Left Coast Press.

CONSENT, CONFIDENTIALITY AND THE ETHICS OF PAR IN THE CONTEXT OF PRISON RESEARCH

James Ward and Di Bailey

ABSTRACT

Purpose – *To consider the unique ethical dilemmas, such as limitations in confidentiality, that research in prison settings is required to address.*

Methodology/approach – *The ethics of prison-based research are explored within the context of a three-year Participatory Action Research (PAR) project which aimed to involve staff and women in prison in the development of care pathways for self-harm.*

Findings – *The ethics of prison research are complex and require the balancing of individual rights with prison security requirements. In keeping with the PAR approach the experience for two of the women of being involved in the research and action for change is discussed through their own accounts.*

Originality/value of paper – *PAR has not been previously used in an English prison; this article provides an account of the ethical considerations of empowering methodologies with people who by their very status as prisoners are disempowered.*

Ethics in Social Research
Studies in Qualitative Methodology, Volume 12, 149–169
Copyright © 2012 by Emerald Group Publishing Limited
All rights of reproduction in any form reserved
ISSN: 1042-3192/doi:10.1108/S1042-3192(2012)0000012011

Research implications – *Although this is just one example within a women's prison the authors assert that PAR as a methodology within a prison environment is not only feasible but also desirable for engaging offenders in the development of services.*

Practical implications – *The engagement of this traditionally 'hard to reach' groups of people can ensure the development of meaningful and effective services based upon service user's experiential expertise (Beresford, 2000).*

Social implications – *PAR offers those in prison a stake in the development and design of services. This not only has personal benefits for the individual but also is likely to increase service uptake and relevance (Foster, J., Tyrell, K., Cropper, V., & Hunt, N. (2005). Welcome to the team – Service users in staff recruitment.* Drink and Drugs News, 21 *).*

Keywords: Self-injury; mental health; forensic; prison; action research; participation

A broad spectrum of research takes place in the prison environment, ranging from epidemiological studies of diseases to outcome studies of offending behaviour programmes. Researchers interested in prison populations reflect this heterogeneity and include forensic psychologists in training, health and welfare commissioners, academics and staff based in independent organisations such as the Howard League for Penal Reform.

It may be unsurprising that prison research is popular as it captures issues relating to a discreet, confined and generally static population. Offenders in custody are costly to care for and have complex needs relating to criminogenic risk factors, mental health and social inequalities. Any research that aims to maximise improvement and efficiency of custodial care must achieve this within a climate of risk management and public safety. This raises complex ethical dilemmas that are compounded by the coercive custodial environment and research interests that often do not benefit the prisoners directly (Crighton, 2006). The varying and different needs of prisoners involved in the research (often labelled as vulnerable, Moser et al., 2004) and the toll taken upon chief investigators trying to manage a variety of ethical considerations add to the complexity. As Towl (2004) highlights while such ethical considerations are not exclusive to prison-based research, the custodial environment does often magnify these issues producing significant ethical constraints that are distinctive to the custodial setting.

This chapter seeks to discuss the ethical issues of conducting a study using a participatory action research (PAR) design in a prison setting. The authors draw upon their experiences of using the PAR methodology in a project that aimed to reduce incidences of self-harm whilst improving outcomes for women who continue to self-injure in custody. The project was funded as a Knowledge Transfer Partnership between offender health commissioners, a university and a women's prison in England.

Particular attention will be given to the key ethical dilemmas of involving the women offenders in this research. Given the nature of the PAR process the chapter will discuss issues relating to informed consent and emphasising and promoting choice in participation amongst disempowered groups such as prisoners. An exploration of the limits of confidentiality and maintaining anonymity in an environment which ordinarily does not prioritise such considerations above security and safer custody will also be provided.

WHY PARTICIPATORY ACTION RESEARCH?

PAR is a methodological process through which the researcher seeks to address or improve identified areas of need by way of action and intervention involving those who are a part of the research process (Dick, 2002; Reason & Bradbury, 2001). This therefore distinguishes it from other epistemological methodologies which seek solely to generate knowledge through observation or effect causal change through experimental means. PAR is a cyclical process involving three distinct phases of planning, action and critical reflection (Lewin, 1946). Fig. 1 illustrates two cycles of the process as realised in the current project; each stage is numerically ordered 1–6. As Dick (*ibid*) describes the PAR cycle is flexible allowing the authors to respond to the needs of all the stakeholders throughout the project lifespan. This was considered vital in a custodial environment where the welfare needs of service users were tempered because of security constraints. Critically, PAR seeks to involve all stakeholders relevant to the identified area for change in all stages of the cycle (Wadsworth, 1998) with potential for democratic and emancipatory outcomes (Whyte, 1991). This methodology was deemed particularly relevant in improving outcomes for women whose self-harming behaviour is likely to be linked with stigma, mediated through social rejection or as an attempt to control threats to self-identity (Balsam, Beauchaine, Mickey, & Rothblum, 2005). For women in custody who experience additional stigma as a result of their offending behaviour and status as a prisoner (Allen, 1987) PAR offered a methodology that

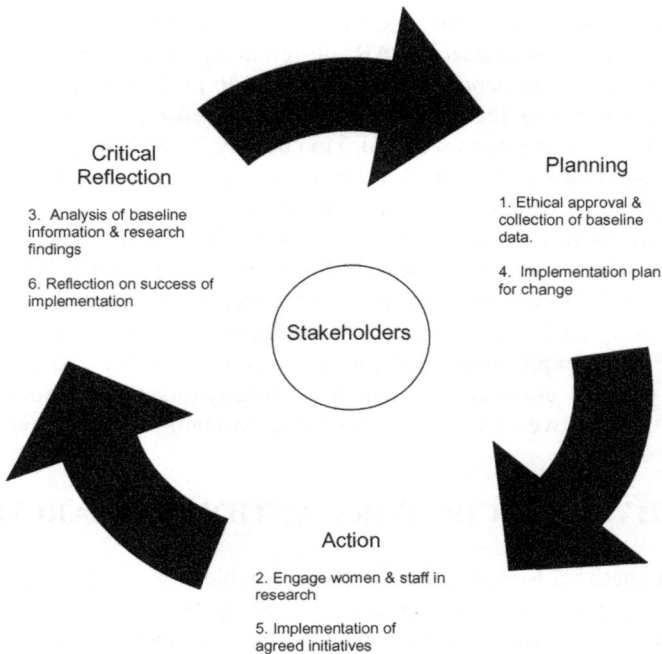

Critical Reflection

3. Analysis of baseline information & research findings

6. Reflection on success of implementation

Planning

1. Ethical approval & collection of baseline data.

4. Implementation plan for change

Stakeholders

Action

2. Engage women & staff in research

5. Implementation of agreed initiatives

Fig. 1. The PAR Process and How This was Realised Through the Project.

would foster engagement and take a needs-led approach to the research and subsequent courses of action. One of the objectives of the project was therefore to involve women in prison in the process of change rather than change being imposed upon them as is often the case in secure environments. The authors aimed to achieve, for the first time in a prison environment, what Faulkner (2004) described as the "epitome of emancipatory research" by "facilitat[ing] the active participation and hence potentially the empowerment of those who are traditionally most disempowered by the research process" (p. 27).

Such an ambition, however, is fraught with difficulty in an environment that is by its very nature disempowering and undemocratic. Prison restricts freedom and access to resources as a method of maintaining security and discipline as well as providing punishment for crimes. In the case of self-harm prison policy does not allow for a harm-reduction approach focussing solely upon prevention. To an extent therefore prison can even be seen to attempt to control what a prisoner can do to their own body. Adopting an approach such as PAR in a custodial setting with the aim of empowering prisoners can raise implications for security; create suspicion as to its motives and possibly raise expectations beyond what is achievable. The methodology may also raise wider questions about the rights of offenders to be involved in the development of services; this, however, is beyond the scope of this chapter. Instead we shall look at three themes that are particularly relevant to PAR and the ethical process. Firstly, we shall discuss preparation for PAR particularly paying attention to the involvement of people in prison, commonly labelled as vulnerable, around sensitive topics such as self-harm. Secondly, the action research process itself will be examined in the light of specific requirements imposed by secure conditions. Finally, the process of effecting change through PAR will be considered.

ETHICAL CLEARANCE AND PLANNING PAR

Obtaining ethical approval for prison-based research can be difficult and time consuming and levels of bureaucracy can prove to be insurmountable resulting in cancellation of studies before they have begun (see Gill, 2009). Given the multi-disciplinary nature of prison it was inevitable that research will involve multiple stakeholders. In all, our project required ethical approval from five organisations with differing agendas:

- The National Health Service Research Ethics Committee (NHS, REC)
- The Ministry of Justice
- The Primary Care Trust (PCT)
- The University
- The Prison

Given the levels of bureaucracy involved a pertinent question would be whether these measures are essential in order to protect research participants and would be Chief Investigator's (CI) and whether the emphasis upon the protection of participants results in missed opportunities due to aversion to risk.

In the case of the current study a lot of emphasis was placed upon procedures to follow should a participant become distressed or self-harm as a result of participation. This was considered to be particularly relevant given that interviews were likely to touch upon distressing events in the woman's life. The reality of the research, however, was that distress during the process was minimal and, to our knowledge there were no incidents of self-harm as a result of participation. Instead many women and staff reported that their experience of participation was beneficial for them personally and that they were optimistic about the impact it could have in facilitating change.

We asked one woman to write about her experiences of being involved throughout the three years of the project. She was keen to contextualise the experience and her use of self-harm with her life experiences. This is what she wrote.

My name is Janet, I am a prisoner. I have an Indeterminate Sentence for Public Protection.

I self-harm and have done since a very young age. I went through a bad time when I was growing up and to me it was bad, but compared to some people's lives it wasn't. I lived with my grandparents from being born I called my Granddad Dad and I couldn't do without them. I was 9 years old when they both suddenly got ill and then died within 6 weeks of each other. I was devastated and my life and world was destroyed within a couple of weeks. On the day of my Nan's funeral I went to live a new life with my Mum, step dad and 4 siblings who I hardly knew, they were strangers to me. I felt uneasy around my step dad and felt him leering over me. I was never comfortable in the company of the strangers that had become my new family. I was always fighting with my brothers and sister, there were also physical fights with my step father neither of us was hurt but it took its toll. One day when I was 11 years old I released the sharp, silver blade from a pencil sharpener and cut a ladder of perfectly, neat rungs down the inside of my left arm. The surprising thing was that it didn't even hurt and I didn't feel that I was doing anything wrong. I knew thought that I had to hide my secret escape-ladder. For the first time since my parents died I felt an immense relief from my tormented world of trauma, upset and grief. I felt alive again. I felt as though I could speak out loud, scream without anyone hearing me, because all that time, I was screaming inside and was about to explode.

A number of years down the line in prison, I met James who was working on research at the prison. He approached me to see if I wanted to take part in some work on self-harm and put a staff training package together.

I had more self control by then and had been diagnosed with Bipolar Disorder and receiving help for that. Still I went away to give myself some time to think about the potential consequences of getting involved in something that was so close to me and was actually a part of me. I wasn't sure if I was willing to let strangers delve into my past and to know so much about the where's and why's of my life. From discussing it, it turned out that it wasn't invasive at all, so I thought I'd give it a shot.

Taking part helped me in many ways including channel some pent up anger. We put together a small group of women who use or who had used self-harm to create a training package. People use it as a way of getting what they want to say across, but cant' express themselves in any other way. We created the training to particularly help staff, but also women in prison, to understand why some people self-harm and to explain what degrees someone is willing to go to for a release from the reality of the world they live in. I also worked with James to put together leaflets and posters with some of my art work and pieces of writing to show and describe what self-harm is all about, what it is and what it isn't.

I feel really proud of what I and others produced. It gave me a feeling of belonging and I didn't feel that I was the only one who had ever harmed myself because that's how self harm made me feel, like an outsider, alone, weak and unable to cope with life. I now feel as though I have got my point across and explained my part and why I do what I do without embarrassment. Taking part also gave me an insight into things I didn't quite understand about myself. I hope that it will help others to understand and maybe have a bit more empathy, not "sympathy" for those who self-harm in the future. I think we also showed that there are many reasons why people use self-harm and many types of ways and that people harm themselves. I am so pleased that I was approached, but mostly pleased that I was given this chance, because now my problems are shared and now halved.

Thank you for taking your time to read this little snippet of my life that's so similar to that of many, many other people.

I am Janet and I am a self harmer, but I am also still human.

Janet's decision to become involved was, for her, a weighing of the potential consequences of what could have proven to be an intrusive process. Her experience, however, reflects a growing body of literature that testifies to the positives of participation provided it is well thought out and ethically sound.

This suggests that ethics committees in their concern to protect research participant may not be up-to-date with emerging findings around the potential benefits of asking about issues such as abuse (Edwards, Dube, Felitti, & Anda, 2007; Read, 2007) or the potential therapeutic benefits for people of involvement in such studies (Rossiter & Verdun-Jones, 2011) if done with sensitivity. Committees may also fail to differentiate between distress and harm adequately, either not considering the possible positive aspects of becoming upset or attempting to shield service users from upset to such a degree as to make them feel patronised (Faulkner, 2004). Choice in participation will itself undoubtedly be empowering for those who are disempowered even if the research process itself does not produce change. For Janet the concern was less about exacerbating self-harm than the intrusion of privacy that taking part might entail. For those exposed to the daily stresses of a prison environment the experience or definition of harm may be different from others in different environments.

PAR's emphasis on 'participants' not being passive subjects in research but equal collaborators can prove vital in the preparation for research. Involving the women in decisions on how they want to be involved, on what terms they want to contribute and the management of risk to themselves offered, in reality, more protection[1] than any amount of preparation for the REC could. This empowerment and discussion about risk led to women choosing to be interviewed with partners and friends or around contact with mental health workers all of whom could offer support should they become distressed. This isn't to say that the REC has no value and its requirements invalid. Instead in the case of research involving sensitive topics such as self-harm it emphasises the importance of involving potential participants in an active way from the very outset, including in safety planning. It is worth noting that current guidelines allow for the active involvement of service users and/or potential research participants in planning process before ethical approval (Involve, 2009).

PAR also provided the means to maintain contact with participants through either chance or planned meetings around the prison. After the research process this was usually to work on service development but also allowed us to check on the participant's welfare and keep them informed of the progress of the project. In the case of the women who had participated this also gave them the opportunity to ask for resources such as puzzles and distraction activities that they found useful in managing self-harm and that we could provide. As such there was plenty of opportunity to continue to meet with the women involved after data collection which allowed us to monitor for any adverse consequences of participation.

When conducting research around sensitive topics the safety, both physically and emotionally, of the CI is also of concern. Whether the researcher will be 'lone working' or accompanied by a member of prison staff has implications for the research findings and security considerations. Research accompanied by prison staff may mean the CI can bypass statutory prison service training such as security awareness and personal protection and may be a safeguard for the CI (and in some cases the participants). However, having a member of prison staff present is likely to impact upon how the person responds or add an element of coercion that a CI independent of the prison service may not. Gaining unaccompanied access to the prison may be desirable to help potential participants feel more at ease during the research process and will provide different data than if prison staff are present. In these cases considerations around personal safety and understanding prison service policy in the event of certain disclosures needs to be attended to (see below). In a similar way to Weiskopf's (2005) description of the prison nurse's needs to balance care and security so too must the CI balance ethical considerations with security requirements.

In addition to physical safety the risk of vicarious (Dunkley & Whelan, 2006) or secondary (Motta, 2008) trauma is a real ethical concern in prison research. Vicarious trauma is often associated with therapists or mental health workers who are exposed to narratives of traumatic events (Sabin-Farrell & Tuprin, 2003) and particularly associated with empathic engagement (Pearlman & MacIan, 1995). This can result in those listening to accounts of traumatic events experiencing similar feelings of distress, fear and other symptoms of post traumatic stress as those recounting the experience. Figley (1995a) described such effects upon the listener as the 'cost of caring' (p. 1). Such an impact may not be limited to those delivering therapies and are equally a consideration for researchers, particularly if the methodology involves life history accounts or is likely to touch upon topics such as trauma, abuse, self-injury and suicide. Even when the focus of research is not upon such emotive areas working with people with complex psycho-social needs, whilst also being able to identify when these needs are appropriate or inappropriate to address, requires detailed planning. As such the appropriate and timely use of supervision, occupational health resources and the CI's ability to monitor and protect their own wellbeing also need to be considered in the planning stages of the research. This all assumes, however, that the research process is a negative experience and plans for worst case scenarios. If the experience is positive for the participants, however, it can be equally positive for the CI and bring the benefits that any collaborative and productive working relationship can produce. This was our experience and there were no adverse consequences for the CI but that is not to say that vicarious trauma does not need consideration.

THE ACTION STAGE – PRODUCING CHANGE

The need for balance in the preparation for PAR in prisons has been highlighted a number of times already. This is equally, if not more, true in the action stages in which participants will become actively involved in the process of effecting change. Specifically, a balance needs to be struck between three competing, although not mutually exclusive, needs. These are

1. The needs of those who become involved in the PAR process. In our project this was both staff and women in prison. It was the responsibility of the project team to properly represent the opinions and needs of those who gave their time to be involved.
2. The needs of the prison to maintain security, fulfil its duty of care to prisoners and staff and adhere to national policy and legislation.
3. The needs of the research. This in itself is a combination of ensuring rigour and objectivity in its methods, being appealing in order to recruit and keep participants engaged and ensure that through adhering to regulations it can continue to have a presence in the prison.

We shall consider these three needs in relation to two crucial aspects of the action stage of PAR, the recruitment of participants and the effecting change in working practices.

Recruitment to Research

Prisons provide a condensation of needs and issues that are present in the wider community. Those who are imprisoned are more likely to experience mental health difficulties, misuse or be dependent upon substances, have greater needs relating to literacy and numeracy, have experienced traumatic events such as violence or sexual violence in their past and are more likely to have been unemployed and/or homeless prior to imprisonment (see Stewart (2008) for a thorough needs analysis of recently sentenced offenders). These complex and multi-faceted needs are often described as vulnerabilities for the potential research participant. Whilst the label of 'vulnerable' has been criticised for being further stigmatising and unhelpful (Corston, 2007) such factors require consideration in the research process even when they are not the focus of enquiry.

Considering the needs of the individual is likely to have the largest impact upon the recruitment to research. The inclusion criteria of our study was for women to have a recorded incident of self-harm whilst in prison as identified through their prison records (all staff who worked directly with prisoners were eligible to participate). This was limited, however, by a number of factors. Whilst the issue of capacity and the person's ability to provide informed consent was relevant, the exclusion of potential participants due to the prison's operational requirements impacted more upon the recruitment to the project. Although the original intention of our study was to approach all the women in the prison who met our criteria compromises had to be made. Agreements were reached with the prison's security department regarding not including women who were of media interest due to concerns about data security and especially recorded interviews. In other cases clinical teams requested that women be 'exempt' from the study because of a clinical judgment that their involvement would exacerbate their self-harm which was already potentially life threatening. The reality therefore was that some women who were eligible to participate, and would have undoubtedly brought a unique and valuable aspect to the research, were not even approached. This creates limits on the research itself and highlights the necessity to sometimes remove power from those in prison to make choices about whether to be involved in initiatives or not. Again however this assumes that the process will be negative and that women won't be able to manage any distress after the event. Whilst acknowledging that this may be the case for some women our experience suggests otherwise for the vast majority who chose to become involved. It is unfortunate that perhaps the women whose self-harm was at its worst and who may have benefitted from involvement the most were not given the opportunity to take part. To approach these women, however, would have required the CI to dismiss the concerns of the responsible clinicians potentially jeopardising the needs of the prison and the project. Ideally, discussions around the nature of the risk posed by involvement could have been held as a part of a care management process involving the women and staff to find an agreeable compromise.

Informed Consent in a Coercive Environment

Whilst for some in a prison setting the ability to choose to become involved is removed for others the issue of coercion to participate is of equal concern.

Coercion is institutionalised within prisons and in many ways contributes to the maintenance of discipline and order within the establishments. This can be seen in the use of adjudications and sanctions against sentenced prisoners refusing to work and the progression of prisoners being dependent upon them conforming to their sentence plan[2]. Whilst Day, Tucker, and Howells (2004) suggest that coercion is not inherently unethical, citing having to pay taxes as an example, we would argue that in relation to research coercion is the antithesis of truly informed consent.

Moser et al. (2004) highlights that with such a marginalised population as those in prison coercion can be very broadly defined to the extent of

"The fact that participation may enable the inmate to leave his or her cell more frequently and interact with people from outside the facility is a form of potential coercion" (p. 2).

Whilst opportunities such as talking to someone new are unavoidably inherent aspects of prison research, care has to be taken that coercion is not implied or unintentionally a feature of the research. The longer-term nature of PAR certainly offers more opportunities for interaction and possibly time out of cells. If this is the case, however, PAR approaches could be argued to provide meaningful activities that should be integral to the prison regime anyway. People in prison may become unaccustomed to being able to refuse to take part in activities due to staff–prisoner relationships often being an "instrument of power" (Liebling, 2001). Prisoners may also be wary of the consequences of refusing to participate (e.g. fearing sanctions for declining) or may want to appear cooperative in the expectation of better treatment or increased privileges (Moser et al., 2004).

Again PAR and the nature of the working relationships between all those involved in the research can go some way to addressing issues of coercion. The traditional roles of researcher and participant have implications for the power relationship casting the *Researcher* as an active agent whilst the *Participant* as passive and controlled. This has lead to a number of criticisms about participant–researcher relationships, most notably by feminist researchers who not only highlight issue of control but also of mastery or expertise being the sole preserve of the researcher (Stanley & Wise, 1983). Such power relationships can be magnified through the prison lens where the researcher may be a member of staff whilst a prisoner's position is disempowered by her very position. As such refusing to become involved or choosing to be no longer involved in research may be a more difficult decision for those in prison. In our study through taking time to explain the options and choices around engagement this did not appear to be a problem.

As Janet testifies she took the time to consider her decision and this was encouraged of all women who we approached to take part.

The issue of payment is also an ethical dilemma that needs to be addressed. There are a number of guidelines, especially for those involved in the service user movements, suggesting payment should be offered to people who give their time to participate in research (Faulkner, 2004; Involve/ DH, 2006). This practice, however, is not supported by the Prison Service (Prison Service Instruction 41/2010) due to concern about the use of the money for illicit purposes (Sneddon, 2005). The use of payment may also introduce a further element of coercion. Most people in prison have the opportunity to earn wages through work; however, these are small sums of money that can be used for buying additional supplies such as toiletries and confectionary. During discussions about our research there was a division of opinion amongst the team about this issue. Whilst some thought there was an ethical obligation to compensate those who gave their time, others had concerns that payment would unfairly disadvantage those who were not eligible to participate. In our experience the issue of payment never arose, even for women who have contributed for the three full years through the service development and evaluation. The exceptionally high rates of return for questionnaires (89%) suggest that an opportunity to be involved and have a stake in change was sufficient.

It is apparent that when used properly PAR provides a strong framework for the development of collaborative working relationships with participants. This is not only based upon the voluntary nature of the relationship but also a basis that acknowledges the experiential expertise that participants can bring to the research (Beresford, 2000). This approach of taking time to discuss the options for involvement with potential participants differs from a lot of research conducted in prisons where questionnaires are put under prisoner's cell doors during times they are confined to their room with the expectation they will be completed and returned with minimal contact from the CI.

The nature of the working relationship in a prison environment can never be truly equal however. This is perhaps best exemplified by the CI's inability to offer total confidentiality to participants. Prison policy requires all incidents or increased risk of self-harm be reported and action taken to place the person under the care of the Assessment Care in Custody and Teamwork (ACCT) process. This is clearly in conflict with the ethical protection of total confidentiality and anonymity usually offered to the participant during research. It also potentially impacts upon the development of relationships within the working collaboration requiring clear 'rules' to be set out as to what can be held in confidence and what will have to be passed on. Again balance is required to be struck between participant confidentiality whilst adhering to the prison service's duty of care and security procedures to allow us continued access to the jail.

Similarly, the CI may be required to structure the expectations of what is achievable in order not to instil false hope. This was perhaps most demonstrable in our project by the CI not taking forward suggestions for additional resources (one example being a Rubik's Cube) to the prison management based upon his knowledge that they had been previously refused on security grounds. Such examples demonstrate an obvious power difference with the CI influencing what suggestions were and were not progressed albeit for pragmatic reasons. We tried to manage this by being honest about what was achievable when suggestions were made but also pushing boundaries to implement initiatives that had not previously been tried and challenging senior managers about what was achievable when.

Effecting Change in Prisons

PAR not necessarily just about collaborative work with those who are most marginalised (e.g. prisoners) but is equally applicable to all involved in the process. Prison staff too can also be marginalised and deserve the same protections from power relationships through research. Liebling (2001) describes the 'intellectual hegemony' (p. 476) of prison research focussing upon prisoners to the detriment of studying the way power is used by those managing the prison system. Her argument that sympathy should not always be reserved for the subordinate prisoners but that managers and governors will also be in some way subordinate and also vulnerable to coercion make them equally deserving of a sympathetic approach. It is perhaps Liebling's affinity with value neutrality, or the suspension of personal beliefs about the way things should be, that leads her to conclude that 'Whose side are we on? The side of prudent, perhaps reserved engagement.' (ibid, p. 483). Liebling certainly isn't the only researcher to compromise (see Martel, 2004) and it can be argued that sensitivity and respect for prison governance is essential in order to inform productive working relationships. Such reserved engagement is perhaps unlikely to produce substantial or comprehensive change that may be required. Such a conservative approach is, at best, more likely to result in evolution of existing processes rather than true empowerment of those involved or the introduction of new methods of work (akin to consultative service user engagement on Hickey and Kipping's (1998) Participation Continuum as opposed to User-Controlled research). The CI is then left with the ethical dilemma of how to negotiate, implement and evaluate change in an institution which does not embrace change readily without coercion. This requires translating the work of the research process with prisoners in identifying problems and developing solutions into business cases. The CI effectively becomes a go between representing the prisoners to the prison senior management and vice versa. Ideally, prisoner councils similar to those set up by the organisation User Voice could be arranged to allow prisoners to directly represent themselves and make suggestions for change. This would, however, necessitate the prison's senior management to allow themselves to be openly led, to some degree, by the ideas of prisoners. It was deemed in our case that a more neutral representative (the CI) would be more effective.

Over the three-year course of our research there were significant changes which impacted upon implementation of change in the jail. These included internal restructuring of the prison's senior management team whilst externally the recession resulted in tight budgetary constraints which contributed to prison staff job losses. Given all this, understandably, driving change through PAR was not a priority for the prison. Again this required the project team to strike a balance. On the one hand we had a responsibility to represent the women and staff who had given their time to the project and attempt to improve care based upon their experiences. A failure to assert the work done would be to let down participants and lose the opportunity to effect change. To be unrealistic or too demanding of senior management, however, would be to lose their respect and build their resistance to change. Liebling (*ibid*) observes that it is of course possible to be sympathetic to more than one side and this is reflected in our approach that is probably best described as 'picking our battles'[3]. We were pragmatic and used 'reserved engagement', for example conceding ideas about involving more multi-disciplinary staff in ACCT case management at a time when there were concerns about job roles and potential losses. At other times we felt a duty to represent participants and this meant more assertively (or doggedly) pursuing initiatives with the support of external stakeholders such as the Offender Health Commissioners. These 'no-compromise' issues included prisoners co-delivering staff training and proposals to allow, in some cases, women to dress their own self-inflicted wounds. The battles we picked to pursue were those that were held to be the most important by staff and the women in the prison and that had been previously untested in the prison environment. In this respect we feel we have gone some way to empowering women and staff in the prison and that this has produced positive change, even in the light of compromise.

It is worth ending with the reflections of another woman 'Claire' who was actively involved in the development and delivery of a staff training package named At Arm's Length. This was successfully delivered to a range of multidisciplinary staff around the prison as one of the 'no-compromise' issues after it was identified as a need by both staff and women in prison.

> I didn't know anything about the 'At Arm's Length' project until I found out that my name had been put forward as someone who had the ability to deliver PowerPoint presentations. Once I was introduced James I had a look over the material and decided that it was something I would like to be involved with. I did have reservations about my ability to deliver presentations to staff, not because I didn't think I was capable, I just doubted myself being able to put aside the irrational assumptions I was thinking in regards to staff opinion of me. But I decided to stick it out regardless. I felt that, as a prisoner, I had somewhat of a responsibility towards the girls who had worked with James to make the project as they had put so much work in to it and in a way I felt like I was representing them. There were times when, mostly due to nerves, I didn't want to turn up but I did and I am glad not that I was as determined as I have gained so much confidence from it. My self-esteem and confidence have grown since getting involved with the 'At Arm's Length' and I have greater understanding of self-harm. The most important thing to me though is that I feel like the presentations are making a difference.
>
> The response from staff has been a lot different than what I expected it to be. When we first started to roll out the presentations I thought that most staff would be sitting there thinking it was wrong for a prisoner to be telling them about anything, let alone self-harm which they deal with first hand on a daily basis. I assumed they would be looking at me with the opinion I had no right to tell them nothing as I was a prisoner. How wrong I was! The staff listen to what I have to say and it appears they appreciate the insight in to self-harm they get being as they get it from a prisoner's point of view. This is also reflected in the questions I get asked after almost each presentation and the comments that are written on the feedback forms. In my opinion I feel that the staff are different towards me as it seems they now feel they can

approach me and me things without them worrying whether or not they are going to offend me.

I think that the awareness sessions have made a big difference and have given the staff a better understanding of self-harm in general. I believe the officers now feel that what they are doing is right which makes making them more confident in dealing with and helping self-harmers. Most importantly I believe it has gone a long way in addressing the prisoner–officer divide and as a prisoner it has been overwhelming the support and the positivity shown towards me. The staff's eagerness to engage and learn more, not just about self-harm but other subjects such as drugs, domestic violence etc. The staff are also utilising the packs[4] and I have seen them using them with confidence. The activity boxes,[5] in my opinion, in the past have been viewed as nothing more than a waste of time, whereas the packs are being used as a legitimate tool that can help not only the women help themselves, but also help the staff help the women. I don't think that there is a prison in this country that wouldn't benefit from the same kind of awareness programmes.

CONCLUSIONS

The PAR process offers a number of opportunities to address the issues that a difficult working environment, such as a prison, raise for conducting ethically rigorous research. The approach offers a framework for engaging with disenfranchised and socially excluded populations by offering them a stake in effecting change that will hopefully prove to be positive. PAR also offers a method for developing and implementing effective systems of checks, balances and protections for those who choose to become involved.

Much of the research that is conducted in prisons can be considered to be applied, however due to lack of generalisability, small sample sizes or resource constraints the application of findings is often found to be lacking (Crighton, 2006; Hoshmand & O'Byrne, 1996). PAR, however, does not attempt to generalise its findings but instead solve specific, local problems through engagement with those with experiential expertise. To date this has been an underutilised approach in prison-based research and whilst the initiatives that have emerged from the current study may not be generaliseable to other prisons, however we suggest that the methodology is.

Whilst the focus of this chapter has been upon the use of a PAR methodology many of the issues raised will be equally applicable to other forms of prison research. Our experience leads us to offer some general do's and don'ts of conducting ethically sensitive research in prison.

Do:

1. Be aware of the limitations of confidentiality and be clear and transparent about these with potential participants.
2. Be prepared for the fact that participants may become distressed, but don't let this stop you asking relevant questions. Knowing how to deescalate situations, review coping strategies and signpost to support appropriately is essential when working with people with complex psycho-social needs. However, don't forget that the research process could also be beneficial for the individual if done with care.
3. Make necessary arrangements to maximise the person's ability to give properly informed consent. This involves both fully understanding the risks of participation as well as being able to choose which aspects of the research they can contribute to. Be prepared to make use of alternative methods of communication such as pictograms and translation services and be prepared to provide additional support where required.
4. Make use of supervision and occupational health resources and take responsibility for your own mental wellbeing.
5. Be flexible and tenacious. The prison environment can often be unpredictable resulting in cancelled appointments, reduced regimes and research coming bottom of the list of priorities. Don't give up!

Don't:

1. Make promises that can't be kept. Ultimately the position of 'researcher' in the prison environment is also a disempowered one. Promising to effect changes that can't be realised is likely to increase cynicism towards research and reduce participation in the future.
2. Exceed the remit of conducting ethical and sympathetic research. De-briefs and empathic listening are important; however, it is not the CIs job to counsel those who give their time to research. Ensure participants are signposted to appropriate sources of support.

NOTES

1. Arguably those who chose to engage with our research didn't want or need protecting but required all the information and choices available to them.

2. A Sentence Plan is a set of targets the prisoner is expected to complete in order to reduce their risk of re-offending. Often these will include educational, therapeutic and offending behaviour interventions. For prisoners on life sentence and indeterminate sentences their progression through the prison system, and their eventual release is dependent upon them completing their sentence plan. That therapeutic and psychological-based interventions are often included is much discussed and whether this constitutes and anti-therapeutic level of coercion is debated (see Day et al., 2004).

3. To describe the discussions we had about certain initiatives as battles is to overstate the confrontation that we encountered and the phrase is used as an illustrative metaphor. The reality in relation to initiatives such as the staff training was more a case of reservation and concern, given that no precedent had existed in the prison. The suggestion of providing women with wound dressings was met with an overwhelming aversion to risk and an understandable concern to protect the women and the prison staff but highlighted the idiosyncrasies of the prison environment.

4. The 'packs' are care planning action packs designed with the aim of empowering women to develop their own care plans and consider what actions they can take, and what they can ask of others, to help maintain mental wellbeing.

5. Activity boxes contain activities for distraction such as puzzles and colouring books.

ACKNOWLEDGEMENTS

We would also acknowledge the work and assistance of the women and staff who gave their time and experience during the course of this research project. Their enthusiasm to contribute to change was very much appreciated.

REFERENCES

Allen, J. (1987). *Justice unbalanced: Gender, psychiatry and judicial decisions.* Milton Keynes, UK: OU Press.

Balsam, K. F., Beauchaine, T. P., Mickey, R. M., & Rothblum, E. D. (2005). Mental health of lesbian, gay, bisexual and heterosexual siblings: The effects of gender, sexual orientation, and family. *Journal of Abnormal Psychology, 114*(3), 471–476.

Beresford, P. (2000). Service users' knowledge and social work theory: Conflict or collaboration? *British Journal of Social Work, 30,* 489–503.

Corston, J. (2007). *The Corston report.* London: Ministry of Justice, HMSO.

Crighton, D. A. (2006). Methodological issues in psychological research in prisons. In G. J. Towl (Ed.), *Psychological research in prisons.* Oxford: Blackwell Publishing.

Day, A., Tucker, K., & Howells, K. (2004). Coerced offender rehabilitation – A defensible practice? *Psychology Crime & Law*, *10*(3, SI), 259–269.

Dick, B. (2002). *Action research: Action and research* [on line]. Retrieved from http://www.scu.edu.au/schools/gcm/ar/arp/aandr.html. Accessed on 18 July 2011.

Dunkley, J., & Whelan, T. A. (2006). Vicarious traumatisation: Current status and future directions. *British Journal of Guidance and Counselling*, *34*(1), 107–116.

Edwards, V. J., Dube, S. R., Felitti, V. J., & Anda, R. F. (2007). Its OK to ask about past abuse. *American Psychologist*, *62*(4), 327–328.

Faulkner, A. (2004). *The ethics of survivor research guidelines for the ethical conduct of research carried out by mental health service users and survivors*. Bristol: Policy Press.

Figley, C. R. (1995a). Compassion fatigue as secondary traumatic stress disorder: An overview. In C. R. Figley (Ed.), *Compassion fatigue: Coping with secondary traumatic stress disorder in those who treat the traumatized* (pp. 1–20). New York, NY: Brunner/Mazel.

Gill, J. (2009). Prison research project is throttled by red tape. *Times Higher Education*. Retrieved from http://www.timeshighereducation.co.uk/story.asp?sectioncode=26&storycode=405434. Accessed on 25 October 2010.

Hickey, G., & Kipping, C. (1998). Exploring the concept of user involvement in mental health through a participation continuum. *Journal of Clinical Nursing*, *7*(1), 83–88.

Hoshmand, L. T., & O'Byrne, K. (1996). Reconsidering action research as a guiding metaphor for professional psychology. *Journal of Community Psychology*, *24*(3), 185–200.

Involve/DH. (2006). *A guide to reimbursing and paying members of the public who are actively involved in research: For researchers and research commissioners (who may also be people who use services)*. Eastleigh: INVOLVE Support Unit. Retrieved from http://www.invo.org.uk/pdfs/payment_guidefinal240806.pdf

Involve. (2009). *Patient and public involvement in research and research ethics committee review*. Retrieved from http://www.invo.org.uk/pdfs/INVOLVE_NRESfinalStatement310309.pdf. Accessed on 20 July 2011.

Lewin, K. (1946). Action research and minority problems. *Journal of Social Issues*, *2*(4), 34–46.

Liebling, A. (2001). Whose side are we on? Theory, practice and allegiances in prisons research. *British Journal of Criminology*, *41*(3), 472–484.

Martel, J. (2004). Policing criminological knowledge: The Hazards of qualitative research on women in prison. *Theoretical Criminology*, *8*(2), 157–189.

Moser, D. J., Arndt, S., Kanz, J. E., Benjamin, M. L., Bayless, J. D., Reese, R. L., … Flaum, M. A. (2004). Coercion and informed consent in research involving prisoners. *Comprehensive Psychiatry*, *45*(1), 1–9.

Motta, R. W. (2008). Secondary trauma. *International Journal of Emergency Mental Health*, *10*(4), 291–298.

Pearlman, L. A., & MacIan, P. S. (1995). Vicarious traumatization: An empirical study of the effects of trauma work on trauma therapists. *Professional Psychology: Research and Practice*, *26*(6), 558–565.

Prison Service Instruction. (41/2010). *Research applications*. Retrieved from http://psi.hmprisonservice.gov.uk/psi_2010_41_research_applications.doc. Accessed on 8 April 2011.

Read, J. (2007). To ask or not to ask about abuse. New Zealand research. *American Psychologist*, *62*(4), 327–328.

Reason, P., & Bradbury, H. (Eds.). (2001). *Handbook of action research: Participative inquiry and practice*. Thousand Oaks, CA: Sage.

Rossiter, K., & Verdun-Jones, S. (2011). Evidence-based ethical decision-making in research: Considerations from trauma-focussed research with women receiving forensic mental health services. Paper presented at the 8th International Association of Forensic Mental Health, Barcelona.

Sabin-Farrell, R., & Tuprin, G. (2003). Vicarious traumatizaion: Implications for the mental health workers? *Clinical Psychology Review, 23*, 449–480.

Sneddon, T. (2005). Paying drug users to take part in research: Justice, human rights and business perspectives on the use of incentive payments. *Addiction Research and Theory, 13*(2), 101–109.

Stanley, L., & Wise, S. (1983). *Breaking out: Feminist consciousness and feminist research.* London: RKP.

Stewart, D. (2008). *The problems and needs of newly sentenced prisoners: Results from a national survey.* Ministry of Justice Research, 16/08.

Towl, G. J. (2004). Applied psychological services in HM Prison Service and the National Probation Service. In A. P. C. Needs & G. J. Towl (Eds.), *Applying Psychology to Forensic Practice.* Oxford: Blackwell Publishing.

Wadsworth, Y. (1998). *What is participatory action research?* Action Research International, Paper 2. Retrieved from http://www.scu.edu.au/schools/gcm/ar/ari/p-ywadsworth98.html

Weiskopf, C. S. (2005). Nurses' experience of caring for inmate patients. *Journal of Advanced Nursing, 49*(4), 336–343.

Whyte, W. F. (Ed.). (1991). *Participatory action research* (Sage Focus Editions, Vol. 123). Thousand Oaks, CA: Sage Publications.

PART III
INTENSIFICATIONS

LISTENING TO VOICES: AN ETHICS OF ENTANGLEMENT

Lisa Blackman

ABSTRACT

Purpose – *To explore an ethics of entanglement in the context of mental health and psychosocial research.*

Design/methodology/approach – *To bring together debates within body and affect studies, and specifically the concepts of mediated perception and the performativity of experimentation. My specific focus will be on voice hearing and research that I have conducted with voice hearers, both within and to the margins of the Hearing Voices Network (see Blackman, 2001, 2007).*

Findings – *The antecedents for a performative approach to experimentation and an ethics of entanglement can be found within a nineteenth-century subliminal archive (Blackman, 2012).*

Originality/value – *These conceptual links allow the researcher to consider the technologies that might allow them to 'listen to voices' and introduce the non-human into our conceptions of listening and interpreting. This directs our attention to those agencies and actors who create the possibility of listening and learning beyond the boundaries of a humanist research subject.*

Keywords: Ethics of entanglement; Hearing Voices Network; affect; embodiment; automatism

Ethics in Social Research
Studies in Qualitative Methodology, Volume 12, 173–188
Copyright © 2012 by Emerald Group Publishing Limited
ISSN: 1042-3192/doi:10.1108/S1042-3192(2012)0000012012

INTRODUCTION

My research over the last two decades has been developing an approach to embodiment and subjectivity at the intersection of the humanities and sciences. More specifically, the trajectory of the dialogue and conversation I have staged has its origins in critical psychology and more lately with debates on affect within cultural theory and body studies (see Blackman & Venn, 2010). The focus of this chapter will be on some of the ethical issues presented by doing such research, particularly as it has been enacted within the area of mental health research. My specific focus will be on voice hearing and research that I have conducted with voice hearers, both within and to the margins of the Hearing Voices Network (HVN) (see Blackman, 2001, 2007). This research presents particular ethical issues, specifically for conducting research with those who within some conceptions of ethics might be considered vulnerable research subjects. The question of vulnerability will be addressed by reposing some of the questions we might ask about the relational dynamics produced between the researcher and the researched. The work that has been important in my own research development is contemporary, but equally connects to epistemological and ontological issues surrounding experimentation which connect the present to the past. The past that I am interested in is what I have termed a 'subliminal archive', characteristic of research carried out in William James' Harvard Psychological Laboratory under the tutelage of Hugo Munsterberg in the late 1890s (see Blackman, 2012).

ENCOUNTERING PSYCHIATRY

My academic and intellectual interests in mental health research were informed by my own experiences of growing up with a Mother who hears voices. I was aware at a very young age of the power of psychiatry, having experienced my Mother being sectioned and hospitalised cyclically, and witnessing her reliance on a repeat prescription of Largactyl that she has taken since being prescribed at the age of 18. In times of crisis the psychotropic drugs did nothing to lessen the distressing voices that she heard. I have written elsewhere about the presumptions that are central to biological psychiatry and the kind of 'hope technology' enacted by the faith in drugs that are central to its practices (see Blackman, 2007). One of the distinct shifts central to the practices of the HVN is to *focus* on the voices, rather than dismiss them as simply meaningless signs of disease and illness (see

Blackman, 2001, 2007). One of the main shifts in the status of voice hearing to emerge from this re-orientation away from a disease-model, with its corresponding language of deficit and pathology, is that voices have something to say, that they should be listened to (see Romme, Escher, Dillon, Corstens, & Morris, 2009). They might be thought of less as irrational perceptions and more as forms of embodied memory or modalities of communication that challenge both our understandings of madness and how we might approach memory and perception (see Blackman, 2001, 2007 for a development of this). Once we start to listen to voices our conceptions of madness and the limits of understanding perception through a singularly, bounded and distinctly human psychological subject might also be subject to challenge (Blackman, 2012; Cho, 2008). This raises questions about how exactly as family members, professionals and researchers we might 'listen' to voices, and what ethical, ontological and epistemological issues this raises.

There are many experiences of 'irrational perception' that are the subject of psychiatric, neuroscientific and humanities speculation, investigation and explanation. One that has similarities with voice hearing is that of phantom limb perception, where a person experiences something that is phenomenologically 'real' for them and yet cannot be seen in the conventional methodological sense. Both phantom limb and voice hearing can be visualised via brain imaging scans and even localised within specific areas of the brain. However, this neuro-reductionism cannot capture or contain experiences which also extend beyond the limits and boundaries of the fixed and static 'Cartesian body'. Vivian Sobchack (2010) has recently proffered a method of 'phenomenological autobiography' to attend to the changed experiences of psychic and bodily morphology that accompanied her own phantom limb sensations. She explores the body's 'doublesidedness' in relation to her experience of changed and changing psychic and bodily morphology following the amputation of her leg and subsequent incorporation of a prosthetic limb.

Many philosophers, including Drew Leder (1990), have written about the paradoxes of embodiment, where the body can be both absent and present and subject and object. Bodies are processes defined by openness to the world, but phenomenologically this capacity to affect and be affected is lived in complex and often contradictory ways. Leder's (1990) concept of dys-appearance captures the way the body can both recede and exist in the background of experience – what he terms the body's absent-presence – as well as coming to the foreground in experiences such as pain. He terms this the dys-appearance of the body, where the body might be experienced as having a 'thing-like' quality and even be experienced as separate from mind/consciousness. Sobchack draws on this work to explore the dynamic, kinaesthetic processes which characterise her attending to such sensations, and the limits of static concepts of body-image to capture the lived experience of what we might call, following Featherstone (2010), the 'body-without-an-image'. Sobchack's concept of 'morphological imagination' attends to the more affective processes which characterise the body's incorporations and extensions and which thoroughly entangle the psychic, bodily, and symbolic in our being and becoming.

This work is useful to characterise the phenomenology of voice hearing that this chapter is attending to. However, it becomes difficult to understand the more inter-corporeal and relational dimensions of voice hearing that exceed the voice hearer's reflexive autobiography. As an example, many voice hearers I have met whilst doing my research hear voices of people they do not know and experience as coming from somewhere and someone else. They might feel as if their thoughts are being directed from elsewhere and indeed experiences of possession and automatism are often central to how the voices are heard. The voices confound distinctions between inside and outside, self and other, material and immaterial and even the dead or alive. One technique that is being used within the HVN that recognises the limits of conventional interviewing to understand this is 'voice-dialoguing'. This technique is interesting because it presumes that the 'researcher', professional or indeed a trusted person willing to hear voices is an active participant or actant within the voice hearing process. Voice-dialoguing is an intervention that creates the conditions for the voices to be heard and distributed beyond the voice hearer. The voice hearer might vocalize the voices so that the 'third person' can speak and respond to the voices and develop their own relationship, experiencing some of what the voice hearer feels, thinks and hears in relation to the voices (also see Blackman, 2010). The ethical motivations for listening presume that hearing voices is an active process that implicates the researcher in dynamic processes of change and transformation. What I want to do is say a little about how I have developed this understanding in my work, and particularly in more recent work published in my book, *Immaterial Bodies: Affect, Embodiment, Mediation* (2012).

LISTENING AND INTERVIEWING

In 1997 I was commissioned by the Inner London Probation Service and two housing associations to make a documentary that could be used for education and training. My role was to direct and produce the documentary, as well as interview the service users who were to take part in the process. We called the documentary '*Inside Looking Out: Personal Perspectives*', which as the title suggests was based on telling the stories of those appearing in the documentary, stories that might usually remain untold or merely used as the basis for diagnosis and intervention. The aim of the documentary was to challenge housing officer's potential prejudices and fears, when working with clients who had been diagnosed with mental health difficulties. We wanted to challenge the bio-genetic model and produce accounts which did not reduce mental health difficulties to a language of bio-genetic disease. I am not a trained film-maker, and although teaching theory to practitioners at undergraduate and Masters Level in Media and Communications theory, I had not considered how useful the editing process might be to thinking about what often gets left out of our research practice. As any film-maker will know, the process of filming produces an archive of data, some of which will end up on the cutting room floor. This archive might extend to hours and hours of tape, analogous to the kinds of transcription data produced from qualitative interviewing techniques, for example. Part of the process of transforming the data into a film is to produce a 'paper edit'. This might be based on story-boarding, where the director will have a clear sense of the story they want to tell and will shape this from an immersion in the data. As with the concept of telling a story, attention will be paid to the kinds of dramatic conventions and techniques that might be used to amplify the material and create the possibility of emotional commitment to the story by the viewer and spectator.

The focus of the editing process is very much on how the not-said can be animated; this is based on the idea that the dialogue or talk always reveals or discloses other forms of communication which carry the story in more affective registers. The attention to affect, or what scholars in television studies refer to increasingly as 'televisual affect', repositions viewers as not simply engaging with television through the structures of language, discourse and signification (see Gorton, 2009; Kavka, 2008). Rather televisual subjects are repositioned as embodied subjects engaging in forms of knowing and interpreting that cannot be reduced to the cognitive or the rational (see Wood & Skeggs, 2011). This raises ethical considerations for the kinds of techniques of listening and interpretation that are classically constituted within qualitative interviewing situations and for the dynamics between the researched and the researcher that might usually be silenced within the writing-up of research. One experience that has stayed with me during and after the documentary process indicative of what I am pointing towards was how much I was affected by what passed between me and the documentary subjects. This was not articulated through the conventions of language or the editing process. This might be equated to the off-screen dynamics that were enacted but were difficult to see or articulate in a conventional methodological sense. It is, however, this register of experience that has become fore-grounded within some forms of psychosocial interviewing and interpretation (see Walkerdine & Jimenez, 2012). The interviewing techniques I am interested in reposition the interview as being more akin to an analytic encounter between therapist and analysand, and draw attention to those processes, cognitive and non-cognitive, which carry meaning in ways that are far more difficult to decipher. Although I am aware of the problems of reducing the interview as an event to an analytic encounter,[1] this research raises some interesting ethical questions for how we might 'listen to voices'.

In the interviews conducted and filmed for the documentary I do not appear on the screen. This is one convention of interviewing where the person guiding the questions whom the subject is responding to is not visible in the process. They are seen as an adjunct to what emerges and unfolds and the dynamic created is one where the interviewer is required to frame this encounter through certain ethical requirements – this might include analytic distance, objectivity, empathy and so forth. Within psychosocial interviewing, the interviewer is encouraged to examine their own more embodied responses to the interview, including feelings and emotions that might not have made sense at the time, and to explore how these might be carriers of what remains unsaid, if we remain at the level of talk and text in our interpretations. Although this humanises the encounter between researcher and research subject, and can be traced back to New Paradigm research in the 1980s (Reason & Rowan, 1981), it is still based on an ethics of listening, which views 'listening' as a distinct human activity. In other words the technologies of listening developed within psychosocial interviewing are modelled upon perception based upon a singularly, bounded and distinctly human psychological subject. The researcher is positioned as one who listens in particular ways, guided by insights derived from analytic encounters, and who develops certain capacities of discernment that might allow what is equated to the transferential exchange to surface. These forms of reflection might direct our attention to the bodily and non-verbal exchange and to the gaps, silences and contradictions within and between the talk and dialogue, for example. However, in the next section I want to extend this work by focusing upon technologies of listening that are not modeled on a distinctly human perceptual system and that come from work on mediated perception and diasporic vision. It is this work that turns our attention to what Grace Cho (2008) terms an 'ethics of entanglement', and it is this ethical commitment that has increasingly become important in my own research practice.

AN ETHICS OF ENTANGLEMENT

It has become anachronistic within the HVN to view voices as irrational perceptions or signifiers of disease and illness. Rather, it is more common, and often useful to the voice hearer, to view their voices as modalities of remembering. The voices communicate with the voice hearer and others, and might enable a connection and proximity to trauma, abuse, loss and love. The relationship between voice hearing and trauma and abuse is one that has been well established within the HVN, and takes us back to Patsy Hague, the voice hearer who first challenged the psychiatrist Marius Romme to take seriously and listen-with-her to the voices she heard. These were voices communicating something of the trauma surrounding her own experiences of sexual abuse. The relationship between voice hearing and historical trauma, both in the context of a person's life history and to experiences of historical trauma that have been foreclosed is something that I have increasingly become interested in. I want to spend some time in this section talking about some work that has become really important in thinking about this for me, and which connects me to my own experience of listening to my Mother's voices as both a child and an adult. My own experiences have parallels with an American cultural studies scholar, Grace Cho (2008) whose Mother also heard voices. She took her own mother's experience of hearing voices as the subject of her PhD which is written up in her fascinating book *Haunting the Korean Diaspora: Shame, secrecy, silence and the Forgotten Korean War*.

In order to listen to her Mother's story Cho had to uncover something of her Mother's story that had never been told, which was never talked about, at least not directly or consciously. Cho's Mother was part of a Korean diaspora of women who had migrated to the United States at the end of WWII as GI brides; that is they had married American soldiers who had occupied Korea along the border between North and South. Cho's Mother never spoke to Grace about her migration story, what surrounded it were patterns of shame, secrecy and silence. Cho's Mother's story was emblematic of many Korean women who in the social work literature had journeyed from rural poverty in Korea to psychosis in America. Cho felt that her Mother's voices were ghostly interlocutors from the past, and in order to construct the possible conditions of their existence and what they might have to say she went on her own journey which she reconstructs in the book.

Cho asks the question in the book; what does it mean to *see* through another's voice.

The emphasis on *seeing* as opposed to hearing or listening, for example, draws our attention to the concept of synaesthesia. The concept of synaesthesia assumes that the senses do not work in isolation, but rather interdependently, co-existing and co-producing the possibility of embodied perception. In this sense it might be possible to *see* through another's voice. Work on synaesthesia has been important within affect studies and particularly the work of the seminal affect theorist, Brian Massumi (2002), who has used this concept to refer to those forms of bodily memory, which lie outside of a person's conscious reflections and deliberations, but which nevertheless orient them in the world. However, in Massumi's work bodily memory is primarily enfleshed within the processes of the central nervous system or proprioception and manifested through bodily forms of habit (see Blackman, 2010). Cho (*ibid.*) takes this concept out of a distinctly human sensory apparatus and turns her attention to those socio-technical processes and practices that transmit memory and shape attention in ways that engender technologies of listening that she equates to forms of mediated perception.

Cho (*ibid.*) presumes therefore that the voices have something to say, that they should be listened to. The question of how to listen is, however, not straightforward or grounded within the practices of the speaking subject. In order to listen she turns to film and art practices, often made by second-generation Korean Americans who had grown up in similar patterns of secrecy and silence and had expressed their own experience of this through artwork. So in other words their experience was primarily represented non-representationally as telling the story using narrative simply was not possible. In some senses it was a story that was unrepresentable. She reconstructs the unrepresentability of what the voices might be saying by turning to secondary histories of the Korean War. She uncovers the profound shame of many Korean women who became GI brides who had worked as prostitutes for American soldiers on Army bases in Korea, a form of militarised sex-work, where some had met their future husbands and eventually migrated to America. The term for this in Korean is the *Yanggongju*, a term which is extremely shameful and denigrating for the women involved. This traumatic secret is concealed by many Korean women, and Cho explores how the unspoken history can become transmuted into a hallucination and haunts the next generation and become distributed across space and time.

Cho (*ibid.*) draws on work on intergenerational haunting in order to explore this. She looks in the book at how films, such as *Soul's Protest*, a film which dramatises an event where a boat carrying Korean prisoners of war back from Japan to Korean was blown up, allegedly by the Japanese crew who had fled the boat just before an explosion was heard and the boat sank. Many people now refer to this event as The Korean Titanic. She argues that media technologies, like film, allow one to see the possible trauma that led to the concealment of this ghost and work with a concept of diasporic vision. Diasporic vision is a form of mediated or distributed perception which allows one to remember a story that has never been told. She argues that distributed perception allows one to bring a trauma that has been foreclosed into the social so that the voices can be listened to. This isn't about historical accuracy but about staging that which has never been spoken and to a certain extent is unrepresentable as official histories have never been documented of the event; it has literally been written out of history. This is also a growing focus of service users, such as Jacqui Dillon, the current chair of the HVN, who have been active in the campaign not only to recognise dissociation as a normative response to abuse but also to make the argument that in order to enable voice hearer's to listen to their voices it is important to be able to connect up their own micro-histories of trauma and abuse with official histories. She recognises how difficult this is for voice hearers when official histories of organised child abuse and paedophilia that she was made to participate in, even by members of her own family, are only now starting to be documented and told.

The connection between the campaigns of service users to tell these stories of shame, secrecy and silence with Cho's study is a way of linking up what Davoine and Guadilliere (2004) term histories beyond trauma. That is, connecting up those histories that have never been told, authorised or documented within official histories, such as the forgotten Korean War, with micro-histories of trauma and shame. Davoine and Guadilliere are analysts who have worked for over three decades with psychosis. Many analysts are reluctant to work with hallucinatory phenomenon, preferring instead to work within the confines of language and ideation. Davoine and Guadilliere have pioneered work within studies of the intergenerational transmission of trauma, particularly approaching psychosis as an attempt to bring into existence a social trauma that has been foreclosed. This is an attempt to explore precisely those carnal generational connections that exist genealogically but which cannot be articulated. For Davoine and Guadilliere the subject is always a subject of history, even though those histories may have been cut out of what they call 'the sanctioned social narrative' (p. xii).

This moves discussion of voice hearing beyond the function of the voice within the context of a person's autobiography, to the role of the voice as a ghost distributed across space and time, revealing perhaps the entanglement between past and present, living and dead, fantasmatic and real, self and other, and human and non-human. Thus to listen, hear or see through another's voice requires a different kind of technology of listening based on seeing through mediated forms of perception, or what Cho (2008) terms an ethics of entanglement.

IMMATERIAL BODIES

The work on an ethics of entanglement that Cho (*ibid.*) develops challenges some of the ethical considerations we might have in working with vulnerable research subjects. It also introduces the non-human into our conceptions of listening and interpreting, and directs our attention to those agencies and actors who create the possibility of listening and learning beyond the boundaries of a humanist research subject. The kind of ethics that Cho develops and that has been central to my current work 'researching affect' has taken me back to what I am terming a subliminal archive in the nineteenth century. This archive brought together the preoccupations of philosophers, writers, artists and scientists who were all interested in phenomena such as voice hearing, delusions, hypnotic suggestion and psychic phenomena such as telepathy and mediumship (see Blackman, 2012). These phenomena were not simply dismissed as abnormal or marginal perceptions, but rather what was of interest was in how these experiences breached the boundaries between the self/other, inside/outside, dead/alive, and material and immaterial. They were approached as trans-subjective phenomena, revealing perhaps something of how communications, in a more embodied sense, can be passed and transmitted across space and time.

What is interesting about this particular archive was the ontological and epistemological position enacted within forms and practices of experimentation conducted at the time. Experimentation was viewed as an active process designed to bring something into being that did not necessarily pre-exist the experimental encounter. This work has resonances with contemporary work on the performativity of experimentation (Barad, 2003, 2007), as well as the suggestion that 'haunting' might be a more appropriate foundational ontology to approach subjectivity from (see Gordon, 2008). In this last section I want to focus on a series of experiments that took place in William James' psychological laboratory at Harvard University, between the avant-garde writer Gertrude Stein and Leon Solomons, both of whom were undergraduate students in psychology at the time. The experiments took place under the tutelage of the psychologist, Hugo Munsterberg, exploring the phenomenon of automatic writing. I develop my analysis of these forms of experimentation in my book, *Immaterial Bodies: Affect, Embodiment, Mediation* (Blackman, 2012), and wish to draw attention to some of the ethical considerations surrounding experimentation which might be useful in taking this work forward.

The experiments were designed to induce the feeling of automatism – that is the experience of being governed by someone or something else. The phenomenology of automatism has been aligned to a range of experiences which all challenge the boundaries and limits of the autonomous selfhood, including voice hearing, hypnosis (see Andriopoulos, 2008) and in the particular examples I will focus on, the experience of hysteria as it was recounted and enacted within the nineteenth century. The aim of the experiments was to explore the extent to which phenomenon associated with hysteria could be created within the laboratory (Solomons & Stein, 1896). The backdrop to these experiments were some of the claims of subliminal psychologists, such as Myers (1903) and Sidis (1898), who were interested in psychic phenomenon, such as telepathy and mediumship, as well as hypnotic suggestion and hallucinations, which they argued were evidence of other forms of consciousness, subliminal and supraliminal, which connected subjects to the other, human and non-human. Solomons and Steins, like many scientists of the time, remained ambivalent about the veridicality of such claims, but were interested in exploring associated phenomenon, such as the concept of 'double personality', under experimental conditions.

THE PROBLEM OF AUTOMATISM

Solomons and Stein (1896) were interested in experiences which produce a sense of automatism, that is, experiences where a subject might feel that they are being directed or governed by an imperceptible force or agency, or even by a secondary personality. The experience of automatism, or divided attention as it is conventionally called within modern psychological interpretation, reveals how permeability can be experienced as connection and also as possession (see Andriopoulos, 2008). Automatism is a phenomenon that describes experiences which are threshold phenomena, that is, they operate across and between the self and other, material and immaterial and inside and outside. Solomons and Stein, like many scientists and psychologists of the time, were interested in theorising these experiences as part of a normal continuum or spectrum of experience. Thus, in this context, Solomons and Stein's experiment was based on drawing parallels between the performance of secondary or double personality aligned to hysteria and experiences of automatism which are often associated with particular habits of attention. They argued that their experiments showed the limits of habit as it was conceived at the time and raised questions as to how to theorise more corporeal forms of knowing (see Blackman, 2008).

Solomons and Stein (1896) took the technique of automatic writing into the psychology laboratory in order to explore the experience of being governed by a foreign will or imperceptible force or agency (see Blackman, 2012). My purpose in discussing the experiments in the context of the ethics of mental health research is to consider the *performative* notion of experimentation that they enacted. They were not simply attempting to disclose an object or entity, but rather to actively produce an object or entity that might be analogous to the experience of hysteria or automatism. The focus was on the techniques, experimental apparatus and practices that were central to creating the possibility of experiencing automatism within a laboratory situation. This focus on the non-human actors and agencies as dynamic actants within the process of experimentation pre-figures Cho's (2008) focus on mediated perception and diasporic vision as integral to hearing voices. Cho (*ibid.*) locates mediated perception within the context of media technologies which allow the 'unspoken' to circulate and be transmitted through non-representational registers. The technologies are not simply 'carriers' but allow dynamic processes to take form and co-emerge between subjects (much like voice-dialoguing techniques, for example). This has resonances with Bracha Ettinger's (2006) notion of a 'matrixial encounter' or 'subjectivity-as-encounter' where the term *matrixial* refers to the role of practices such as artwork in actively producing the possibilities of such encounters (see Blackman, 2011).

The focus on experimentation that I am developing here links the arts to sciences and the past to present. It is one that provides continuity with the scientific practices we find in psychological laboratories, such as William James' Harvard Psychological Laboratory, in the late nineteenth and early twentieth centuries. The history of experimentality might shift focus to the non-human actors and agencies producing particular forms of intra-action (also see Blackman, 2010). This might be written in relation to the specific artifacts, devices and experimental apparatus, which in some instances were designed specifically with the purpose of bringing something into being that did not pre-exist the experimental encounter. This has resonances with the work of the Belgian anthropologist, Vincianne Despret (2008), who argues that meaningful communication (in this case with animals) is dependent upon the success of the apparatus in redistributing the parameters and terms of what is meaningful for the species in question. She uses the concept of affordance to refer to the capacity of the experimental apparatus to be sensitive to what is meaningful to the 'experimental subject' in question. This ethical requirement shifts our focus to the kinds of method and creative forms of experimentation that allow such obligations to take form.

The examples that I have given within this chapter particularly focus on experiences or phenomena that pose questions for how to meaningfully communicate when the phenomena in question exceed the boundaries of more conventional methodological senses of knowing. This might be in the context of modalities of communication such as voice hearing, or cross-species communication, or equally might direct us towards experiences which might remain 'unknowable' if one remains at the level of the representational and the competences of the 'speaking subject'. One question might be to imagine how these considerations might operate in an experimental form within sociology and related disciplines. There is already an archive of work exploring the relationship between culture and performance which is instructive in this sense (also see Bell, 2007). The work I am interested in looks at the performance of amnesia in the context of trauma and forgetting and the limits of the interview for accessing these registers (see Blackman, 2011; Hamera, 2005). The interviewer was directed towards what she termed the 'ghostly interlocutors' that were communicated via more embodied forms of knowing and practice (in this instance through traditional forms of Khmer dance and movement).

Avery Gordon (2008) has also invoked the concept of haunting as of important methodological significance for sociological theorising. In the foreword to her book, *Ghostly Matters. Haunting and the Sociological Imagination*, Janice Radway concurs with Gordon's calls for a renewed attention in humanities research to how certain things, entities, processes or ideas have become 'marginalised, excluded or repressed' (p. 4). Gordon shifts the focus on the 'visible and the concrete' (*ibid.*) characteristic of empiricist methodologies to those aspects of our 'complex personhood' (p. viii) that have been lost. In a reconfiguration of genealogical research shared by other feminist sociologists such as Vikki Bell (2007), Gordon makes an argument that disrupts the usual focus in Foucauldian genealogical study on historical discontinuities, arguing that what is missed in such methodological framings are those aspects of historical continuity that are passed and transmitted through silences, gaps, omissions, echoes and murmurs. It is this *hauntology* which connects with the intensification of work across the humanities on affect, and how one might research registers of experience which are non-representational and arguably require mattering processes to take form (see Blackman and Venn, 2010).

CONCLUSION

To return to the subject of this chapter – the person who hears voices – and how to listen and hear voices in the context of mental health research which aims to de-stabilize the foundations of psychiatric forms of knowing. The paradigms I have opened up in relation to this question move our ethical interests and obligations beyond the speaking subject and the normative model of humanist ethics grounded upon this. It suggests that our actions as researchers are always interventions that, in the case of 'good' research, allow us to become attentive to the practices of experimentation which allow articulation and meaningful communication to take place. This takes us beyond the importance of reflexivity towards an ethics which is attentive to the connections between the psychosocial, historical and technical and which requires trans-disciplinary co-operation and collaboration. I argue that these models were already in circulation and enacted within nineteenth-century experimental practices which brought together philosophers, artists, literary writers, scientists and medical doctors interested in a subliminal archive. As I argue elsewhere, histories of trans-disciplinary co-operation and collaboration are central to histories of scientific innovation and development (see Blackman, 2010, 2012). Recognition of this and attentiveness to the ethical, epistemological and ontological requirements this entails is all the more urgent given the current attack on the humanities vis-à-vis scientific forms of experimentation by UK and other neo-liberal governments. Despite these attacks, the 'turn to affect' and the interest in more marginal forms of knowing are taking form in the common ontologies emerging across the humanities, and the natural, social and human sciences (see Blackman & Venn, 2010). It is this context which provides the ideal milieu for reposing our ethical interests, commitments and obligations and which I hope my contribution can be part of.

NOTE

1. In a recent special issue of the journal *Body & Society on Affect*, Couze Venn and I draw attention to some of the potential problems with psychosocial interview

methods, which produce data which arguably are not the same kind as those that are produced within an analysand/analyst relationship (see Blackman & Venn, 2010, p. 19).

REFERENCES

Andriopoulos, S. (2008). *Possessed: Hypnotic crimes, corporate fiction and the invention of cinema.* Chicago, IL: University of Chicago Press.

Barad, K. (2003). Posthumanist performativity: Toward an understanding of how matter comes to matter. *Signs: Journal of Women in Culture and Society, 28*(3), 801–831.

Barad, K. (2007). *Meeting the universe halfway: Quantum physics and the entanglement of matter and meaning.* Durham, NC: Duke University Press.

Bell, V. (2007). *Culture and performance. The challenge of ethics, politics and feminist theory.* Oxford: Berg.

Blackman, L. (2001). *Hearing voices: Embodiment and experience.* London: Free Association Books.

Blackman, L. (2007). Psychiatric cultures and bodies of resistance. *Body & Society, 13*(2), 1–24.

Blackman, L. (2008). *The body: The key concepts.* Oxford: Berg.

Blackman, L. (2010). Embodying affect: Voice-hearing, telepathy, suggestion and modelling the non-conscious. *Body & Society, 16*(1), 163–192.

Blackman, L. (2011). Affect, performance and queer subjectivities. *Cultural Studies, 25*(2), 183–199.

Blackman, L. (2012). *Immaterial bodies: Affect, embodiment, mediation.* London: Sage.

Blackman, L., & Venn, C. (2010). Affect. *Body & Society, 16*(1), 1–6.

Cho, G. (2008). *Haunting the Korean Diaspora: Shame, secrecy, silence and the forgotten war.* Minneapolis, MN: University of Minnesota Press.

Davoine, F., & Guadilliere, J. M. (2004). *History beyond trauma.* New York, NY: Other Press.

Despret, V. (2008). The becomings of subjectivity in animal worlds. *Subjectivity, 23*, 123–139.

Ettinger, B. (2006). *The matrixial borderspace. Theory out of bounds* (Vol. 28). Minneapolis, MN: University of Minnesota Press.

Featherstone, M. (2010). Body, image and affect in consumer culture. *Body & Society, 16*(1), 193–221.

Gordon, A. (2008). *Ghostly matters: Haunting the sociological imagination.* Minneapolis, MN: University of Minnesota Press.

Gorton, K. (2009). *Media audiences: Television, meaning, emotion.* Edinburgh: Edinburgh University Press.

Hamera, J. (2005). The answerability of memory: "Saving" Khmer classical dance. In A. Abbas & J. N. Erni (Eds.), *Internationalizing cultural studies: An anthology.* Oxford: Blackwell Publishing.

Kavka, M. (2008). *Reality TV, affect and intimacy: Reality matters.* Basingstoke: Palgrave.

Leder, D. (1990). *The absent body.* Chicago, IL: The University of Chicago Press.

Massumi, B. (2002). *Parables for the virtual: Movement, affect, sensation.* Durham, NC: Duke University Press.

Myers, F. W. H. (1903). *Human personality and its survival of bodily death* (Vol. 1). New York, NY: Longmans, Green and Co.

Reason, P., & Rowan, J. (Eds.). (1981). *Human inquiry: A sourcebook of new paradigm research.* Chichester: Wiley.

Romme, M., Escher, S., Dillon, J., Corstens, D., & Morris, M. (2009). *Living with voices: 50 stories of recovery.* Ross-on-Wye: PCCS Books.

Sidis, B. (1898). *The psychology of suggestion: A research into the subconscious nature of man and society.* New York, NY: D. Appleton and Co.

Sobchack, V. (2010). Living a 'Phantom Limb': On the phenomenology of bodily integrity. *Body & Society, 16*(3), 51–67.

Solomons, L., & Stein, G. (1896). Normal motor automatism. *Psychological Review, 3,* 492–512.

Walkerdine, V., & Jimenez, L. (2012). *Gender, work and community after de-industrialisation: A psychosocial approach to affect.* Basingstoke: Palgrave.

Wood, H., & Skeggs, B. (Eds.). (2011). *Reality TV and class.* Basingstoke: BFI and Palgrave.

THE AGENCY OF ETHICAL OBJECTS

Joost van Loon

ABSTRACT

Purpose – *Using Whitehead's notion of prehension in a critical reappraisal of phenomenology, a different kind of understanding of subjectification and objectification is being proposed in which subjectification is that which enables action as a multiplicity or virtuality, and objectification enables actuality.*

Approach – *A critical engagement with literature on objects, including Gabriel de Tarde, Alfred North Whitehead, Martin Heidegger and Graham Harman, is used to develop an original conception of objectification and subjectification. This is applied to debates about objectification in pornography.*

Findings – *This approach enables us to better understand the theoretical underpinnings of empirical philosophies such as Actor Network Theory in support of the argument that objects are capable of action. While subjectification is folded within the process of prehension as the opening of the virtual, it is logically possible to argue that objects are a matter of concern for ethics. This also means that in terms of the pornography debate, the pornographic object as such can be held accountable. We do*

Ethics in Social Research
Studies in Qualitative Methodology, Volume 12, 189–205
ISSN: 1042-3192/doi:10.1108/S1042-3192(2012)0000012013

not have to accept the instrumentalist argument that 'what you do with it defines its ethics'.

Originality/value – *The argument that objects are capable of action has thus far not been pursued in relation to questions of ethics as opposed to politics.*

Keywords: Objects; affect; prehension; pornography; ethics; action

THE PORNOGRAPHIC OBJECT

Objectification is a not only a dirty word but also a dirty practice. A host of critical social scientists would immediately swarm around any attempt at objectification because it is seen as eliminating (human) agency. For example, in her essay on objectification, Martha (1995, pp. 249–50) explains how through the works of radical feminists such as Dworkin and Mackinnon, the term sexual objectification (in pornography) has become associated with a negative process of degrading and dehumanising women. However, in an attempt to provide a more differentiated interpretation of pornographic objectification, she carefully distinguishes between seven different ways in which a human being can be treated as a thing: (1) instrumentality, (2) denial of autonomy, (3) inertness, (4) fungibility (interchangeability or replaceability), (5) violability, (6) ownership and (7) denial of subjectivity (*ibid.*, p. 257). Although these categories are used to differentiate between different *types* of objectification, they are still unified by the common denominator of being 'mediated forms of sex'.

For all its sophisticated distinctions, however, crucial to Nussbaum's work remains the unity of objectification; it treats that which is not a thing as a thing. That 'no-thing' is the subject. That is, for Nussbaum and most feminist critics, objectification concerns subjects only. The objectification of objects is in her view not possible, because things are already objects. Indeed, the objectification of objects is a little redundant as objects are things that are always-already objectified.

As her analysis moves from the treatment of objects (which are always-already objectified) to the treatment of plants and animals, to the treatment of human beings in work and finally in pornography, it becomes clear that objectification also becomes increasingly problematic. In this sense, it has become a moral variable (with a range from neutral to negative). It enables her to say that not every act of objectification is morally problematic,[1] but at best it remains morally neutral, that is, *indifferent*. She makes a link between the moral philosophy on sex and marriage in the work of Kant (1997) and the objections of radical feminism to objectification, which focuses on only three of the seven aspects: instrumentality, denial of autonomy and denial of subjectivity. Nussbaum herself struggles to remain consistent in terms of her valuation of objectification in terms of morality because her sense of 'what is acceptable objectification?' becomes infected with another virus, namely that of sexual pleasure. Hence, the chapter ends up as an assertion of a critique of judgment based on taste rather than ethics. That is, Nussbaum experiences a dilemma between sexual pleasure and moral justification in certain forms of pornography and is seeking to differentiate the concept of objectification to such an extent that it enables her to 'rescue' certain forms of mediated sex (in literature) from being thrown into the abyss of condemnation.

However, perhaps it is simply the case that after Kant, we will always have problems speaking about objects in terms of ethics, because he has prohibited thought from engaging with 'things as such'. What is also clear is that by equating things with objects and depriving objects of any capacity to act, the Kantian universe would never really welcome a consideration of 'ethical objects' in the first place. Objects are incapable of practical reason. Nussbaum does not really reject or go beyond Kant on this point. She does not demand from objects that they are to be ethical; she only rejects the point blank condemnation of all forms of sexual objectification as evil. Certain forms of consensual, artistic and playful objectification should not be prohibited by the morality police. Nussbaum too remains a liberal at heart.

The pornographic dilemma that, even though all objectifications are morally wrong or at best morally indifferent, some objectifications are experienced as pleasurable and therefore difficult to deny (at least in a universe based on a liberal pluralism of taste), highlights that Nietzsche (1886) was right to state that after Kant moral philosophy always appears as a pompous masquerade of personal prejudice, that is, an assertion of *a* will-to-power that in its singularity remains arbitrary. This explains the need of Nussbaum to separate 'bad' objectification (e.g. *Playboy*) from 'good' (or 'still acceptable') representations of sexual desire (e.g. D.H. Lawrence) and relocate the root of evil in heterosexual patriarchal structures of domination. Objectification then becomes bad when it serves to reproduce existing relations of domination (via expressions of sexual desire). This, however, remains itself tied to a will to power that can only validate its own moral philosophy as long as it remains subordinate; hence, it is a slave morality.

How Can Ethical Objects be? Or Toward a Theory of Ethical Objectification

However, it is not my intention to beat Nussbaum or radical feminism at their own game of moral philosophy, and even less to devalue their critique of pornography which in my opinion has many merits. Instead, I propose to shift our attention to a more fundamental issue that prevents Nussbaum's critique of (bad) pornography from becoming more than an assertion of slave morality. I want to claim that Nussbaum's concept of objectification is logical only if we assume that there are subjects and objects in the first place.

Whereas I am not going to dispute the practical viability of talking about subjects and objects as different entities, I am going to engage with a questioning of this 'in the first place'. This is nothing original and new and has already been worked through in a most thorough fashion by Heidegger in *Sein und Zeit* (1986 [1927]). According to Harman, for Heidegger the main issue has been the equation of Being with 'presence at hand' or *Vorhandensein*. This metaphysical trick from Plato's cave, which Derrida (1974) later dubbed 'the metaphysics of presence', enabled the western metaphysical tradition since Plato to assume that there is such a *thing* as 'being-as-such' or worse, that 'the thing' is a 'being-as-such'.

Instead of being-as-such or *Vorhandensein*, Heidegger posited a notion of being as a relationship between *Dasein* (being there) and *Zuhandensein* (being ready-to-hand). Readiness-to-hand makes it clear that there is already a relationship between entities that enables us to 'be there'; Harman usefully explains that this, thus, means that for Heidegger *tools* are not a mere example of objects among others (as Arendt (1958) maintained in her critique of Heidegger that forms the core of *the Human Condition*). Instead, all objects are tools because it is in their readiness to hand that they become objects. In pornography, representations of sex are deployed as tools to create experiences of sexual desire.

Tools enable. That is, tools allow us to 'do things'; in other words, they enable us to be. Latour (2005) thus repeats Heidegger's point when he says that 'action is already overtaken' because if in order to be, we have to be enabled, it means that all that 'is' has already been enabled. Foucault's Nietzsche (Foucault, 1977) might have been hinting at a very similar idea when he suggested that we should stop thinking historically in terms of *Ursprung* (source or origin) but instead work with a more pragmatic notion of *Herkunft*, which in English would also be translated as origin, but its usage in German has greater affinity with a place where one comes from; it is a 'pointing back towards' or a 'descent' rather than a vantage point.

If we understand Being in terms of tools, as Harman proposes, then we can already dismiss the assumption that subjects and objects exist 'in the first place'. Subjects and objects have to be made. However, contrary to the 'critical' reading of objectification, which stems from a legacy inscribed by Plato's cave, we should not read objectification as a process that grants 'no-things' object-like qualities; it is not a process by which some-no-thing becomes 'as if' it is an object, like the shadows on the wall appeared to Plato's hapless prisoners 'as if' they were the things themselves. If taken in this 'critical' sense, objectification remains just a deception and nothing more; it would be a synonym for simulation; a force that denies any engagement between signification and realisation (Baudrillard, 1993). They would be prisoners of mythology, self-referential products of 'stolen language' (Barthes, 1993).

We have to reject, *a priori* if we must, this conception of objectification because it is itself highly misleading. To use it in this way would force us to presuppose what real objects are, as opposed to shadows, what real objects are before they are ready to hand. This can only be done if we already presuppose something that is to hold out against it, something that remains beyond the objects that are being drawn into the shadowplay of simulations. This something is, of course, the subject.

Plato could dismiss the shadows only because his subject (it could have been an angel) was miraculously freed from his or her chains to leave this position and enter into the real world. Because violence was used to free the subject from his/her chains, force him/her into the world and enable him/her to convince upon return those left behind of the real world beyond the shadows, this heroic and ultimately totalitarian subject is required to engage in a priori violence to distinguish between the real object and the simulacrum. This presupposition of what an object and what a subject already are would require a metaphysical leap that privileges *Vorhandensein* over *Zuhandensein*. One is of course free to choose the cave as the *Urmythos* of metaphysics. Most scholars have implicitly or explicitly taken this option. A few have not. This is perhaps because the idea of having to be locked inside a cave first, in order to be able to say anything about reality, is somewhat odd. It is those claustrophobics whom I wish to follow.

It was Marx who, in his early critique of Feuerbach (in the *German Ideology*, Mark & Engels, 1969), exposed a hidden idealism in this version of materialist philosophy. Feuerbach's materialism was a *'beobachtender Materialismus'*, a spectatorial materialism. Against this, Marx posed a praxiological materialism, one in which realisation is not a matter of perception but of action. Leaving aside some huge problems regarding Marx' own conception of praxis that especially in these earlier writings can be traced back to 'unfinished business' regarding his inherent Hegelianism, the lesson is clear. Any form of materialism that relies on an ontology of perception remains a form of idealism and generates a philosophy that remains self-referential and, most problematically from an ethical standpoint, self-valorising.

However, Marx was far from original in this respect. Heidegger argues that a critique of the ontology of perception, which is the ontology of *Vorhandensein* and the crux of what he referred to as 'the western metaphysical tradition', goes as far back as the Presocratics, against whom the cave was initially dug out as a form of rhetorical critique. Likewise, Aristotle's version of empirical philosophy may have had some inconsistencies in terms of its own metaphysics; it does pose some critical footnotes at the 'perceptionist' bias of the Platonic tradition. Epicurus and Lucretius were also quite 'praxiological' in their philosophical orientations, if only because they drew so much attention to the physiology of thinking, something that Nietzsche imitated even though his corporeality of thinking was less driven by enjoyment and pleasure and more by discomfort and irritation. Finally, Spinoza's monism and Leibniz' monadology were equally making significant inroads into developing a nonperceptionist alternative to the western metaphysical tradition, before these roads were being barricaded by the Kantian- and Hegelian-thought police of the modern – allegedly 'postmetaphysical' (Habermas, 1994) – era.

I apologize for the sketchy and panoramic engagement with a beautifully complicated history of ideas, but this only serves the purpose of a reminder that not every philosopher was a complacent prisoner of Plato's cave and that there have been a steady stream of voices who have whispered different poetry. I could have simply asserted that I am not going to accept the starting position that there are subjects and there are objects. I want to do more, however. I want to argue that it is *better philosophy* and *therefore better social science* to make the question about 'what subjects and objects are' an empirical one. I also want to argue that *because* the question of what subjects and objects are is an empirical one, its pursuit leads to opening the possibility not just of engaging objects ethically (which is what Nussbaum's moral philosophy is concerned with) but also of engaging ethical objects.

PERCEPTION VERSUS PREHENSION?

It would be mistaken to see this turn as a simple rejection of the phenomenological tradition. I prefer to see it as a temporary suspense of a particular line of phenomenological inquiry and the birth of another one. The three main problems with the main phenomenological tradition are connected, but not therefore reducible to each other: (1) the aforementioned presupposition of subjects and objects; (2) the *ontological* primacy of perception,[2] and (3) its anthropocentrism (in terms of the idea that both 'sense' and 'reflection' are the exclusive domains of the human subject which is the Kantian legacy).

Subjects and Objects as Categories Defined in Opposition to Each Other

The general idea behind the subject/object distinction is that subjects act and objects are acted upon. In many languages, this can be traced back to a grammatical structure which points toward mood and transitivity (Halliday, 1985). This separation of subject and object is not in itself problematic. Surely, one should be allowed to make a distinction between different modalities of 'being'. For example, the master of monism, Spinoza (1677) used the term 'attributes' and distinguished between modalities of thought and extensions. However, both were still attributes of the same substance. With subjects and objects as a priori categories, the underlying assumption is not the unity of substance, but the duality of essence.

Of course, one modality of being could be identified in terms of 'degree of activeness'. Certainly, in any given situation, it will be possible to distinguish between more and less active entities. However, that remains an empirical identification, not a matter of presupposition. It is a quantity, not a quality. Moreover, if an entity is completely inactive, what difference does it make when one does not pay any attention to it at all?

The a priori – that is a non-empirical separation between subjects and objects as essentially two different substances – makes two mistakes at once: (a) it assumes subjectivity and objectivity are caused by something that belongs to the 'being' of an entity and (b) it assumes that this 'essence' is an absolute modality of being: one is either active or passive. The first problem relates to the Kantian rejection of Leibnizian monadology which he, unjustly in my opinion, relegated to the generic fallacy of 'rationalism'. A quick return to Spinoza may help here. As has just been mentioned, for Spinoza both 'extension' and 'mode of thought' were attributes of substance (or monad), not two different substances. If we want to force the issue and equate mode of thought with subject and extension with object, we would still have to find a way to dismiss Spinoza's logical premise that they are not of a different substance because there can only be one substance, they are only different attributes of substance. Kant's separation of 'reason' from 'intuition', however, implies two different substances. Reason consists of a conceptual abstraction, a purely cognitive process; while intuition still relates to experience, and thus to an encounter with objects.

Clearly, these problems are much less pertinent if we would simply stop thinking in terms of being and replace it with 'having'. Having is much more amenable to thinking in terms of more or less, that is, quantities and intensities (Latour, 2002). Moreover, having is relational, temporal and situational. One could have something at some point, but it can be given or taken away a moment later. Finally, having allows one to think in terms of identification as movement, nothing is ever exactly the same; temporality, for example, already marks the tiniest of differences if we consider decay.

Phenomenology has thus far always presented itself as a philosophy of being. It is an activity done by subjects in respect of objects. It does not matter in the slightest that these subjects are conceived of as material instead of ideational identities (i.e. that subjects are embodied rather than 'mere spirit', which is of particular importance when considering transcendence) as long as this materiality is then again subsumed under the special label of 'subject'. As long as the 'I' of phenomenology is not treated as being of the same quality as the 'it', we are forced to accept the exceptional status of the I as being capable of something that the 'it' is not capable of. Furthermore, we need to assume that this special status is transmitted from situation to situation, that it belongs to something that the 'I' is, *in essence*.

If we do not want to accept this; if instead we want to suspend judgment on special qualities until we have found traces, until we can be convinced that these traces constitute a difference that matters, we simply cannot commence our thinking in terms of a dualism of I/it. However, at the same time, we can presuppose that some entities are more active than others, that some entities are more subjective and others are more objective. Yet, these must remain a matter of 'empirical' realisation: an entity's degree of activity is relative to the specific situation or event it emerges in. Furthermore, there is always some degree of activity, of movement, of difference, if we want to make sense of existence.

It is more fruitful to shift from a focus on modalities of being to modalities of having, which means the same as 'modalities of realisation'.

It is for this reason I propose that in terms of ethnographic research, we need to look for subjectifiers and objectifiers instead of subjects and objects. Subjectifiers are 'enablements of action', whereas objectifiers are 'enablements of actuality'. It is in this sense that we could reinvoke Spinoza and argue that subjectifiers are that which engender virtuality and suspense between a causal force and its effect. It enables us to think of multiple forces and effects as connected events; or said differently: it enables us to 'prehend time'.[3] Time is then that which emerges as a process of emergence/perishing and not separate from occasions (actualities), but only constituted by them. Subjectifiers are therefore forces of multiplicity and create possibilities that are not-yet actualities, by means of which temporalities come into being. These could also be referred to as 'political occasionings'.

The Ontological Primacy of Perception

What happens when we prioritise having over being? It shifts attention to material attachment rather than detachment. Thinking in terms of being creates a static world in which 'what is' exists as such out of and for itself. Although in English, the word 'being' can be seen as a 'present continuous' and this is temporal, this is quickly moved to the background in a process that Heidegger described as 'the forgetting of being'. In contrary to Latour's (1993) rather scathing dismissal of Heidegger's critique in *We have never been modern*, in which he accuses Heidegger himself as having forgotten being, the forgetting of being is what hits the nail on the head as far as early phenomenology is concerned. Latour's mistake is quite simply that he has misunderstood 'the forgetting of Being' as 'the forgetting of beings' (objects). Heidegger meant the verb, however, and quite literally too: the forgetting of existence as time-bound.

Latour is of course right to defend phenomenology[4] against the accusation of having forgotten beings, as it has always been concerned with objects. However, this 'concern' has been practiced in a rather limiting (rather than limited) fashion, namely in terms of only one type of activity: perception. Classical phenomenology simply copied the Kantian notions of 'sense' as sense-experience, which is the cornerstone of analytic thought, and reflection as purely mental activity as the cornerstone of synthetic thought. Sense-experience, however, is then already subsumed under the mastery of cognition; it becomes a purely 'mental' activity as well. Sense no longer stems from an encounter between two different entities, but becomes the product of cognition and from then on only inhabits the exclusive province of thought.

However, if we take Heidegger's point against classical phenomenology as having forgotten the question of Being-*as-process*, then we are on very similar grounds[5] as Alfred North Whitehead's Philosophy of Organism (Whitehead, 1978). Being becomes an unfolding in time, a process that is irreducible to the (emergent) beings that are being processed, and a concern for Being then means a non-exclusive concern: sense is not the province of thought but of experience (Dewey, 1925). For something to make sense, we need to follow some 'thing' in the unfolding of its being and see ourselves as part of this unfolding, that is, as part of 'the thing'. Thought becomes an afterthought that enables a specific form of sense-making, namely that of synthetic abstraction. It neither 'fixes' the essence of the thing nor its 'concept'; it merely adds to its virtualisation.

If we reject the a priori separation of subjects and objects, then it logically follows that we have to reject the ontological primacy of perception. Thinking Being-as-process leads us away from experiencing in terms of perception of phenomena, but instead invites us to think in terms of 'events'; what 'appears' as brought about by the sun is an emergence, not something that is simply 'there' lurking in the darkness of ignorance, waiting to be uncovered. A process-oriented mode of thinking being refuses to separate between entities and forces that move these or other entities, but instead conceives of both in terms of monads (Tarde, 2009; Whitehead, 1978).[6] This is the basis of Whitehead's notion of prehension; through prehension occasions are actualised; prehension does not take place in addition to entities: entities only exist in prehension.

This, however, is exactly what a phenomenology based on perception does not allow. The world of objects as such cannot be known, but only become subject to understanding by means of being brought into the light of sense-making through perception. Perception is thus elevated to the unique status of being the portal between the world of 'things as such' that we cannot know and the world of sense-making and reflection, that is, the world of consciousness.

William James (2010 [1912]) once made a simple but effective intervention into forms of psychology that presuppose the existence of 'consciousness as such' by pointing out that it is logically impossible to be conscious-as-such because we cannot be conscious of nothing (although we can be conscious of nothingness, which is not the same *thing*). When we are said to be conscious, we are always conscious of *some*thing. How are we then to logically argue that this 'thing' only *makes* sense because we have a consciousness that makes sense of it?

There is therefore no logical ground to presuppose that the primary form of experience is a perception that is embedded in consciousness. What could perception be before an object engages in consciousness? Referring to its original use in the work of Whitehead, Harman proposes to use the term '*prehension*' as the basic form of experience. Prehension always takes place between at least two entities that are occasioned by it, neither of which have a preordained 'special status' to mark the sense of what is being apperceived with an a priori 'qualification' (Harman, 2010, pp. 37–39). The event of experience as prehension is thus an emergence. It could be an emergence of consciousness, and this could be called perception, but this is not the only form of intelligibility that can be engaged in prehension.

Anthropocentrism

It has been an insight from Actor Network Theory that subjects and objects are not to be equated with active versus passive entities, let alone humans and non-humans respectively. Subjective and objective are in the first instance adjectives that point to specific modes of engagement. A subjective mode of engagement is oriented towards *virtualisation*; it is the creation of multiple possibilities between the no-longer and the not-yet, a zone of potentiality in which 'things could take place'. An objective mode of engagement is geared toward *actualisation*, the limitation of possibilities that we can associate with a 'becoming real' as a mode of resistance. Objectification is the creation (or invention) of objects, entities that resist and therefore become real; subjectification is the enablement of action, of inaugurating possibilities and thereby, for example but not exclusively, the need for decisions.

When we compare such a notion of objectification with what Tarde (1899) referred to as 'Adaptation', it becomes clear that we are dealing with a quantitative conception of difference:

> Between the absolute confirmation of one proposition by another, and an absolute contradiction between the two, there are an infinite number of partial contradictions and partial confirmations, without counting the infinite number of degrees of affirmative and negative belief. Invention is a question followed by an answer. But for each question set a thousand answers are possible, of all possible degrees of completeness and exactness (1899, p. 125).

Objectification, the creation of objects, has thus very little to do with 'rendering passive' or the 'depleting of agency'. The alleged agency of subjectivity, by contrast, is enabled by objectification. It is because of the work of objectification that there are actualities in relation to which actions become possible. Because objectification is the process by which 'the real' becomes actualised, we can no longer work from the primacy of the (meta-physical) active subject. It has been a major stumbling block for pheno-menology that it always had to assume as a starting point the individuated general human being who perceives 'a' world as it emerges. Not only was it thereby forced to adopt a cognitivist understanding of reason, but it also had to assume that thought emerges from perception. Knowing was always bound to sense-perception that was initiated by the unique character of the perceiving subject.

In an exchange of disagreements, Don Idhe tried to maintain, in the face of Bruno Latour's critique of the anthropocentrism of phenomenology, that phenomenology was not necessarily idealist, but that, for example by embracing the body (as Merleau-Ponty has done), it becomes more 'materialised' or perhaps even 'actual' (Idhe & Selinger, 2003). Whereas it is clear that placing the body before the subject enables us to understand other forms of sense-perception than those of observation, that is, the dissociation of 'the eye' and 'the I', it still remains a human body that is supposed to be the locus of perception.

Of course, philosophers and social scientists tend to be humans most of the time as well. It is very easy to develop definitions in which sense-perception, experience, cognition, intelligence, thought and so on are exclusively human. After all, subjects and objects have a base in many grammar systems too. However, just because we are able to establish definitions, impose logos and discuss abstractions, it does not mean we are the exclusive creators of all that can be called 'real'. Only die hard solipsists would want to claim this, and a solipsist rarely has followers.

In other words, the choice is between two different understandings of reality. The first treats it as 'split from the beginning' into two substances: subject and object, and the second treats it as one substance with different attributes: subjective and objective. For the first, the object remains unin-telligible as such. Latour (2002) rightly asks why those who believe nothing intelligible can be said about things as such (or objects) continue to talk about these things. We can, however, maintain a sense of 'objective intelli-gibility' if we understand the emergence of occasions (time) as 'prehension', as actualities that are enabled (by objects 'doing things') as 'coming into being'. As attributes, subjective and objective merely reflect the doubling of virtuality and actuality: things are and can be different at the same time. This is thus not a radical and absolute unintelligibility, but merely the fullness and vitality of life itself.

INTEROBJECTIVITY

If objects do things (prehension) then the question might be asked: can objects be ethical? Before we can engage with a question like that, we need to take a closer critical look at what we consider 'ethics' to be. I am going to assume that the 'gold standard' of modern ethics is the Kantian principle of practical reason: 'Act so that the maxim of thy will can always at the same time hold good as a principle of universal legislation.'[7]

The presupposition here is that an ethical act is ethical only if it has been processed as a rational decision based on 'practical reason'. It requires consciousness. However, this postulate is axiomatic as it has been exclusively derived from a definition and it thus only obeys the logos of its own authority (cf Nietzsche, 1992, p. 440). In the Kantian logic, ethics precede action, but are still connected to action; without a concept of action, there is no concept of practical reason. Were we to obey this logic, there would be no such thing as an ethical object since ethics presuppose decision and objects do not act upon a decision: their action is itself *decisive*.

If there were to be such a *thing* as an ethical object, we would need to either redefine ethics or redefine objects. As Heidegger (1986 [1927]) has been at pains to show in *Sein und Zeit*, the thing itself is a curious being. As a gathering of everything that evades specificity, that is, a universal mark of identification, the thing is an association or assemblage. For a thing to hold together, it requires 'affect', the power to compose and decompose. The 'ability to be affected' or 'pathos' could be seen as the critical power that enables a thing to emerge. This idea is linked to what Stengers (2005) referred to as 'cosmopolitics'. Being affected is thought of by Stengers as the ability to 'serve the public' and to be fully accountable to every*thing* that is being affected.

Could this pathos be the singularity that enables us to redefine 'the decision'? That is, rather than contrasting pathos and decision, as in, for example, the contrapositioning of affect and cognition or pathos and logos, could we not be a little more Spinozist and see 'modalities of thought' as affective from the beginning as attributes of substance? Then decision becomes a modality alongside affect, a 'type' of affect if you wish – a being-affected.

To return to the problem of sexual objectification in pornography, we could ask whether the 'tools' of pornographic sexual desire can be ethical objects. When we accept that an ethical object is that which has the ability to be affected, we are immediately thrown into the empirical. Rather than defining the pornographic as a general type, we would have to engage with each pornographic event as it emerges, not just as a piece of text or description, but as a mediated practice. We could ask: what does this or that 'thing' gather in this specific instance? However, for the sake of not having to do an empirical study of porn, I wish to simply shift attention to its 'logic'.

The logic of porn is to provide mediated representations of sex (van Loon, 2008). It is from this point of view that we may ask whether mediated representations of sex could cultivate ethical objects. It is here where attention could shift to what ethical objects can do: they can subjectify. When they do, they are tools that enable action. For ethical objects to subjectify they need to open up the virtual, multiply possibilities and occasion temporalities. Ethics as 'being enabled to become-affected' means that that which is being objectified is fully and unconditionally 'taken into account'.

It is not such a challenge to reflect on what kind of subjectifications pornographic objects are able to generate. Theoretically, they could enable a wide range of possibilities ranging from sexual rapture to utter disgust; they can be mediators for a wide range of political movements and collective actions. However, when we consider the logic of porn as to provide mediated representations of sex, this limits the realm of possibilities to a considerable extent. Porn makes sexual acts 'present again', however, only by making itself disappear. The technologies of porn, the camera, the sound recorder, the script, remain absent, indifferent, as if they are mere inter-mediaries as opposed to mediators.[8] Yet at the same time, porn engages in repetitions of the same: the mediated representations of sex are imitations of a limited repertoire of actions that are interspersed with relatively obsolete interruptions that only serve to set the scene for the next instance of mediated sex. In this sense, the pornographic object 'normally' engenders self-satisfaction[9]; it actually diminishes the ability to be affected, it de-subjectifies.

It is with this criterion that we could make a useful distinction between ethical objects and non-ethical objects. From this point of view, it is hard to see how pornography could ever involve ethical objects, since – as a cultural industry and as a form of politics – its objects are deprived of the ability to be affected; instead they are produced to be effected. Pornographic objects are not being engaged in associations (as affect); instead they are manipulated, used and made obsolete (as effect).[10] This problem is not simply exclusive to the field of pornography, but is an issue that permeates large sections of the cultural industries: design, marketing, advertising and so on. To speak with Baudrillard (1993), these practices are not engaged in symbolic exchanges where there is a risk of being affected, a vulnerability of having to encounter something that cannot be subsumed, but has to be 'associated with'. Instead, they are practices of simulation: of codes referring to codes in a self-enclosed and self-referential universe. Without the ability to enter into exchange, the pornographic object remains indifferent. The outcomes are already known; no new associations are being enabled; no associations are required for it to 'do its job'. This is why it will be difficult for a pornographic object to instigate what Schillmeier and Pohler (2006), following Stengers, have referred to as 'a cosmopolitical event', simply because it does not allow that which it objectifies to be fully taken into account, and it does not hold itself accountable to what has been objectified.

NOTES

1. Although it is commonly accepted in both humanities and social sciences that critique cannot go beyond being a matter of opinion, there is not enough critical discussion of the ontological status of the boundary that serves as a threshold between what is to be accepted and what is to be prohibited.
2. It is of course true that it is inaccurate to accuse Merleau Ponty, for example, of a perceptionist bias as far as his concern for embodied experience is concerned. However, what is constituted by this embodied experience remains a subject, an 'I' that is ontologically separated from the materialities that modulate experiences.
3. Prehension is a concept derived from Whitehead's seminal work *Process and Reality* (1978) and understood as 'the most concrete element in actualities' (p. 19; on time, see page 29).
4. I am fully aware that Latour completely rejects being associated with phenomenology. This rhetorical move is only done to stress that his rejection of Heidegger's premise is unnecessary and contradicts his own metaphysical position, which he developed more explicitly in his later works.
5. This link was made by Harman (2010).
6. A similar idea can be found in Section 13 of the first essay in Nietzsche's (2003) *Genealogy of Morals:* 'For, in just the same way as people separate lightning from its flash and take the latter as an *action*, as the effect of a subject, which is called lightning, so popular morality separates strength from the manifestations of strength, as if behind the strong person there were an indifferent substrate, which is *free* to express strength or not. But there is no such substrate; there is no "being" behind the doing, acting, becoming. "The doer" is merely made up and added into the action – the act is everything. People basically duplicate the action: when they see a lightning flash, that is, an action of an action: they set up the same event

first as the cause and then yet again as its effect. Natural scientists are no better when they say "Force moves, force causes," and so on.' With thanks to Kevin Love for pointing out this passage.

7. Kant, I. (1997). *Critique of Practical Reason*, Book 1, Chapter 1, §70, can be found online at: http://www.gutenberg.org/cache/epub/5683/pg5683.html

8. This distinction has been derived from Latour (2005).

9. This includes moral self-satisfaction for example in the form of repugnance as an assertion of self-valorization and domination (including assertions of moral superiority).

10. In the language of moral theology: pornography entails the purging of lust from any remnants of love.

ACKNOWLEDGEMENTS

I would like to thank Kevin Love for his feedback and comments on an earlier version of this paper. All of the ideas developed in this chapter are the product of lively conversations with many people within and beyond academia. The responsibility for mistakes is, of course, solely mine.

REFERENCES

Arendt, H. (1958). *The human condition*. Chicago, IL: University of Chicago Press.
Barthes, R. (1993). *Mythologies*. London: Vintage.
Baudrillard, J. (1993). *Symbolic exchange and death*. London: Sage.
Derrida, J. (1974). *Of grammatology*. Baltimore, MD: The Johns Hopkins University Press.
Dewey, J. (1925). *Experience and nature*. New York, NY: Dover Publications.
Foucault, M. (1977). *Language, counter-memory, practice. Selected essays and interviews*. Oxford: Basil Blackwell.
Habermas, J. (1994). *Postmetaphysical thinking: Between metaphysics and the critique of reason*. Cambridge: Polity Press.
Halliday, M. A. K. (1985). *An introduction to functional grammar*. London: Edward Arnold.
Harman, G. (2010). *Towards speculative realism. Essays and lectures*. Washington, DC: Zero Books.
Heidegger, M. (1986 [1927]). *Sein und Zeit*. Tübingen: Max Niemeyer Verlag.
Idhe, D., & Selinger, E. (2003). *Chasing technoscience: Matrix for materiality*. Bloomington, IN: Indiana University Press.
James, W. (2010 [1912]). *Essays in radical empiricism*. New York, NY: Cosimo.
Kant, I. (1997). *Critique of practical reason*. Cambridge: Cambridge University Press.
Latour, B. (1993). *We have never been modern*. Cambridge: Polity.
Latour, B. (2002). Gabriel trade and the end of the social. In P. Joyce (Ed.), *The social in question. New bearings in history and the social sciences* (pp. 117–132). London: Routledge.

Latour, B. (2005). *Reassembling the social: An introduction to actor network theory.* Oxford: Oxford University Press.

Mark, K., & Engels, F. (1969). *Die deutsche ideologie.* Werke, Band 3, S. 5–530. Berlin: Dietz Verlag.

Martha, N. C. (1995). Objectification. *Philosophy and Public Affairs, 24,* 249–291.

Nietzsche, F. (1886). *Jenseits von Gute und Böse,* Sections 187-91. Retrieved from http://gutenberg.spiegel.de/buch/3250/5

Nietzsche, F. (1992). *Der Wille zur Macht.* Frankfurt: Suhrkamp Verlag.

Nietzsche, F. (2003). *Geneaology of morals.* New York, NY: Courier Dover Publications.

Schillmeier, M., & Pohler, W. (2006). Kosmo-politische Ereignisse. Zur sozialen Topologie von SARS. *Soziale Welt, 57*(4), 179–199.

Spinoza, B. (1677). *The ethics.* Retrieved from http://users.erols.com/nbeach/spinoza.html

Stengers, I. (2005). The cosmopolitical proposal. In B. Latour & P. Weibel (Eds.), *Making things public: Atmospheres of democracy* (pp. 994–1003). Cambridge, MA: MIT Press.

Tarde, G. (1899). *Social laws: An outline of sociology.* New York: Macmillan.

Tarde, G. (2009). *Monadologie und Soziologie.* Frankfurt: Suhrkamp Verlag.

van Loon, J. (2008). *Media technology: Critical perspectives.* Maidenhead, Berkshire: McGraw Hill – Open University Press.

Whitehead, A. N. (1978). *Process and reality. An essay in cosmology.* New York, NY: The Free Press.

TOWARD A SPECULATIVE ETHICS

Kevin Love

ABSTRACT

Purpose – *To develop an alternate metaethical framework based upon a specific modality of difference.*

Methodology/approach – *A radicalisation of Moore's naturalistic fallacy and the application of the open question argument within the broader context of the continental tradition allow one to direct the ethical question away from non-naturalism and towards a speculative ethics.*

Findings – *Suggesting an ethical modality irreducible to ontological description or political prescription, the chapter argues for a metaethics of 'exhortation'.*

Originality/value of chapter – *The chapter opens a new space for thinking ethics, and further encourages the continuing rapprochement between continental and analytical traditions in philosophy.*

Practical implications – *Questions of practical ethics will find new modes of engagement and expression in the context of a hortative metaethics.*

Keywords: Ethics; speculative realism; naturalistic fallacy; non-naturalism

Ethics in Social Research
Studies in Qualitative Methodology, Volume 12, 207–230
Copyright © 2012 by Emerald Group Publishing Limited
All rights of reproduction in any form reserved
ISSN: 1042-3192/doi:10.1108/S1042-3192(2012)0000012014

INTRODUCTION

Beginning with G. E. Moore's famous naturalistic fallacy, I aim to indicate that the common reduction of ethics to an ontological basis in fact denudes and renders impotent the question of ethics. The three main points that I finally draw from the encounter with Moore are as follows: (1) that for Moore 'the good is' *somehow*, despite not being existent in any empirical or metaphysical sense; (2) since mental phenomena are also natural objects, when we intuit, feel or think the good we do not grasp it in itself, forcing it to appear in time as a natural object. Rather we intuit, feel or think a *relationship* to the good; (3) by contrast, it is Moore's attempt to answer the ontological question concerning the being of the good itself that indirectly returns him to the naturalism. Arguing that (2) above, far from rendering Moore's project self-defeating, in fact redirects the enquiry away from non-naturalism and towards a speculative ethics, I suggest an ethical modality irreducible to ontology. Conceiving the bearing and character of the relation to the good in terms of *exhortation*, and drawing upon elements of contemporary continental philosophy, I conclude in contemplating the absolutisation of this principle as an alternative ground for meta-ethics.

GAUGING THE HUMEAN DIVIDE

I cannot forbear adding to these reasonings an observation, which may, perhaps, be found of some importance. In every system of morality, which I have hitherto met with, I have always remark'd, that the author proceeds for some time in the ordinary way of reasoning, and establishes the being of a God, or makes observations concerning human affairs; when of a sudden I am surpriz'd to find, that instead of the usual copulations of propositions, *is,* and *is not,* I meet with no proposition that is not connected with an *ought,* or an *ought not.* This change is imperceptible; but is, however, of the last consequence. For as this *ought,* or *ought not,* expresses some new relation or affirmation, 'tis necessary that it shou'd be observ'd and explain'd; and at the same time that a reason should be given, for what seems altogether inconceivable, how this new relation can be a deduction from others, which are entirely different from it. But as authors do not commonly use this precaution, I shall presume to recommend it to the readers; and am persuaded, that this small attention wou'd subvert all the vulgar systems of morality, and let us see, that the distinction of vice and virtue is not founded merely on the relations of objects, nor is perceiv'd by reason. (Hume, 1978, pp. 469–470)

With this celebrated identification of immediate logical incompatibility between 'is' and 'ought', Hume inaugurates for the modern era a paradigmatic metaethical framework. Echoing a parallel bifurcation in metaphysics, the debate plays out across various realist and non-realist moral

positions that distend from this juncture, aiming mostly to elide, less frequently to preserve as categorical, this 'imperceptible' difference of 'last
consequence'. Recent philosophy is replete with examples. Tracing for a
moment the lines of debate in the Anglo-American tradition, moral naturalisms, perhaps most characteristic of the realist comportment, attempt to
span directly the Humean divide. Purportedly explicating logically secure
threads of argumentation that conjoin the realm of scientifically verifiable
fact with that of ethical judgments, moral naturalisms precisely *do* aspire to
derive an 'ought' from an 'is'. Non-naturalisms, by contrast, insist upon the
distinction between normative and non-normative contexts, and typically
secure the former by backing into forms of moral intuitionism and the
apprehension of non-natural properties that supervene on less contentious
natural properties. More antirealist in disposition, moral non-cognitivism
and error theory are united in the view that moral properties do not exist at
all, but that moral statements reveal only linguistic, performative or
psychological dispositions of varying degrees of sincerity. Subjectivism by
comparison may well allow the existence of moral facts, but only in an ideal
(i.e. mind-dependent) form. Already, then, one might note how quickly
ethics is striated by metaphysics; note that despite setting out in all good faith
to ask questions about ethics, one swiftly finds the enquiry articulated in
ontological terms.

Ontology thus seems to trump ethics on every occasion, the latter being
interpretable as little more than a symptom or expression of some deeper
ontological fundament. Whether real or ideal, natural or linguistic, the
ethical invariably situates downstream of ontology in a causal or (at a very
minimum) epiphenomenal mode. Even non-naturalism I will argue, after
establishing some distance from the ontological by dint of the naturalistic
fallacy, typically accedes (to both metaphysics and naturalism) in the final
analysis. Thus one finds Hume's observation increasingly vexing. Whatever
detours the arguments might take, the finer points of reality/irreality
notwithstanding, the ethical appears to be founded each time on a prior
facilitative moment that, in providing 'sufficient reason' for ethics, affects
the assimilation of the ethical 'ought' into the broader architecture of an
ontological 'is'. And how could it be otherwise? However adamant one
remains about the distinction between 'is' and 'ought', how could the ethical
not owe its existence to the ontological?

In configuring the relationship between ethics and ontology, it is
important to note that on occasion the contrary tendency manifests itself,
the ethical resisting (for a time at least) the immediate reduction to ontology.
A more detailed consideration of these moments of ontological reticence will

therefore prove informative, affording an opportunity to examine the indicative logic in its most acute form. To this end the chapter will attempt to analyse non-naturalism in fairly precise terms, but before embracing the detail it should be noted that it is not without good cause that one encounters examples of the latter propensity less frequently. The guiding questions of metaethics have invariably been couched in onto-epistemological terms. We enquire, for example, what ethics *is* or through what *cognitive processes* one acquires moral knowledge. Beset by the clamour of being and seemingly unable to articulate itself otherwise, axiology swiftly succumbs to aetiology, except, that is, on those philosophically awkward occasions where the ethical obstinately stands its ground – even when there should be no ground. At best these dogged attempts to preserve or respect the difference between 'is' and 'ought' tend to result in a form of metaethical aposiopesis, proponents appearing to lack both method and vocabulary, and thus often feeling it necessary to continue to articulate their defiance in epistemological terms (the notion of 'self-evident truth' and the like). More commonly, as I illustrate below, a move is made that finally concedes the ethical to ontology in one form or another. Despite this, and while as a rule I try to be wary of philosophies that 'glimmer', it seems to me that one does on these occasions catch a glimpse of something beyond onto-epistemology. It may be argued that such imaginings are fanciful, and that little can remain for an ethics that aspires to elude both ontology and epistemology as we know them. Nonetheless here I will entertain the thought that these moments of aposiopesis indicate the edges of *logos*[1] rather than the limits of an ethics. In our opening passage, that is to say, I take Hume to have touched on something beyond mere grammatical quirk, semantic differentiation or the projection of sentiment onto an otherwise impassive onto-epistemological surface. 'Imperceptible' and yet 'entirely different', this distinction is indeed of 'last consequence' because ontologically it is of no consequence, and if this radicalisation of the naturalistic fallacy can be sustained, then the way we conceive ethics as both discipline and practice will require reformulating.

The term 'naturalistic fallacy' is of course attributable to G.E. Moore's seminal *Principia Ethica*, which (perhaps reluctantly) offers one such example of ontological hesitance. Principally this effect is due to the consequences that follow from its famous summation of the simple, unanalysable, indefinable form of the good (Moore, 1971, p. 21). I will shortly turn to this text, both for a measure of encouragement and to initiate a more determined consideration. I take Moore to have recognised the stakes Hume's innocent observation establishes, for which reason he determines to invest his considerable analytical ability in more precisely configuring the problematic. The *Principia* opens in fact by proffering the following heuristic:

> It appears to me that in Ethics, as in all other philosophical studies, the difficulties and disagreements, of which its history is full, are mainly due to a simple cause: namely to the attempt to answer questions, without first discovering precisely *what* question it is which you desire to answer. (Moore, 1971, p. vii)

To me oddly reminiscent of the introduction to *Being and Time*, one might imagine Heidegger and Moore, strangest of bedfellows, agreeing on the importance of the framing question, if then agreeing on nothing further. Heidegger's hermeneutic understanding of the relationship between question and answer (1962, pp. 2–35) is not too far removed from Moore's position at this point, and in part it is the latter's commitment to a rigorous formulation of the question of ethics (as opposed most explicitly to the ontological question of reality) that already prefigures the naturalistic fallacy and his final axiomatic rendering of 'the good'. The question, more specifically the famous 'open question', will figure prominently in the following discussion. In itself I consider it to be a methodological instantiation of a more fundamental 'question of ethics', which projects itself in a manner other philosophical questions do not, and which for this reason lends force to both Hume's remark and Moore's naturalistic fallacy. Beyond the guiding projection of the opening question, however, the *Principia* is further constrained by certain methodological and epistemological loyalties. Supposing ethics to be first and foremost an instance of moral epistemology (rather than, say, a more fundamental mode of engagement with the world) and assaying the question through an analytical lens alone, Moore arrives at the limits of his enquiry. The resultant metaethics, however, remains largely circumscribed by the onto-epistemological context and specific trajectory of the analytical method. Only by altering the horizons of engagement will Moore's intuitive distension of Hume's imperceptible difference progress beyond the parameters of analysis. While agreeing with Moore's prefatory heuristic, therefore, I will extend the logical remit of the open question in order to disrupt the onto-epistemological context in which Moore deploys it. I further suggest that it is possible to do justice to the differentiation of ethics and ontology only if analysis recombines with a more speculative approach to the question of ethics. This speculative moment occurs at the limits of Moore's analysis and requires a step the analytical approach will resist as long as it remains wedded to its particular epistemological *modus operandi*. Accordingly, if a little ambitiously, this chapter is intended as

something approaching a prolegomena to a more expansive, speculative
ethics, as opposed to a prolegomena to a scientific ethics (Moore, 1971,
p. ix). I imagine a project that allows space for the ethical to develop its own
trajectories, logics, methods and parameters. To this end, the following
essay ventures to reassess and radicalise Moore's analytical axiom in
conversation with elements of the continental tradition, indicating the
historical extent and philosophical degree of the reduction of ethics, before
proposing an alternative course. As a first step in the broader project it will
be important to liberate Moore's reiteration of Hume, not only from the
native environment of the analytical approach but also from the equally
dominant onto-epistemological climate found within the continental
tradition. I will maintain that the distinction between 'is' and 'ought', the
ontological and the ethical, has a foundational quality we have not yet
adequately appreciated. It is a necessary but insufficient step to pose this
difference as 'categorical', if this term is understood to imply that the ethical
is yet housed in some overarching natural, linguistic, psychological or
idealist framework. The phrase 'existential difference' might serve one
better, were it not for the clear historical and semantic contradictions, more
obvious but no more acute. The articulation of this difference in existential
terms will also prove valuable, but ultimately the difference between ethics
and ontology can be neither ethical nor ontological in character, a demand
that may possibly exceed even the quasi-ontological forms of *differance*
familiar to readers of Derrida.

So whereas the form of articulation between 'is' and 'ought' must
certainly be reconfigured, this can only occur once Hume's simple observation has been allowed to run its course. *Principia Ethica* represents a key
staging point in this reconfiguration, as here Moore assays and formulates
the problematic with admirable precision. For this reason our excursus on
Hume's observation begins in the context of an emerging analytical
tradition, before opening itself to the broader vistas of continental
philosophy, noting that whatever may yet divide the two traditions it is
certainly not a propensity to defend ethics from ontological reduction.

ETHICS AND THE ONTOLOGICAL

It has long been recognised that the naturalistic fallacy is poorly named.
Moore himself makes clear that the fallacy in its most elemental form has
little to do with the reduction to naturalism per se (1971, p. 14), as detailed
later. The fallacy proper concerns the reductive identification of *any* object

with any other. Likewise the 'open question argument' is not simply, or even primarily, a refutation of moral naturalism per se but at base represents a refusal to accede to a reductive definition of the good, in the first instance specifically for Moore a reduction to natural properties. Moore holds that the good is a simple, unanalysable and indefinable ethical concept (1971, p. 21), and for this reason resists its unreserved association with any natural object, complex or simple. It is the open question (Moore, 1971, pp. 15–17) that implicitly measures this irreducible logical gap between the ethical (goodness itself) and the ontological (things that are good). As Moore poses it, the open question assigns itself to every attempted definition of ethics, disputing the presumed association of the good with a specific instance of the natural/empirical. For example, if one defines the good as pleasure, it remains entirely appropriate for an individual competent in moral discourse to enquire whether (in this instance or generally) pleasure *really is* good. In any given case one may agree that it is indeed pleasant, but continue to question whether it is good. Similarly, some activity or other may well be one's duty, but again (as history attests with especial vigour) the reduction of the good to the performance of duties is not unproblematic. The precise mechanism of the fallacy will feature below, but note that Moore explicitly extends the critique beyond naturalism to include those 'Metaphysical Ethics' (1971, pp. 110–141) that envelop the good within the body of a hierarchically prior, supersensible reality, and in so doing meaningfully extends his critique within a much wider onto-epistemological context than analytical philosophy would normally warrant.

> To hold that from any proposition asserting 'Reality is of this nature' we can infer, or obtain confirmation for, any proposition asserting 'This is good in itself' is to commit the naturalistic fallacy. And that a knowledge of what is real supplies reasons for holding certain things to be good in them is either implied or expressly asserted by all those who define the Supreme Good in metaphysical terms. This contention is part of what is meant by saying that Ethics should be 'based' on Metaphysics. It is meant that some knowledge of supersensible reality is necessary *as a premise* for correct conclusions as to what ought to exist. (Moore, 1971, p. 114)

To argue, for example from some a priori position, that a metaphysical prime mover such as volition, Spirit or God defines the essential nature of the good, remains as problematic for Moore as a crude scientific naturalism positing the good in the empirical facts of human existence. Not because the metaphysical thesis lacks scientific verifiability, but again primarily because it reduces the simple form of the good to some other conceptual frame. The good is no longer defined in and of itself, but instead remains good strictly to the extent that it agrees with the metaphysical absolute. The

open question argument accordingly rematerialises in the metaphysical
sphere (consider the question of theodicy for instance), interjecting the same
ethical singularity into the onto-epistemological totality. One should not
conclude, therefore, that it is the term 'metaphysics' which is particularly
problematic here. Moore's objections would weigh just as heavily against a
Heideggerian ontology, no matter how assiduous one's crossing-through.[2]

It is worth emphasising the form of relation the *Principia's* ethical moment
performs in its exchanges with the ontological. The good, it seems, demonstrates a tendency toward ontological immiscibility: it does not found or
displace and perhaps cannot even be said to disrupt or disturb. Rather the
good simply and quietly *evades* onto-epistemology. Despite the meticulous
analysis of what the good *is not*, the positivity of the good remains entirely
wrapped up in itself, immune to analysis, aloof almost. The figure of the good
performs no rational critique or formal deconstruction of any given
philosophical ontology, naturalist or otherwise. Seemingly indifferent to the
'to and fro' of realism/idealism, and certainly not concerned to engage in
elaboration or explanation, the 'subject-matter of Ethics' remains largely
opaque to onto-epistemological inquiry. Thus, not denying any palpable
capaciousness one might intuitively wish to affirm for the ethical dimension,
the open question nonetheless transects the ontological plane in singular
fashion. This oblique relationality – *a luxation not entirely without character* –
will prove increasingly central to my argument, but already for Moore there is
a sense of obstinacy about the ethical: the 'good is good and nothing else
whatever' (1971, p. 144) and analytically that is all there is to say. It matters
not whether the ethical is up against a hard-nosed, scientifically rigorous
naturalism or a grand-theoretical metaphysics, it remains immune under the
protective logic of the open question.

Now for the analytical philosopher such a frustratingly impenetrable
formulation flirts with the trivial and the truistic, rubbing up as it does
against the paradox of analysis. The latter, a reformulation of Meno's
paradox of inquiry, would thus demarcate the limits of Moore's analysis by
suturing the ethical interruption of the ontological on the basis of an
epistemological maxim: that no analysis can be both correct and informative. The proposition resulting from the operation of the open question
('the good alone is good') is thus taken to be nothing more than an
unremarkable example of the limits of analytical epistemology. Accordingly,
any fanciful glimmer of non-ontological positivity the formulation might
have suggested is closed off by a hierarchically prior logico-linguistic
ontology, and ethics again becomes a causally dependent element of a
broader ontological architecture.[3] The founding maxim of the paradox,

however, not only is predicated upon specific conceptions of identity and difference, but also testifies at a deeper level to the *preferred onto-epistemological trajectory* of the analytical tradition.[4] Positing alternative trajectories, or indeed imagining alternative modalities of thought, renders it entirely conceivable that ethical inquiry might yet extend both correctly and informatively elsewhere. Moore is interesting in this respect, being situated at an early point in the divergence of two 20th-century philosophical traditions: undeniably analytical in method, yet he not only extends his critique to deal with those grand metaphysical philosophies (explicitly, Spinoza, Kant and Hegel) that remain influential at this time, but also avoids running into the analytical dead via an appeal to self-evidential truth and intuition. For the *Principia*, the proposition 'good is good' is not an instance of the paradox of analysis but a founding axiom of ethics.

In truth, there is probably little to distinguish the parameters to enquiry established by the paradox of analysis from the parameters of enquiry established by the appeal to self-evident truth. Both mark the limits of epistemology, albeit at different locations, and neither will provide our preferred route for further consideration of the ethical. Moore precisely identifies, analytically measures and later argues stubbornly to maintain the immediate distinction between the ethical and the ontological. Unable to fathom this difference *as a difference*, however, the good finally succumbs to naturalism via Moore's attempt to accommodate the ethical within ontology. The next section will detail the process of this second-order reduction while noting that the open question itself does not suffer the same fate. Obdurate, the open question continues to occupy the Humean divide in such a way as to preserve the distinction, drawing its force from the ever possible dissociation of the good from the ontological facticity of a given place holder. Resisting the reductive intent of the ontological, preserving *at a minimum* an 'ontologically reticent' realm of normativity,[5] I will argue that the operation of the open question in fact extends analysis in alternate directions.

With the paradox of analysis, then, one observes the same programmatic return to ontology which, I have suggested, characterises much ethical reasoning: 'there is nothing special about 'the good', it is just another concept governed by the onto-epistemological principles of analysis'. To be clear, this is not a critique of the paradox itself, which undoubtedly delimits the analytical project in one important aspect. Rather, the observation is intended to prepare the ground for a more sustained consideration of the ontological reduction itself. Now one might immediately object that it is simply the role of moral philosophy to find reasoned, ontological premises on which to ground an ethics, so deriving defensible solutions to the

question 'What ought one to do?' Accordingly, even normatively inclined
ethical theories, appealing to notions such as fairness, justice or individual
liberty, tend to ground themselves on ontological premises (human nature
and the like).[6] Exactly what is the problem with this gesture? Why should I
remain so exercised by the attempt to found ethics ontologically? By way of
reply it is worth considering Moore's conception of the good in greater
detail, and in the context of recent trends in naturalistic explanations.

Curry (2006), for instance, argues for a 'Humean-Darwinian metaethics',
rejecting in the process what he reads as various articulations of the
naturalistic fallacy. His basic argument follows the same pattern of
ontological reduction identified above:

> The Humean-Darwinian argues that humans are equipped with a suite of adaptations
> for cooperation, that these adaptations constitute what have been called the moral
> passions or moral sentiments, and that these adaptations determine what people deem
> morally good and bad. If one accepts this argument, it makes no sense to complain that
> evolution may have *explained why* humans find certain things morally good, but it
> cannot tell us whether these things are *really* morally good or not. It follows from the
> premises of the argument that there is no criterion of 'moral goodness' independent of
> human psychology, and hence this question cannot arise. (Curry, 2006, p. 242)

With a now familiar gesture the Humean–Darwinian thesis establishes the
ontological status of moral values and in so doing effectively seeks to close
down the open question, the insistence on the primacy of ontological inquiry
denying any ethical riposte: 'the normative question presupposes, incor-
rectly, that it makes sense to morally evaluate moral values. Given that it is
not possible to answer a senseless question, the failure of Humean-
Darwinian meta-ethics to answer the normative question does not count
against the thesis' (p. 242). Interestingly, the open question may precisely be
considered an attempt to morally evaluate moral values, as will become
apparent. In principle, however, the Humean–Darwinian thesis is no
different to a social constructionist view of ethics, informed by the genealogical approach of, say, Nietzsche or Foucault: what we take to be ethics
is in fact some hidden, ontological prime mover (evolutionary principles or
ubiquitous fields of power), that induces us to think the things we think and
feel the things we feel. In this sense we are fooled by ethics, indeed there are
no ethics, not as such: what we have come to call ethics is more properly an
ontological modality, or even an ontological ruse the better to ensure
compliance with the fundamental nature of reality, whatever one consider
that to be. All reductive ontologies evacuate the ethical with this gesture,
and the effect is not limited to the ethical alone. One might first extend the

argument to the axiological in general (hence beauty is no longer really beauty but simply, for example, a neurochemical reaction to certain physical stimuli or an ideological production reflecting power relations, etc.), until finally even consciousness itself is overrun (such that the very thought of X is itself simply an instance of X).[7]

Ontologies that posit a non-temporal essentialism (an unchanging form of human nature, say) are able to provide some refuge for a derivative ethics, but ontologies of becoming such as Darwinian evolution offer little purchase for any form of moral philosophy. The cooperative adaptations Curry initially valourises are finally conceivable only as instrumental modalities of a more fundamental ontological principle[8] or, in the case of a truly unprincipled becoming, utterly contingent phenomena. Thus Curry's appeal to 'the common good' (2006, p. 235) remains either an appeal to some underlying ontological principle (biological diversity or the selfishness of genes) given ethical clothes, or a meaningless category: there being no 'common' other than the totality of all living (and possibly all material) things, and no 'good' only becoming. To my mind Moore has already provided the resources to dispatch arguments of this sort, in extending the open question to metaphysical ethics. Nonetheless, Curry's direct discussion of Moore's notion of the good affords an opportunity to highlight the final trajectory of the open question.

There is some inaccuracy in Curry's interpretation of Moore at this point. In the first place he argues that Moore never made the argument for the good being a non-natural property:

> If Moore had conclusively demonstrated that *good* was a non-natural property in this sense, then Humean-Darwinian meta-ethics would indeed be in trouble. However, Moore made no such argument. And there is no such argument to be found in the pages of *Principia Ethica*. This mistaken interpretation of Moore can be traced to his somewhat idiosyncratic use of the term 'natural'. For Moore, the opposite of 'natural' is 'intuitive', not 'supernatural'.

Moore did not of course 'conclusively demonstrate' that the good was a non-natural property, but he certainly suggested as much: 'For I do not deny that good is a property of certain natural objects: certain of them, I think, *are* good; and yet I have said that "good" itself is not a natural property' (1971, p. 41).[9] Nonetheless, it is undoubtedly the fraught issue of the 'non-natural' that continues to beset the *Principia*, and which will provide for the present work a route out of the analytical tradition in an engagement with elements of 20th- and 21st-century continental philosophy.

NON-NATURALISM

Before attempting to coordinate a bearing for a speculative ethics, I will first indicate how non-naturalism generally, after separating itself in some measure via the naturalistic fallacy, nonetheless accedes to ontology and so returns inexorably to naturalism via relations of dependence and supervenience. For Moore, as noted, attempts to guard against both naturalistic *and* metaphysical ethics. The apparent conclusion, at least at the time of the *Principia*, that the good was a 'non-natural property' is symptomatic of this dual aversion. Although finely balanced between the two faces of the ontological reduction, however, the relation is not as even-handed as it first appears. Addressing the question of 'the being of the good', Moore finally sides not with the metaphysicians but (to steal a phrase) with 'that other class of philosophers – "empirical" philosophers – to which most Englishmen have belonged' (Moore, 1971, p. 111). To appreciate the consequences of this decision it will be necessary to consider the ontological format of non-naturalism in more depth. In so doing I will draw upon Shaver (2000) and Hochberg (1962) in particular, to argue that Moore's category of the non-natural will finally reduce to naturalism via its dependence (Moore's term), or supervenience, on the natural. One will observe the same Humean divide emerges in a supervenient form, before again dissipating against the backdrop of an all-encompassing ontology. In other words, Moore's non-naturalism takes the difference between 'is' and 'ought' to be an ontological difference: a difference in the modes of being of the good. This decision seals the fate of non-naturalism and also elides a more interesting *ethical difference*, on which the present section closes. The final part of the chapter will then demonstrate how a speculative approach to this ethical difference promises an alternative metaethical framework.

Non-naturalism, then, is characterised by an epistemological symmetry between normative and non-normative planes. Just as an object's natural properties are elicited from the world via the operation of particular mental faculties, so *non*-natural moral properties are typically held to be intuitable through the operation of a special moral faculty. In this way the non-naturalist is able to preserve the normative specificity of the 'ought' from the merely descriptive tendencies of the 'is', but at some cost. For the non-naturalist both types of property (natural and non-natural) are *real*, but remain metaphysically distinct. Immediately, then, the question concerning the status of, and relationship between, these two planes of reality arises.

Shaver (2000, p. 264), quoting Warnock (1967) amongst others, captures the essence of the non-naturalist position:

> For example, Moore pictures 'a realm of moral qualities ... floating, as it were, quite free from anything else whatever, but cropping up here and there, quite contingently and for no reason, in bare conjunction with more ordinary features of the everyday world'.

It would be fair to say that Moore's decision to posit the 'existence' of a non-natural property is amongst one of the most controversial in the history of analytical philosophy. Clearly some work is required to defend such a view, as a series of pertinent questions attend the nature of the relationship between natural and non-natural. For instance, if metaphysically distinct, how is that particular assemblages of natural properties consistently give rise to normative contexts, whereas others consistently do not? If one imagines two scenarios identical in all natural properties, can one still imagine a variance in non-natural properties? What does a non-natural property specifically add to reality?[10] In response to the issue of the relation between natural and non-natural, Moore has goodness *qua* non-natural properties *depend* on natural properties (Hochberg, 1962). The form of this relation of dependence means that while the good is not of course a natural, empirical or perceptual reality,[11] neither does it exist independently as some type of supersensible reality or Platonic form. Here one needs to finesse the argument a little.

The *Principia* operates with a distinction between being and existing, or as Hochberg (1962, p. 373) has it: 'Good is somehow—even though it doesn't exist.' Those things that exist are found in time as natural properties; particulars of natural objects or themselves simple objects. The good, by contrast, does not exist in time and is more properly considered a universal rather than an empirical particular. The way it attaches to natural objects is via *exemplification* (Hochberg, 1962). So when we say that some natural object (whether that be a traditional object, a state of affairs or a mental object such as a thought or feeling) is good, we are not, for Moore, asserting that goodness is somehow part of its substantial or material form, as say the properties 'yellow' or 'square' might be. Rather we assert that this thing *exemplifies* the good and accordingly an ontological disjuncture is introduced between the natural and the non-natural. Dependence in Moore's context, however, means that it is the particular combination of natural properties in a thing that gives rise to the possibility of exemplification.[12] Nonetheless, if the *possibility* of the good *qua* non-empirical, universal arises from natural properties, the *being* of the good lifts off from these humble origins to form a concept that can no longer be reduced *to* those origins. Hence the assertion of goodness itself is not based upon our apprehension of those natural properties alone. We apprehend something other than those natural properties when we 'intuit' the good. More precisely, what we apprehend is the fact that this particular assemblage of natural properties, as well as being yellow, square, here and now (i.e. existent), is *also* good. If one removes or alters one of its natural properties the object may well cease to be good, but this is not to say that goodness was *contained* by the object as a property, or that the good was identifiable with that particular property per se. Rather, shuffling the properties in this way results in an object that no longer *exemplifies* the good. Thus when we apprehend the good in an object we are not apprehending goodness itself (which would be to commit the naturalistic fallacy once again), but a relation to a universal that does not itself exist in time.

Now whereas Curry is correct to point up Moore's equivocation over the term 'naturalistic', and also correct to identify a hesitation in the *Principia*, over whether 'the good' is to be considered a natural object or not. He loses himself a little in the convolutions of Moore's text – but usefully so. The general form of the fallacy is certainly the reductive identification of any one object (simple or otherwise, natural or not) with another: 'If I were to imagine that when I said "I am pleased", I meant that I was exactly the same thing as "pleased", I should not indeed call that a naturalistic fallacy, although it would be the same fallacy as I have called naturalistic with reference to Ethics' (Moore, 1971, p. 13). At an ontological level, therefore, the fallacy concerns the reduction of relations of *containment or association* (A being a part of B or otherwise empirically associated with B) to those of identity (A = B). The fallacy becomes specifically 'naturalistic' in Moore's sense of the word when the ontological relation of *exemplification* is reduced to a relation of identity. The problem, then, rests with the specific sense of the copula in the axiom, and the open question would more precisely open the space between two different forms of relation to the universal: exemplification and identity. Of greater significance for the present work is that these relations remain ontological in character and the same geometry would therefore apply to *any* universal: truth, say, or being even. Thus again, there is nothing particularly special about 'the good', and as yet we have no principle on which to ground ethics in its own terms. This can be demonstrated in greater detail as follows.

Retaining the notion of exemplification, we can continue by rejecting Curry's assertion that for Moore the '*good* is a subjective psychological entity and not an objective feature of the world' (Curry, 2006, p. 239). In fact it is *neither* a subjective psychological entity *nor* an objective feature of the world. Moore's definition of natural objects is clear enough to include all mental phenomena[13]:

> By 'nature', then, I do mean and have meant that which is the subject-matter of the natural sciences and also of psychology. It may be said to include all that has existed, does exist, or will exist in time. Moore (1971, p. 40)

As a result, goodness as a psychological phenomenon would indeed be a natural object and itself subject to the intervention of the open question:

> If indeed good were a feeling, as some would have us believe, then it would exist in time. But that is why to call it so is to commit the naturalistic fallacy. It will always remain pertinent to ask, whether the feeling itself is good; and if so, then good cannot itself be identical with any feeling. (Moore, 1971, p. 41)[14]

It is certainly the case that Moore, *when discussing the nature of the fallacy*, deploys a form of words one might read as a possible hesitation in relation to the status of the good, a moment Curry (2006, p. 239) alights upon: 'Even if it were a natural object, that would not alter the nature of the fallacy nor diminish its importance one whit' (Moore, 1971, p. 14). It is apparent, however, even from the immediately preceding passages, that Moore intends the good to be considered non-natural, which following Hochberg (1962) we now understand to indicate a *universal substantive exemplified*, not existing in time but nonetheless *dependent*:

> But if he confuses 'good', *which is not in the same sense a natural object*, with any natural object whatever, then there is a reason for calling that a naturalistic fallacy; its being made with regard to 'good' marks it as something quite specific, and this specific mistake deserves a name because it is so common. As for the reasons why good is not to be considered a natural object, they may be reserved for discussion in another place. (Moore, 1971, pp. 13–14, emphasis added)

The good then is not, or at least not in the same sense, a natural object. Here the *Principia* is caught betwixt two poles of its own making, in a dilemma related intimately to the form of being of the good. On the one hand the good cannot exist empirically in time as a natural object (a subjective psychological entity or objective feature of the world) and neither can it exist eternally as some supersensible, metaphysical reality or Platonic form. Moore accordingly reaches for a mode of being that *depends upon* the natural, empirical world, while itself remaining irreducible to that world by reason of its specific ontological tie: exemplification. The ensuing problem, as Shaver (2000, p. 269) points out, however, is that on such a model the being of the good can only be thought to have arisen *a posteriori*, that is, *from* the natural world. This being the case, non-naturalism not only has to explain the necessary emergence of a special form of ontological tie (*exemplify* as opposed to the presumably more natural, less abstract *contain*), but more seriously finds itself thrown into a historical process in which the formation of a universal good occurs in time (whether the time of an individual, a culture or a species). Hence, not only running the gauntlet of ontological accounts of ethics from Hume, through Hegel, Marx, Darwin, Nietzsche, Freud and social constructionism generally (to name but a few), more immanently this move places the good *itself* in question. If above all else the *Principia* strives to preserve the good, Moore's ontological decision in fact closes the circle on the open question *most* emphatically: not asking whether this or that natural or metaphysical reality is truly good, but if the good, *qua universal, is* at all, or whether its pretensions to universality simply reflect psychological necessity, cultural contingency or evolutionary convenience.

So it is that Moore's attempt to establish a non-natural, non-metaphysical good finally cedes itself to the natural via ontological dependence, and once again ethics seems to evaporate under the intense scrutiny of ontology. This is not to argue that ontological *independence* would serve Moore any better. The latter in any traditional form will simply play the non-natural, universal form of the good the opposite way, toward metaphysical reality. The initial gambit of this chapter, then, appears to have run aground. It seems that one is unable to radicalise Hume's distinction in a sufficiently stable form to preserve the difference between 'is' and 'ought'. It is at this point that we must prepare to leave the climate of Moore's work and look elsewhere for inspiration. Before doing so, however, I should identify the exact point of interjection. One will recall the following passage: 'But if he confuses "good", which is not in the same sense a natural object, with any natural object whatever, then there is a reason for calling that a naturalistic fallacy' (Moore, 1971, p. 13). With any natural object whatever: we have already noted that mental objects generally and feelings explicitly are held to be natural objects. The perturbing consequence of this fact, then, is that if the 'good cannot itself be identical with any feeling' (Moore, 1971, p. 41), neither can it be identical with any thought. Most immediately, the thought of the good *itself* remains in disjunctive relation with 'the good itself'.

One can summarise the salient points from the encounter with Moore in the following way: (1) For Moore, let us say, the good *is* somehow, but is not existent in any empirical or metaphysical sense; (2) When we intuit, feel or think the good we do not grasp it in itself, forcing it to appear in time as a natural object. Rather we intuit, feel or think a *relationship* to the good, for

Moore (via Hochberg) a relation of exemplification; (3) It is Moore's attempt to answer the ontological question concerning the being of the good that finally (and perhaps unsurprisingly) returns him to the naturalistic fallacy, in the following way: (a) dependence introduces a form of supervenience which, although not immediately reductive; (b) only permits a formulation of the being of the good *a posteriori*, which thus; (c) reduces the good once more to an existence in time, explained by any number of ontological variants. In the final section I attempt to orchestrate these three moments to articulate a point of departure for a speculative ethics informed by elements of the continental tradition.

SPECULATION AND EXHORTATION

On the basis of (2) alone, Moore's project might well appear self-defeating, at least at first glance. If the open question allows a 'scientific ethics' to catch sight of a non-naturalistic good, it also, to the same measure, undermines the attempt to think it systematically. Under the continuing influence of the open question, that is to say: the good *qua* non-natural universal immediately dissociates itself from the thought of the good *qua* natural object. The same will hold for any other mode of cognition, non-cognitive feeling or intuition, all of which appearing in time must be considered natural objects. As a consequence the axiom 'good is good' does not operate in a straightforwardly self-evidential form, as both Moore and Sidgwick would have it (Moore, 1971, pp. 142–144; Shaver, 2000). Rather, at best one might imagine a cognitive noncongition or 'negative intuitionism' that intuits the fact that one cannot intuit the good. This is doubtless an inconvenient but unavoidable consequence of the logic Moore's open question entails. Any attempt to think a non-natural good scientifically, fails on its own terms: we cannot *know* the good.

Taking (1) and (3) together, we find the rather odd situation that although the good 'is somehow', as soon as one attempts to specify the being of the good one slips inevitably into the ontological reduction, whether in naturalistic or metaphysical form, and ethics seemingly dissolves into an ontological milieu. The reduction, however, does not silence the open question in any principled way. Say for instance we take the Humean–Darwinian thesis, and follow the reduction of ethics to a 'suite of adapt-ations'. It is not as though faced with this explanation the open question recognises the logical absurdity of its claim, meekly ceasing to question the identification of any particular adaptation with the good. Clearly it still has purchase. Like the sceptical thesis the open question continues unabated, as though its refutation sounded in a different register to its operative logic (Levinas, 1998, pp. 165–171). In fact, as we saw with Curry (2006) the only way the ontological argument is able to silence the open question is in ruling it out of court by ontological fiat: 'It just *is!*' If the good continually runs up against the boundaries of epistemology (via the paradox of analysis, the notion of self-evident truth, or as above via the internal logic of non-naturalism), it also causes some trouble at the limits of ontology – it is this radical freedom of the good in relation to the ontological that the open question performs.

Let us recall, however, that for (2) above it would be more precise to say that when one encounters (as we undoubtedly do) good in an adjectival form, one in fact encounters a *relationship*, which to this point we have represented by 'exemplification'. To think, feel or intuit a relationship of exemplification is not to think, feel or intuit the good itself but rather a *difference* of a certain character, the difference between the natural and the non-natural good. The theme of difference has of course been a staple of the 20th-century continental tradition since Heidegger configured (1962), and then reconfigured (1999), difference in an ontological form. Doubtless readers of Heidegger will have already noticed the obvious comparisons with Moore as I have presented him: where Heidegger insists upon the ontological difference, Moore insists upon an 'ethical difference': the difference between substantive and adjective (Moore, 1971, p. 9), or universal and particular (Hochberg, 1962); where the question of being calls to Heidegger, the open question seems to exert a similar influence on Moore; where early Heidegger seeks the meaning of being itself across the ontological difference, before noting the priority of that difference itself, so Moore pursues the good itself but, as now noted, is able only to access the *difference* between adjective and substantive.

A number of avenues of potential enquiry arise from the recognition of difference in the context of Moore's analysis. One might follow Derrida and examine the possibility of a 'universal ideal of the good', based upon an original repetition that finds material expression in empirical instances of the good (Derrida, 1973). This would not straightforwardly constitute a return to naturalism, since: (i) the *difference* between this and that natural object is not itself a natural object and (ii) an ideal based upon original repetition does not arise in a linear historical mode. As subtle as quasi-ontologies of this sort may be, however, there remains a sense in which the ethical is yet derived from a hierarchically prior configuration, achieved in pursuit of the question of being.[15] In other words, the ethical question has still not been asked on its own terms. If we agree with Moore that the good is the subject matter of ethics, then the open question can be considered an instantiation of a more fundamental question of ethics. Moreover, we have seen how the operation of the open question itself leads to a specific form of relationality. One cannot simply speak of the contingencies of grammar, linguistics or a particular philosophical tradition at this juncture, without once again performing an ontological reduction and resurrecting the open question argument. Accordingly the *form* of relationality that emerges through the operation of the open question can be considered immanent to the outworking of that question. What, then, might one glean from a closer examination of the specific relationality inaugurated by the open question?

If the relation to the good is configurable in differential terms, it is not I argue the equanimous difference of Heideggerian *Seyn* or Derridean *differance*. Here we have a form of relation that possesses a specific character of its own, one which thus orchestrates ethics accordingly. What is at stake in this claim? My suggestion is that by correctly identifying the relation to the good propagated in the operation of the open question, *one can derive an irreducible ethical principle*. In other words, although quite out of character, I am claiming that one might identify *an ethical absolute* on which to base a non-ontological meta-ethics. To indicate how it might be possible to attempt such a feat I will close with reference to recent, parallel developments in continental metaphysics.

> Let us call 'speculative' every type of thinking that claims to be able to access some form of absolute, and let us call 'metaphysics' every type of thinking that claims to be able to access some form of absolute being, or [which is the same thing] access the absolute through the principle of sufficient reason. If all metaphysics is 'speculative' by definition, our problem consists in demonstrating, conversely, that not all speculation is metaphysical, and not every absolute is dogmatic – it is possible to envisage an *absolutizing* thought that would not be *absolutist*. Meillassoux (2009, p. 34)

This is not the place to engage systematically with the work of Quentin Meillassoux, or indeed with that wider philosophical movement that has come to be called speculative realism. For the purposes of the present work I will simply conclude with a few comments regarding the viability of a speculative ethics, in contrast perhaps to a speculative ontology. There are some obvious comparisons. Positing the good as an accessible universal, for instance, would mirror the metaphysical move Meillassoux rightly rejects, and we have seen the fallacious tendencies that result. Positing the good in differential terms, however, already appears more speculative in nature. I do not imagine Derrida would disagree with Meillassoux's sentiment here. In fact *differance* might well provide an exemplar of a non-absolutist absolutizing thought, were it but a thought.[16] Notwithstanding, the speculative gesture arises in Meillassoux via the absolutisation of the empirical facticity of existence, leading to the rejection of the principle of sufficient reason and the development of the thought of necessary contingency. From a purely ontological perspective, much remains to be said in this respect,[17] but here I simply wish to take this speculative gesture and apply it in the context of ethics by signalling the possible absolutisation of a foundational ethical principle. The problems we have encountered around the open question, however, indicate that 'exemplification' cannot provide us with that foundational absolute, since it remains overly apprehending in character. If one is able to discern a relation of exemplification between A and B, then one is engaged in a moment of comparison. Certainly there is more flexibility as far as the naturalistic fallacy is concerned, B may exemplify A more or less in an economy of goodness that never, for all that, naturalises the good, but still there remains the sense that one must somehow *know* the good in order to make the comparison. The good, I have argued from Moore, will not give itself to epistemology in this way, thus before attempting the speculative gesture our ethics will need to analyse the relation to the good with greater determination.

Already we understand that no relation specifying a *particular* good can be valid. To this we must add the fact that the good itself maintains a relationship of exteriority (as the 'ex' of exemplify already seems to indicate). It is, though, *the specific character of the relationality, not the mere exteriority of the good* that is crucial here. The good accessed by cognition, feeling or intuition, say, is clearly not conceivable as some kind of *sample* of an inaccessible universal good: a material part of a material whole. Nor is it conceivable as an *example*, if by this we again imply some formal contiguity, trait or property that mysteriously informs the empirical realm. We *have not* already seen the eternal form of the Good, in order that we might then recognise its mark in the empirical; if the open question has validity we do not intuit, feel or cognise the good at all. Exemplification, therefore, seems a less than suitable term to describe the relation to the good. In asking 'what ought I to do?' one is not seeking to map one's actions onto a universal pro forma – such formulations remain overly wedded to an epistemological model of ethics. Neither can one properly represent this relation in a prescriptive, that is to say political, form. The ethical 'ought' disassociates from the political 'ought' to such an extent that one might question the use of the term altogether in the ethical context. The 'ought' of ethics does not sit in a continuum of prescription, ranging through obligation and requirement to meet finally with an imperative that itself resembles in its necessity a descriptive ontology (hence notions of 'natural law'). The political has its own remit and form and mode of engagement with ethics, but not even the pyschopolitics of *internal* power relations (where one cajoles and reprimands oneself) can be considered an adequate description of the relation to the ethical glimpsed via the open question.

To this extent it is indeed the *difference* between 'is' and 'ought' that detains us, since once articulated the 'ought' seems immediately to engender prescription and the political. If one is committed to the idea of a comportment that is ethical in and of itself, it will be necessary to avoid prescription as well as description – avoid the imperative *and* the indicative. Thus, in the difference between 'is' and 'ought' can one identify a subjunctive mood that might be thought proper to ethics? Such an articulation of the relation to the good must allow the ethical to maintain an element of freedom from either ontological or political reduction, and must further capture something of the character of the good: its irreducible, non-particularity and exteriority.

I propose the hortative mood of the subjunctive as a candidate. That is to say, our relation to the good is not one of exemplification, description or prescription, but one of *exhortation*. We do not intuit, cognise or feel the good; rather, we are exhorted. In this sense, ethics simply *is* the question: 'What ought I to do'? It is, as it were the *fact* of that question. The ethical modality, if we are to maintain ethics at all, is that dimensional modality that *in itself* exhorts to the good. Not an exhortation to do 'this' or 'that', questions of conduct will of course remain complex negotiations of many modalities, but nonetheless an exhortation that somehow structures each situation. Neither an exhortation that comes and goes, applying itself mysteriously to some scenarios and not to others, but an exhortation that resides as a discoverable facet of every scenario: an exhortation to exhortation. I do not intend any kind of crypto-religious rendering of this relation, which would return one to ontology and prescription just as squarely, but propose instead a more detailed consideration of metaethics *as* exhortation. If such a proposition were to be considered favourably, the effect would not only be to preserve the ethical from the insistently reductive tendencies of ontology, but also provide a principled, non-absolutizing, ethical absolute upon which the work of a practical ethics might commence.

NOTES

1. Specifically, an onto-epistemologics.
2. See Derrida (1976). Neither does the naturalistic fallacy attempt an inversion of the normal priority accorded to the ontological. In this respect Emmanuel Levinas would make interesting comparison. Like Moore he undeniably wishes to preserve a

measure of ethical autonomy, recognising the potential tyranny of the ontological, particularly in Heideggerian form. In establishing the ethical as first philosophy, however, he simply inverts the problematic, hoping to derive an 'is' from an 'ought' as it were. Here the reduction of ontology to ethics would be as unjustified as the reverse tendency, not to mention philosophically fraught. Embroiled in these hierarchical tussles, Levinas in fact finally delivers the ethical back to being via the operative necessity of the 'il y a' (Love, 2007).

3. The same fate would result if the good were determined to be an attributive predicate modifier as opposed to a predicate adjective, or indeed if the sense of the good is simply exhausted by one or both of these terms (see Geach, 1957).

4. 'A thing becomes intelligible first when it is analysed into its constituent concepts' (Moore, 1993, p. 8). 'The fundamental epistemological principle in the analysis of propositions containing descriptions is this: *Every proposition which we can understand must be composed wholly of constituents with which we are acquainted.*' (Russell, 1959, p. 219).

5. See for instance Gibbard (2002) and Shaver's discussion of Sidgwick (2000).

6. Here I have in mind Rawls, Nozick and the like.

7. The circularity of these realist onto-epistemologies (the logic of which entails an a priori (meta)physical structuring of the inquiry by X, an inquiry which then engages with a world to unsurprisingly find X) will have to be reserved for discussion elsewhere, but I would request it be noted that I take this circularity to be matched by a similar geometry afflicting their idealist counterparts.

8. Curry appears to support his position with reference to Dawkins 'selfish gene' which if not amounting to a 'direction' for evolution (c.f. Curry, 2006, p. 240) certainly constitutes a *telos*.

9. Indeed Curry (2006, p. 247) himself provides a supporting passage from Frankena (1957), where the latter defines intuitionism as the 'ascription to something of an indefinable and non-natural (or non-empirical) property'.

10. Smith (1994) in Shaver (2000).

11. '[...] Moore does not think of goodness as an "empirical" property, in that it is not sensible or an object of perception. In this sense it is more like mathematical properties than like red.' (Hochberg, 1962, p. 390).

12. Here one might compare Heidegger's ontological difference, where the play of difference between Being and beings is more complex, middle-voiced and not so easily decidable in favour of an ontic production of Being (Heidegger, 1999).

13. Although Hochberg (1962) points out the confusion that persists between concepts and simple objects.

14. '"Metaphysicians" have, therefore, the great merit of insisting that our knowledge is not confined to the things which we can touch and see and feel. They have always been much occupied, not only with that other class of natural objects which consists in mental facts, but also with the class of objects or properties of objects, which certainly do not exist in time, are not therefore parts of Nature, and which, in fact, do not *exist* at all. To this class, as I have said, belongs what we mean by the adjective "good". It is not *goodness*, but only the things or qualities which are good, which can exist in time—can have duration, and begin and cease to exist—can be objects of *perception*.' (Moore, 1971, p. 110–111).

15. 'One must therefore go by way of the question of being as it is directed by Heidegger and by him alone, at and beyond onto-theology, in order to reach the rigorous thought of that strange nondifference and in order to determine it correctly' (Derrida, 1976, p. 23).

16. Rightly and importantly Derrida would no doubt wish to complicate matters in respect to the absoluteness of the thought that thinks the absolute. This is, I feel, a valid observation in respect to onto-epistemological realism, and one which will provoke more detailed work in terms of the ethical 'thought' I am seeking to develop here.

17. Not least in relation to the empirical basis of Meillassoux's absolute, that announces itself most noticeably with the theme of touching: 'What you experience in your thought draws its redoubtable power from the profound truth which is implicated within it – you have "touched upon" nothing less than an absolute, the only veritable one, and with its help you have destroyed all those false absolutes of metaphysics, those of idealism as well as those of realism' (Meillassoux, 2009, p. 59). This discussion will form the subject matter of a forthcoming paper, *Touching the absolute: The radical empiricism of Quentin Meillassoux*.

REFERENCES

Curry, O. (2006). Who's afraid of the naturalistic fallacy. *Journal of Evolutionary Psychology, 4,* 234–247.

Derrida, J. (1973). *Speech and phenomena* (D. Allison, Trans.). Evanston, IL: Northwestern University Press.

Derrida, J. (1976). *Of grammatology* (G. Chakravorty Spivak, Trans.). Baltimore, MD: The John Hopkins University Press.

Frankena, W. K. (1957). Ethical naturalism renovated. *The Review of Metaphysics, 10,* 457–473 (in Curry, O. (2006). Who's afraid of the naturalistic fallacy. *Journal of Evolutionary Psychology, 4,* 234–247).

Geach, P. (1957). Good and evil. *Analysis, 17,* 33–42.

Gibbard, A. (2002). Normative concepts and recognitional concepts. *Philosophy and Phenomenological Research, 64,* 151–162.

Heidegger, M. (1962). *Being and time* (J. Macquarrie & E. Robinson, Trans.). Oxford: Blackwell.

Heidegger, M. (1999). *Contributions to philosophy (from enowning)* (P. Emad & K. Maly, Trans.). Bloomington, IN: Indiana University Press.

Hochberg, H. (1962). Moore's ontology and non-natural properties. *Review of Metaphysics, 15*(3), 365–395.

Hume, D. (1978 [1739–1740]). *A treatise of human nature.* Oxford: Oxford University Press.

Levinas, E. (1998). *Otherwise than being or beyond essence* (A. Lingis, Trans.). Pittsburgh, PA: Duquesne University Press.

Love, K. (2007). Emanuel levinas and the question of theophany. *Angelaki. Journal of Theoretical Humanities, 12*(3), 65–79.

Meillassoux, Q. (2009). *After finitude: An essay on the necessity of contingency* (R. Brassier, Trans.). London Continuum.

Moore, G. E. (1971 [1903]). *Principia ethica.* Cambridge: Cambridge University Press.

Moore, G. E. (1993 [1899]). The nature of judgement. In T. Baldwin (Ed.), *Selected writings* (pp. 1–19). London: Routledge.

Russell, B. (1959 [1910]). Knowledge by acquaintance and knowledge by description. In B. Russell (1959 [1917]) *Mysticism and logic* (pp. 209–232). London: George Allen and Unwin Ltd. Retrieved from http://archive.org/stream/mysticism00russuoft#page/n11/mode/1up

Shaver, R. (2000). Sidgwick's minimal meta-ethics. *Utilitas, 12*(3), 261–277.

Smith, M. (1994). The moral problem. Oxford: Oxford university Press (in Shaver, R. (2000). Sidgwick's minimal meta-ethics. *Utilitas, 12*(3), 261–277).